IRISH WRITERS

EDWARD O'REILLY

A Chronological Account of nearly Four Hundred Irish Writers
with a
descriptive catalogue of their works

Introduction by
GEARÓID S MacEOIN

BARNES & NOBLE, INC.
New York
Publishers & Booksellers since 1873

First edition Dublin 1820

Published in the United States, 1970
by Barnes & Noble, Inc.

© 1970

Irish University Press Shannon Ireland

Microforms

Microfilm, microfiche and other forms of micro-publishing
© Irish University Microforms Shannon Ireland

SBN 389 01032 4

PRINTED IN THE REPUBLIC OF IRELAND AT SHANNON
BY ROBERT HOGG PRINTER TO IRISH UNIVERSITY PRESS

INTRODUCTION

Edward O'Reilly belonged to a group of Irish literati who in the year 1818 formed the Iberno-Celtic Society in Dublin, one of many such societies founded in the course of the eighteenth and nineteenth centuries for the purpose of studying and publishing the historical records of Ireland. As far as publishing went, the Iberno-Celtic Society could hardly be described as a success, for its only publication was O'Reilly's *Irish Writers*. But it numbered among its members many distinguished scholars, Sir William Betham, George Petrie, James Hardiman, Paul O'Brien, and Edward O'Reilly who was Assistant Secretary.

O'Reilly had come to Dublin, probably from County Meath, before 1794. Irish was for him an acquired language and, to judge from the many incorrect translations of Irish passages or quotations in this book, his knowledge of it was not altogether accurate. But he was an industrious worker and published, in 1817, his Irish-English Dictionary with a 'compendious Irish grammar' which ran to three editions. He also edited Gallagher's sermons (1819) and saw the second edition of Donlevy's catechism through the press (1822). In 1825 he won a prize in a competition sponsored by the Royal Irish Academy for an essay on the Brehon Laws and this was published in the Academy's Transactions. This essay appears to have been his last work and he died in 1829.

In 1820 O'Reilly published his *Chronological Account of Nearly Four Hundred Irish Writers*. In it he attempted to catalogue all the writers in the Irish language known to him from the beginning of time to his own day. In this task he was following in the footsteps of Sir James Ware and Charles O'Conor of Belnagare. But he had the advantage over these in that he not only knew Irish, which Ware did not, but was also thoroughly familiar with the great manuscript collections of Dublin. In the century and a half since its publication *Irish Writers* has proved a useful guide, although present-day scholars will turn rather to the bibliographies of Best and Kenney and to the catalogues of the important manuscript collections for the information they require.

For a literature like that of medieval Irish, in which the greater number of compositions are anonymous or of uncertain authorship, a chronological account of writers can be only of limited value. It will be noticed that the great majority of writers named by O'Reilly are poets. This reflects the medieval Irish scribal practice of frequently naming the authors of poetic compositions but hardly ever those of prose works. This is why so very little of Irish prose literature is mentioned in this book. Not that one could trust the ascriptions found in the manuscripts either! Many poems were attributed to early historical or legendary characters by poets who intended the compositions to form part of a saga. In other cases false ascriptions may have been added to poems to lend them an undeserved venerability, such as the many poems ascribed to St Columba (died c. 592). Other false ascriptions are the result of genuine error, while a great many are wild guesses on the part of scribes who would not admit to ignorance. One of the faults of O'Reilly's *Irish Writers* is that he accepts almost all ascriptions as genuine. Modern scholarship would reject as of later date everything which O'Reilly places before the year 800, except the *Amra Coluim Chille* (no xlvi). On the other hand there are many anonymous poems, as well as poems which were unknown to O'Reilly, which are today dated to the seventh and eighth centuries. By way of extenuation one must say that O'Reilly was writing before the foundation of the science of Celtic studies. Zeuss's *Grammatica Celtica* did not appear for more than thirty years after the publication of *Irish Writers*, and the great grammarians who mapped out the historical development of the Irish language did not commence work until late in the century. One cannot, then, blame O'Reilly if he was unable to identify false ascriptions, as modern scholars do, by linguistic criteria. He had, however, read enough Irish to note that the language varied at different periods and he sometimes rejects a composition as being of later date. But this did not save him from important errors, such as his dating of the *Dindshenchas* to the sixth century and his acceptance of Benén, disciple of St Patrick, as author of *Lebor na Cert*, an eleventh-century compilation, according to its latest editor, Professor Myles Dillon. On the other hand, O'Reilly dates the composition of *Lebor Gabála* too late when he attributes it, hesitatingly, to Adam ua Cuirmín, c. 1418 (no clx).

O'Reilly frequently errs in his dating of historical persons. The most serious error of this type is when he places Blathmacc macc Con Bretan, an eighth-century poet, whose work has recently been edited by Professor James Carney from a manuscript in the possession of O'Reilly when he was compiling this book, for some unknown reason, at A.D. 1400, although his father is correctly noted at 722. Other dating errors are only a matter of a few years and need not be mentioned here.

O'Reilly's book is also limited by the interests of its compiler. Sometimes he excuses himself from giving a full account of some poems on the ground that they 'are not illustrative of the history and antiquities of our country' (no lxxxiv; cf. nos xlv, ccclxviii). On the other hand he fills three and a half pages with a catalogue of the devotional poems of Donnchadh Mór ua Dálaigh (†1244), perhaps because he happened to own a copy of them. In general, however, his interest in history and antiquities was the deciding factor and set the tone for the work, which is antiquarian rather than literary in spirit.

But when all its errors have been picked out and pilloried there remains the achievement of this book, the fruit of one man's intimate acquaintance with the manuscript literature of a thousand years. O'Reilly planned the history of Irish literature and the plan he conceived still holds good. Modern scholarship has succeeded in filling some of the gaps but still leaves unwritten the complete history of Irish literature for which O'Reilly laid the foundations.

Gearóid S Mac Eoin
University College, Galway

February 1969

TRANSACTIONS

OF THE

IBERNO-CELTIC SOCIETY

FOR

1820.

VOL. I.—PART I.

CONTAINING

A CHRONOLOGICAL ACCOUNT OF NEARLY FOUR HUNDRED

IRISH WRITERS,

COMMENCING WITH

THE EARLIEST ACCOUNT OF IRISH HISTORY,

AND CARRIED DOWN TO THE YEAR OF OUR LORD 1750;

WITH

A Descriptive Catalogue

Of such of their Works as are still extant in Verse or Prose, consisting of upwards of

ONE THOUSAND SEPARATE TRACTS.

BY EDWARD O'REILLY, ESQ.

Author of the Irish-English Dictionary and Grammar, &c. &c. &c. and Assistant Secretary to the Society.

Dublin:

PRINTED, FOR THE SOCIETY,

BY A. O'NEIL, AT THE MINERVA PRINTING-OFFICE, CHANCERY-LANE.

1820.

LIST OF MEMBERS

OF THE

IBERNO - CELTIC SOCIETY.

Patron,

HIS EXCELLENCY EARL TALBOT.

President,

HIS GRACE THE DUKE OF LEINSTER.

VICE PRESIDENTS,

Most Noble the MARQUIS of SLIGO,
Most Noble the Marquis of THOMOND,
Right Honorable EARL O'NEILL,

Right Honorable LORD VISCOUNT
FRANKFORT DE MONTMORENCY,
Right Hon. LORD VISCOUNT MONK.

Right Hon. Earl of Rosse.
Right Hon. Earl Mount Charles.
Right Hon. Lord Viscount De Vesci.
Right Hon. Lord Carbery.
Right Hon. Lord Castlecoote
Right Hon. Lord Clonbrock.
Right Hon. Lord Garvagh.
Right Hon. John Radcliff, Judge of the Prerogative.
Hon. James Hewitt.
Hon. Windham Quinn, M. P.
Sir Robert Langrishe, Bart.
Sir Neale O'Donnell, Bart.
Sir Capel Molyneux, Bart.
Sir Henry Meredyth, Bart.
Sir William Burdett, Bart.
Sir John Bourke, Bart.
Sir William Betham, Secretary & Treasurer.
Right Rev. Doctor John Murphy, R. C. Bishop of Cork.
Right Rev. Doctor Mac Nicholas, R. C. Bishop of Achonry.
General Cuppage
Henry Adair, Esq.
William Ball, Esq.
Edward James Baynes, Esq.
Francis Beatty, Esq.
Wrixon Becher, Esq. M. P.
Ezekiel Davis Boyde, Esq.
Rev. Dr. Bartholomew Crotty, President of the Royal College, Maynooth.

Eccles Cuthbert, Esq.
Rev. Morgan D'Arcy, D. D.
John D'Alton, Esq.
Richard Downes, Esq.
William Fletcher, Esq.
John Fowler, Esq.
Sheffield Grace, Esq.
Rev. Mr. Goff.
William Gorman, Esq.
Robert Gunne, Esq.
James Hardiman, Esq.
Mathew Weld Hartstonge, Esq.
Rev. William Liddiard, Chaplain to His Excellency the Lord Lieutenant.
Samuel Litton. Esq. M. D.
Rev. M. P. Kinsela.
William Monck Mason, Esq.
Hen. J. Monck Mason, Esq. L.L.D. M.R.I.A.
Richard Malone, Esq. Palace Park.
Henry M'Dougall, Esq.
John M'Namara, Esq.
William Shaw Mason, Esq.
Randal M'Donell, Esq.
James M'Donell, Esq. M. D. Belfast.
Rev. Marcus Monck.
J. H. North, Esq.
Rev. Paul O'Brien, Professor of the Irish Language, Royal College of Maynooth.
Mathew O'Conor, Esq.
Colonel O'Kelly.
Rev. Cornelius O'Mullan.

LIST OF MEMBERS.

Neale John O'Neill, Esq.
Rev. Mr. O'Nolan.
Edward O'Reilly, Esq. Compiler of the Irish-
    English Dictionary, Assistant Secretary.
Andrew O'Reilly, Esq.
Miles John O'Reilly, Esq.
Brian O'Reilly, Esq.
William Parsons, Esq.
George Petrie, Esq.
Rev. William Phelan, F. T. C. D.
Richard Power, Esq.
Henry T. Redmond, Esq.
James Miles Reilly, Esq.
James Roche, Esq. Cork.

Rev. Francis Sadlier, D. D. F. T. C. D.
Lieut. Colonel Merrick Shaw.
Rev. Joseph Singer, M. A. F. T. C, D.
Captain John Skinner, R. N.
Rev. Charles Stronge.
Richard Wogan Talbot, Esq. M. P.
Walter Thom, Esq.
Henry Townsend, Esq.
Rev. George Vesey, D. D. Chaplain to His
    R. H. the Duke of Kent.
Thomas Wallace, Esq.
Rev. Robert Walsh, D. D.
Edward Walsh, Esq.
Mathew West, Esq.

Acting Committee for the Year, ending 17th March, 1820.

1 John D'Alton, Esq.
2 General Cuppage.
3 William Fletcher, Esq.
4 John Fowler, Esq.
5 Sheffield Grace, Esq.
6 Rev. Mr. Goff.
7 James Hardiman, Esq.
8 Mathew Weld Hartstonge, Esq.
9 John M'Namara, Esq.
10 William Monck Mason, Esq.
11 Henry Monck Mason, Esq.

12 Rev. William Liddiard.
13 Rev. M. P. Kinsela.
14 Rev. Paul O'Brien.
15 Rev. Cornelius O'Mullan.
16 Neale John O'Neill, Esq.
17 Rev. F. Sadlier, F. T. C. D.
18 Rev. Joseph Singer, F. T. C. D.
19 Rev. C. Stronge.
20 Rev. Robert Walsh.
21 Edward Walsh, Esq.

To the above are to be added the President, Vice Presidents, Treasurer, Secretary, and Assistant Secretary, Members of the Committee, in virtue of their respective offices.

RULES AND REGULATIONS,

&c. &c.

I.

THE Society shall consist of an unlimited number of Members, ordinary and corresponding, governed by a President and six Vice Presidents.

II.

Persons desirous to become Members of the Society, shall be proposed by a Member, either at a General Meeting or a Committee Meeting, and balloted for at the next General Meeting; but if proposed at a Committee Meeting, it must be at least one month before the General Meeting. The balloting to commence exactly at one o'clock, or as soon after as fourteen Members (including the President, or Chairman) shall have assembled, and one black bean in every seven shall reject the proposed Candidate. The ballot to continue one full hour.

III.

Members, upon their admission, shall pay one Guinea as entrance subscription, and thirty Shillings per annum towards the general fund of the Society.

IV.

The Society may elect honorary or correspondent Members, by ballot, in the same manner as ordinary Members are to be balloted for. The honorary or corresponding Members may attend all meetings, offer opinions, and make communications, but have no privilege of voting, or of being elected to offices: they may, however, be admitted as ordinary Members, without any further ballot, upon their paying similar contributions with those paid by the ordinary class.

V.

The payment of ten Guineas at one time, shall constitute a Member for life, free of any annual subscriptions.

VI.

The ordinary business of the Society shall be conducted by a Committee, to be annually chosen, consisting of twenty-one Members, besides the President, Vice Presidents, Treasurer, Secretary and Assistant Secretary, Members of the Committee ex officio ; three Members of the Committee shall be a quorum. The President or Chairman of the Committee to have no vote, on any question, except in case of equality of votes. All Members of the Society, though not of the Committee, shall have the privilege to attend at Committee meetings, but are to have no vote.

VII.

The Committee shall meet on the first and third Tuesdays of every month, and occasionally as business may require, on intimation of the President or Secretary of the nature of the business to be laid before them, at least two days before the intended meeting ; and no business but that which shall be so intimated, shall be decided on at that meeting. They shall keep a record of their Proceedings, to be laid before the General Meeting, for their consideration and approbation ; and shall have a power to call extraordinary General Meetings, whenever occasion shall require, of which previous intimation shall be made, by notices to that effect, served on the Members at least one week before the meeting.

VIII.

The Society shall hold four annual meetings ; one on the 17th of March, except it shall happen on Sunday, and in that case, on the Monday following ; the second on the first Tuesday in June ; the third on the first Tuesday in September ; and the fourth on the first Tuesday in December. Besides these stated meetings, the Society shall hold extraordinary meetings as often as they shall be called thereto by a vote of the Committee.

IX.

Every future election of Officers to this Society shall be held at the March meetings ; the President and Vice Presidents to serve for life ; the Treasurer, Secretary, Sub-Secretary, and Committee shall fill their respective offices for one year. Before March meeting 1819, and every future March meeting, each Member shall pay in his annual contribution of thirty Shillings, or otherwise forfeit his place in the Society.

X.

The election of Officers shall be conducted in the following manner, viz.—Each Member shall be furnished with a slip of paper, on which he shall write the name or names of the persons whom he may judge proper to fill the respective offices of the Society; and when all the Members present have written on their slips, they shall be handed to the Chairman, who shall read them with an audible voice, and the Secretary shall take an account of them in writing, and he or they whose name or names shall appear on the greater number of slips, shall be considered as duly elected to fill such office or offices.

XI.

No religious or political debates whatsoever shall be permitted at any of the meetings of the Society; such subjects being foreign to the objects of the Institution.

XII.

The subscriptions shall be paid to, and the funds deposited in, the hands of the Treasurer, subject to the disposal of the Committee, as hereafter specified. His accounts shall be annually audited by the Committee, at their meeting immediately preceding the General Meeting in March; at which they shall be regularly produced, and also at every meeting of the Committee, for the inspection of Members.

XIII.

All accounts furnished to the Society shall be examined by the Committee; and if found correct, the Chairman shall certify the same, by affixing his initials, and give an order on the Treasurer for payment.

XIV.

Besides the occasional expenditure to be disbursed by the Treasurer, the Committee shall, at any one meeting, have power to order the application of a sum, not exceeding ten Pounds sterling, for the purchase of Books or Manuscripts, or for any of the general objects of the Society. The order on the Treasurer for payment of such money, shall express the purport of such application, and shall be signed by the Chairman of the Committee. For the disposal of any greater sum, the authority of a General Meeting shall be obtained.

XV.

Whatever balance of the annual funds of the Society, exceeding fifty Pounds, shall remain unexpended, together with any donation or bequest made to the Society, shall be formed into a capital, and laid out, on proper security, with the approbation of the Committee. No part of such capital to be afterwards applied, but by authority of a General Meeting; previously to which, intimation shall be always made at two meetings of the Committee.

XVI.

The Secretary shall have custody of the Records, Papers, and Books of the Society, to which all the Members shall have access, at any reasonable time. And all letters and communications for the Society shall be directed to him, and he shall lay the same before the Committee forthwith.

XVII.

The Society shall have it in their power to alter old, and enact new Regulations, at any General Meeting, provided that such intended Regulation shall be notified at a meeting of the Committee, previously to the General Meeting at which such is proposed to be made.

PREFACE.

———•••◦◦◦◦⟨◈⟩◦◦◦•••———

AMONGST the various modes adopted by most modern nations for the advancement of Science, and the investigation of natural and civil History, that of establishing literary Societies seems to be as effectual as it is prevalent. There are few nations in Europe that have not associations to promote Arts and Sciences; to encourage philosophical research; to illustrate local antiquities, and perpetuate national History. Ireland, also, has had her Societies, some of whom laboured, by their publications, to rescue from oblivion and decay, some of the vast quantities of her ancient Annals, her Laws, her Poetry, and her Music.

In the year 1740 a number of literary Gentlemen associated under the name of the Physico-Historical Society, under whose patronage were published the Histories of Cork, Kerry, and Waterford. In the year 1752, another Society was formed in Dublin, whose views were confined to the publication of tracts in the Irish language. It was known by the appellation of Cóimċionnal Ʒaoiḋilʒe, or Irish Society, but does not appear to have ever published. About this time, indeed, the first edition of O'Connor's " Dissertations on the History of Ireland" appeared, but we have no cause to infer that the work was ever encouraged by either of those Societies. The publication, however, attracted a good deal of notice, and drew from the celebrated Doctor Johnson a letter to the author, on the subject of Irish literature, from which the following extract may not be considered impertinent.—" I have long wished that the Irish literature were cultivated. Ireland is known by tradition to have been the seat of piety and learning; and surely it would be very acceptable to those who are curious either in the original of nations, or the affinities of languages, to be further informed of the revolutions of a people so ancient, and once so illustrious. I hope you will continue to cultivate this kind of learning which has lain so long neglected, and which, if it be suffered to remain in oblivion for another century, may perhaps never be retrieved." In the year 1777, Doctor Campbell, author of " Strictures on the Ecclesiastical and Literary History of Ireland," was the bearer of another letter from Johnson to Mr. O'Connor, from which, as it has been since wilfully misquoted by Campbell, it becomes necessary to give the following extract, as it appears in the Life of Johnson, by Boswell, who may be presumed to have fairly given the letter as it was written by its illustrious author.—" What the Irish language is in itself, and to what languages it has affinity, are very interesting questions which every man wishes to see resolved, that has any philological or historical curiosity. Doctor Leland begins his History too late. The ages which deserve an exact inquiry, are those times, *for such times there were*, when Ireland was the School of the West, the quiet habitation of sanctity and literature. If you could give a history, though imperfect, of the Irish nation, from its conversion to Christianity, to the invasion from England, you would amplify knowledge with new views and new objects. Set about it, therefore, if you can ; do what you can easily do without anxious exactness. Lay the foundation, and leave the superstructure to posterity."

After the extinction of the Irish Society, nothing appears to have been done towards the publication of our History or Antiquities by any collective body, until about the year 1782 or 1783, when some essays having appeared under the name of " Collectanea de Rebus Hibernicis," induced the highly-talented authors to co-operate and found the Society of Antiquaries. The principal person in the formation of this Society, and the publication of those tracts, was the late General Vallancey ; and the specimens he gave of some of our ancient laws excited much curiosity, and a desire for further information on so interesting a subject. Amongst those who were particularly charmed with its novelty and importance, was the late celebrated Edmund Burke. That Gentleman felt the matter of such vast moment to literature, that he prevailed on Sir John

Seabright to restore to this country many of her ancient records that had fallen into his hands, and he accordingly presented to the library of Trinity College, Dublin, an invaluable treasure of Irish MSS. that had been collected from various parts of Ireland about the beginning of the last century, by the learned and indefatigable antiquary Edward Lhuyd, author of the Archæologia.

What were the views of Mr. Burke in this interference, and what his expectations from the University and the Society of Antiquaries, will best appear from his letter of 15th August, 1783, addressed to General Vallancey. In this he says, " I shall tell you what a judicious antiquary, about twenty years ago, told me concerning the Chronicles in verse or prose, upon which the Irish histories, and the discussions of antiquaries are founded, that he wondered that the learned of Ireland had never printed the originals of these pieces, with literal translations into Latin or English, by which they might become proper subjects of criticism, and by comparison with each other, as well as by an examination of the interior relations of each piece within itself, they might serve to shew how much ought to be retained, and how much rejected. They might also serve to contrast or confirm the histories which affect to be extracted from them, such as O'Flaherty's and Keating's. All the histories of the middle ages, which have been found in other countries, have been printed. The English have, I think, the best histories of that period. I do not see why the Psalter of Cashel should not be printed, as well as Robert of Gloster. If I were to give my opinion to the Society of Antiquaries, I should propose that they should be printed in two columns, one Irish and the other Latin, like the Saxon Chronicle, which is a very valuable monument, and above all things, that the translation should be exact and literal. It was in the hope that some such thing should be done, that I originally prevailed on Sir John Seabright to let me have his MSS. and that I sent them by Doctor Leland to Dublin. You have infinite merit in the taste you have given of them in several of your collections. But these extracts only increase the curiosity and the just demand of the public for some entire pieces. Until something of this kind is done, that ancient period of Irish history, which precedes official records, cannot be said to stand upon any proper authority. A work of this kind, pursued by the University and the Society of Antiquaries, under your inspection, would do honour to the nation."

Dean Swift, also, (though fond of abusing the Irish) in a letter to the Earl of Oxford, gives much praise to our ancestors for the care with which they preserved the "memory of times and persons" so much greater than is used "in this age of learning, as we are pleased to call it;" and in a letter to the Duke of Chandos, dated 31st August, 1734, he requests that nobleman to restore to Ireland, by presenting to the library of Trinity College, Dublin, then newly erected, a large quantity of her ancient records, on paper and parchment, then in his Grace's possession, that had been formerly collected and carried off from this country by the Earl of Clarendon, during the time of his government here. The Duke, however, did not comply with the Dean's request, and the manuscripts still remain in an English library.

That the ancient Annals of Ireland are of vast importance and value to the Historian, is an opinion not confined to the natives of these islands. Several learned men on the Continent have felt and acknowledged their credibility and utility. The Journal des Sçavans for October 1764, has these words: " C'est un principe incontestable, que, sur l'histoire de chaque pays, les annales nationales, quand elles sont anciennes, authen-tiques, et reconnues pour telles par les etrangers, meritent plus de foi que les annales etrangeres."—" Plusieurs sçavans etrangers, reconnoissent que les Irlandois, ont des annales d'une antiquité très respectable, et d'une authenticité à toute epreuve." The author proceeds to quote upon this point, the authority of Stillingfleet and Innes, " qui ná jamais flatté les Irlandois."

However, neither the Society of Antiquaries nor the University have attempted or encouraged the publication of any of those pieces which Swift, Johnson, Burke, and others, thought of so much importance to literature, and to the credit of Ireland. Indeed very shortly after this period the Society of Antiquaries became extinct. From that institution, however, sprung up the Royal Irish Academy, which, notwithstanding that in the early volumes of its transactions, some little has been done for Irish Antiquities, as well as in the last volume, seems to have directed its principal attention to Science.

This neglect of Irish history and antiquities induced a few individuals, early in the year 1807, to form the Gaelic Society of Dublin. That Body, within a year after their formation, published a volume, containing some observations on the Irish language; Teige M'Daire's Instructions to a Prince, in the original language and character, accompanied by a literal translation into Latin, and an English translation in verse : and the tragic tale of the Children of Usnach, also in the original language and character, with a strictly literal translation into English.

Besides the volume now mentioned, the Gaelic Society has published nothing, as a Body, but individual Members have published works which furnish the means for a complete elucidation of the History, Laws, Manners, and Customs of the ancient Irish. The Reverend Doctors O'Brien and Neilson, the late Mr. Patrick Lynch, and the late Mr. Haliday, a youth of extraordinary talent and acquirements, members of that Society, have each published a Grammar of the Irish language, and Mr. Edward O'Reilly, who was also one of its members, has lately published an Irish-English Dictionary, consisting of upwards of fifty thousand words, collected from ancient and modern manuscripts, and from printed books.

Subsequent to the formation of the Gaelic Society, an association, under the name of the Archæological Society, was commenced in Dublin, for the same purposes as the former, but its exertions have as yet effected little.

Ungrateful and useless would be the task for us to inquire, why so little effectual has yet been done towards the preservation and elucidation of our national records and antiquities, whilst those of almost every other European nation have been sedulously attended to by their respective people. Yet we cannot but regret the fact, that our ancient Manuscripts, the monuments of our country's fame, still remain on the shelves of libraries, covered with the dust of ages, and disregarded by our natives.

The example of other nations should stimulate us to exertion. The Highland Societies of Edinburgh and London have done a vast deal for their nation. By them, and by their encouragement, several volumes have been published on Gaelic literature and antiquities; many of them are in the original language of their country, between which and our native tongue there is scarcely any difference, being only a provincial variation. Within a few years past the people of England have reprinted such of their old Chronicles as in any manner tended to throw a light upon the ancient state or history of their country; and while England and Scotland apply a suitable attention to the antiquities and ancient literature of their respective nations, shall it be said that Ireland alone in the empire, remains without an exertion of her sons to revive her ancient fame, and assert the justness of her claims as the nurse of Science, and the patron of Literature, to whom she afforded an hospitable asylum, when outcast and alienated from every other nation in Europe!

Prompted by all these considerations, a few Irish Gentlemen have formed themselves into an association, under the name of the Iberno-Celtic Society, for the national objects set forth in their Resolution of the 28th of January, 1818, in these words:

" Resolved, That the principal objects of this Society shall be the preservation of the venerable remains of Irish Literature, by collecting, transcribing, illustrating, and publishing the numerous fragments of the Laws, History, Topography, Poetry, and Music of ancient Ireland; the elucidation of the Language, Antiquities, Manners and Customs of the Irish people; and the encouragement of Works tending to the advancement of Irish Literature."

The list of the Members of this Association has lately been enlarged by the addition of some of the most illustrious and learned characters in the country. From such a community much is to be hoped; and much that impeded the progress of former Societies is happily removed from the course of this. No deficiency of members sufficiently skilled in our native language, is here felt; no want of the free and open means to study and attain a competent knowledge of it, longer dispirits. There are now published Grammars and a Dictionary, by the aid of which any gentleman may acquire a knowledge of one of the most ancient and most expressive languages in the world.

To the attainment of its end, the intention of the Iberno-Celtic Society is, to publish such works of merit in the Irish language, as are still preserved in ancient manuscripts, deposited in public libraries, or in the hands of individuals. Of these venerable remains of Irish learning many are of great merit, and all deserve to be rescued from oblivion, as they are fully illustrative of the history, genius, manners and customs of the Irish people. Some of these manuscripts are in the hand-writing of their respective authors. Others, the larger part we must admit, are only copies, but they are copies of considerable antiquity, and preserved in the compilations of writers of great celebrity, such as the authors of the Din Seanchas, the Psalter of Cashel, the Book of Leinster, the Book of Glendalough, the Ulster Book, the Munster Book, the Book of the Eoganachts, the Book of Meath, the Book of the Conallians, the Book of the Oirgiallans, the white Book, the Book of Leacan, the Book of Ballimote, the Book of Fermoy, the Book of Hua Conghabhala, the Book of Mac Partholan, the Book of Conquests, the Book of Cavan; &c. &c. &c. and in the Annals of Tigernach, of Senat Mac Magnus, of Inisfallen, of Boyle, of Conaght, of the four Masters, &c. &c. &c. and also in the Reim Rioghraidhe, and in the Registries of several ancient families, still preserved by their descendants.

That originals of most of our earliest Records should now be lost, may be easily accounted for, when we consider;

First, That, immediately after the Introduction of Christianity, most of the then existing books were burned, in order to destroy the vestiges of Pagan superstition contained in them. Several, however, were completely copied into the Psalter of Tara, and from it into the Psalters or Registries of the principal churches and religious houses in Ireland.

Secondly, That the Danish and Norwegian invaders, who infested and obtained a temporary power over our country in the ninth and tenth centuries, committed great devastation on our ancient Records. Barbarous and ignorant themselves, they took delight in the destruction of every thing connected with learning and science.

Thirdly, That ever since the invasion of the island by the Anglo Normans, under Henry the Second, the destruction or loss of the ancient historic monuments of the country has daily increased, partly from the policy of Princes; partly from the indifference of new settlers to the subjects recorded; and partly by removal of the natives to other lands.

After the reign of James I. of England, when numbers of the Irish chiefs and clergy were deprived of their ancient inheritance and obliged to fly for refuge to France, Spain, Germany, and Italy, they carried with them the records of their families and the archives of their churches and religious houses. Hence works, in the hand-writing of their respective authors, are not now numerous in Ireland; and it is rather a matter of wonder, that so many vestiges of our ancient celebrity still remain, than that there are not more original documents now to be found, in a country which, though acknowledged to have been the sanctuary of science, was subject to the depredations of barbarous invaders for a number of centuries.

But though many of the originals of our ancient books are dispersed through the libraries of other nations, we have still some amongst ourselves, besides numerous authentic copies, of great antiquity, treating of History, Law, Topography, Poetry, Music, Astronomy, Medicine, &c. of which the most common are those on History and Medicine.

The copies of our ancient Laws now extant are not numerous, though we are told by Archbishop Usher, that in his days the Irish had large volumes of their Laws in their own language; and so late as the beginning of the last century, copies of them were common in Ireland, as we are assured by Thady O'Rody, an excellent scholar, who, in the year 1699, shewed several volumes of those Laws to Sir Richard Cox, who had entertained an opinion that our law was arbitrary, and not fixed or written. However, though our Law-books are not now so numerous as formerly, enough still remains to show the manners and customs not only of the Irish people, but also much of those of the other Celtic nations: for Ireland never came within the pale of the Roman empire, nor was she ever subjugated by any of the hordes by whom that empire was overturned; she was not even invaded by any foreign nation for several ages before Christianity, nor until the ninth and tenth centuries, when, in common with France, England, and other countries, she was exposed to the predatory incursions of the Danes and Norwegians. But although these barbarians were able to establish themselves in other countries, and to make some considerable settlements on the coast of our own, their power here was neither of extent nor permanency sufficient to produce any material change in the manners of the people, or the laws of the country. The invasion of Ireland by Henry II. of England, and the partial dominion exercised over the island by his successors, had scarcely any influence on the people, or produced any change in the laws, until the reign of James I. The Irish chiefs, therefore, succeeded to their principalities, and governed their tribes according to the ancient laws enacted by their ancestors, in the early period of their monarchy ; and many of the Anglo-Normans who had obtained settlements amongst them, adopted the laws and manners of the inhabitants. Hence Ireland might furnish, what perhaps no other European nation is able to afford, a complete view of ancient Celtic legislation.

To ascertain the period at which each of our laws was enacted, is, perhaps, at the present moment impossible : both the language and the subject matter of these prove their great antiquity. Many of them were undoubtedly composed before the introduction of Christianity, and others immediately after, and certainly before the Danish invasion. That they were intended for the government of the entire kingdom, and not confined to particular districts, as is supposed by some ingenious writers, may be proved from the Law-books of the different Breithimhs, or Judges, still existing. Those written or preserved by the M'Clancys of Thomond, the O'Breslin's of Fermanagh, the O'Doran's of Leinster, and the M'Egans, who were the hereditary Judges of the O'Brien's of Ormond, the O'Reilly's of Breifne, and several other tribes, are in substance the same, and scarcely differ in any thing, except in the words of their respective glosses.

Having shewn the ends for which the Iberno-Celtic Society is associated, and the utility of laying before the Public some of the most valuable of our ancient Manuscripts, we proceed to exhibit a chronological account of Irish writers, and a descriptive catalogue of their works ; which shall be followed by another catalogue of works whose authors are not now known, but which are of equal value and importance to the Celtic scholar with those whose writers we are able to ascertain. From these works the Society, if encouraged by the Public, propose to publish a Selection of Annals, Laws, Poetry, &c. in the original Language, either accompanied by literal Translations or not, as their means may in future enable them to determine.

In the following account, the Libraries in which each book, tract, or poem is to be found, are pointed out; and the Society earnestly requests that any Gentleman having copies of these, or of any other pieces not here mentioned, will communicate the same to the Secretary, that the Celtic scholar may know where those Works may be consulted.

A

CHRONOLOGICAL ACCOUNT

OF

Irish Writers,

AND

Descriptive Catalogue of such of their Works as are still extant

IN

VERSE OR PROSE.

———————

By *EDWARD O'REILLY.*

Chronological Account,

&c. &c.

ANNO MUNDI 2935.

AMERGIN, son of Golamh, sirnamed *Mile Spainneach,* (the Spanish hero,) was brother to Heber, Heremon, and Ir, from whom the Milesian families of Ireland are descended. He accompanied his brothers, and the other Gathelian chiefs, in their emigration from Spain to Ireland, and was the poet of the colony. In the *Leabhar Gabhaltus,* or Book of Conquests, compiled in the fourteenth century, from much more ancient books, and in the book of the same name, composed by the O'Clerys, who were employed in the compilation of THE ANNALS OF THE FOUR MASTERS, at the commencement of the seventeenth century, are preserved three poems, said to be written by Amergin; the first of these, consisting of only two *ranns,* or eight verses, begins " Fιη τοραċτα τηηõe," and contains the decision of Amergin upon the proposal of the *Tuatha-de-Danan,* that the *Milesians* should retire from the shores of Ireland ; the second consists of twenty verses, beginning " Ꝺlιu ιaċ η'Ɛηɛнõ." This is a particular kind of Irish versification, called CONACLON, in which the last word of every verse is the same as the first word in every succeeding verse. The third poem consists of six *ranns,* or twenty-four verses, beginning " Ꝺιm ɜoeċ ι mτηη," said to have been composed by Amergin, upon his landing at Inver Colpa, near Drogheda.

Amongst the Seabright collection of Irish manuscripts, in the library of Trinity College, Dublin, class H. 54, folio 53, is preserved a small tract on the qualifications of a Bard, beginning " Ꝺɩocoɩηe coɩη ɜoɩηɩaτh ɜoη ηoнɩη õιa õam a õηlιb õemηɩb." In the third line the author informs his readers, that he is "Amergin Glungel, of hoary head and gray beard."— " Oη me Ꝺɩmaηɜeη ɜɩηнɜel, ɜaɩη ɜɩaη, ɜηɛlιaċ."

These compositions are written in the Bearla Feini, and accompanied with an interlined gloss, without which they would be unintelligible to modern Irish scholars. The gloss itself requires much study to understand it perfectly, as the language is obsolete, and must in many places be read from bottom to top.

That these poems were really the productions of Amergin, may be very reasonably doubted. Tarah, the chief residence of our ancient monarchs, is particularly mentioned in the second poem; and therefore, unless we suppose this author to have possessed the spirit of prophecy, as well as the inspirations of poetry, it could not have been written by him; as our ancient historians agree that the palace of Tarah was not erected, nor the name imposed on the hill on which it was built, until after the establishment of the Milesian dynasty. They are, however, of the highest antiquity, and their language and peculiar versification, independent of any other merits they may possess, claims for them the attention of the antiquary, and entitles them to preservation.

II. Cotemporary with Amergin, was LUGHAIDH, son of Ith, and nephew of Golamh, or Milesius.

In the books of Conquests or Invasions, already mentioned, is preserved a poem, said to be composed extempore by Lughaidh, upon the death of his wife *Fail*, the daughter of Milesius. This poem begins "Sᵹḋem ꞅunḋ ꝼoꞃ ꞅan ꞇꞃaċꞇ," "*Here we sat on the beach*," and is given entire at the word Ainbṫeaċ, in O'Reilly's Irish-English Dictionary lately published. The language of this poem does not appear to be so old as those attributed to Amergin, but it is undoubtedly of very great antiquity. It is valuable, as it shows in a strong light an amiable picture of female modesty, and proves how highly that virtue was estimated by the ancient Irish.

A. M. 3236.

III. OLLAMH FODHLA, monarch and lawgiver of Ireland, established the *Feis* of Tarah, or triennial assembly of the states of Ireland, as is asserted by *Ferceirtne file*, a famous poet, who flourished about the time of our Saviour's incarnation. The laws promulgated by this prince, are quoted in Cormac's Glossary, written into the ninth century; but we are not able to say where copies of them are now to be found; perhaps some fragments of them may still exist in the large collections of Irish laws preserved in the library of Trinity College.

A. M. 3596.

IV. CIMBAETH, monarch of Ireland, wrote some laws, fragments of which are to be found in ancient vellum MSS. in the library of Trinity College, Dublin. , Class H. 53 and 54.

A. M. 3619.

V. ROIGNE Rosgadhach (Royné the Poetic) son of Ugoine mór, flourished in the time that his brother MAL was monarch of Ireland.

In the book of Invasions we find a poem ascribed to this author, giving an account of the peregrinations of the Gathelians, and the names of their chiefs, from their departure from Egypt, until their arrival in Spain, and afterwards in Ireland; with an account of the partition of that country amongst the sons of Milesius. The poem begins "Ɑ mec ɑın Ugɑıne." "*Oh praise-worthy son of Hugony,*" and contains an answer to some enquiries made by his brother *Mal,* upon the origin of the Irish people.

If every other proof of the antiquity of this piece were wanting, the language alone would be sufficient to evince its early composition. In fact, it would be nearly unintelligible to Irish readers of the present day, if it were not for the interlined *gloss* that accompanies the text, and even the Gloss is so obsolete, that none but those who have made Irish MSS. a particular study, are able to interpret it. Some laws, said to be written by this prince, are still to be found in some of our old books. A copy of the poem is in the collection of manuscripts in possession of the Assistant Secretary to this Society.

A. M. 3900.

VI. EOCHAIDH, son of Luchtna, King of Munster, flourished at this time, and wrote some laws, fragments only of which are now to be found.

A. M. 3902.

VII. SEAN, son of Agaidh, flourished at this time. He wrote a code of laws called *Fonn Seanchas mor.* A complete copy of a law tract bearing this title is to be found in the Seabright collection of Irish MSS. in the Library of Trinity College, Dublin, H. 53, pag. 13. and another in H. 54. pag. 358.

A. M. 3940.

VIII. CONGAL, son and poet to Eochaidh Feidhlioch, Monarch of Ireland, flourished at this period. He wrote some laws quoted in our Fenian Institutes, and a poem of thirty-four verses, beginning " ᴄol ᴅaṁ aiᵹió ᴇꞃca ᵹniṁ," upon the deaths of the seven MAINES, celebrated in the historic tale of *Tain bo Cuailgne.* Copies of this poem are to be found in the collections of different Members of the *Iberno-Celtic* Society.

One copy, written on vellum, A. D. 1430, by Adam O'Cianan, a famous scribe, is in possession of the Assistant Secretary.

A. M. 3950.

ix. Adhna, chief Poet of Ireland, flourished in the early part of the reign of Conor Mac Nessa over the province of Ulster. Some fragments of laws, said to be the joint production of him and others, are still in existence in the library of Trinity College, Dublin.——He was the father of Neide, who maintained the celebrated contest with Ferceirtne the poet, for the Ollamh's (Professors) Chair of Ireland.

x. At the same time with Adhna, flourished Athairne, of Binn Edair, (Howth) who, under the general proscription of the poets, in the reign of the monarch Conaire the first, fled with the rest of the bards of Ireland into Ulster, where they received shelter and protection from Conor Mac Nessa, king of that province, and the Mæcenas of Ireland. Here Athairne, Forchern, Ferceirtne and Neide, compiled a code of laws, which, in common with the institutes of other *Reachtaires*, (lawgivers,) are called by the general name of *Breithe Neimhidh*, or laws of the nobles, improperly translated by O'Flaherty, O'Connor, and others, " *Celestial Judgments.*"

xi. At this time also flourished Forchern, the poet, who, O'Flaherty, the venerable Charles O'Connor, Columbanus, and others, say wrote the *Uraicepht na n Eigeas,* or primer of the learned. But this cannot be true, unless we suppose that Forchern and Ferceirtne are the same person. For in the account prefixed to the oldest copies (and indeed to all the copies that we have seen) of this work, it is ascribed to Ferceirtne; thus " Libop Fepcéiptne punda. Iocc dó, Eman Maca; áimpip dó áimpip Conco-baip mic Nerra; Peppa dó Feipcéptne File; atucṅd, dan, do bpeiṫ aero paiñ Fop Fer," " the Book of Ferceirtne here. Its place, Emania of Macha, (now Ardmagh); its time, the time of Conor, son of Nessa; its person,

Ferceirtne the poet; its being done, moreover, to bring ignorant people to knowledge."

XII. FERCEIRTNE *file,* (the poet,) upon the death of Adhna, the chief Bard of Ireland, was appointed to the vacant professor's chair by Ollioll and Meidhbhe, king and queen of Conaght. We have seen above, that he was the author of the *Uraicept,* or *Uraicecht.*

In the Seabright Manuscripts in the Library of Trinity College, class H. 54. fol. 49. is preserved Ferceirtne's eulogium of Curaidh, son of Daire, or " ᴀⅼⅿⱤⱥ ConⱤoı," beginning Nı hⱥⱒⱥ ⱒoⅿⱥⱀⅿᵹⱀ," and in the same book, at folio 152, is a law tract, attributed to the same author.

In the Book of Invasions, contained in the Book of Leacan, and in the Book of Invasions compiled by the O'Clerys, in possession of the Assistant Secretary, is preserved a poem, consisting of thirty-two verses, written by this author. It begins " Ollaⅿ ꝼoⱒlⱥ, ꝼeoⱍⱥıⱤ ᵹⱥl," " Ollamh learned, a fighter valiant," and accounts for the establishment of the Feis of Tarah, the erection of the *Muir Ollamhain,* or College of Professors, by Ollamh Fodhla, and gives the names of six monarchs of his race, who succeeded him without the intervention of a prince of any other family; a thing very uncommon in those days. It also accounts for the origin of the names of Munster, Leinster, Ulster, &c. There is a copy of the Uraicept (or Uraicecht, as some copies have it) in the Book of Ballymote, in the library of the Royal Irish Academy, written about the year 1390; another in the library of Trinity College; a third, in a large and very valuable vellum book, the property of Sir William Betham; and a fourth in the collection of MSS. belonging to the Assistant Secretary of this Society.

XIII. NEIDE, the son of Adhna, though younger than Ferceirtne, Forchern and Athairne, was their cotemporary. He was in *Alba* (Scotland) at the time of his father's death, and hearing of that event, and that Ferceirtne had been appointed to the Ollamh's chair, he determined upon returning to his native country, and asserting his right to the professorship. Upon his arrival in Ireland, he instantly proceeded to Emania, and, Ferceirtne being absent, seized on the *Tuidhean* or Ollamh's robe, and took possession of the chair. Ferceirtne, hearing of this incident, instantly returned to Emania, and meeting with Neide, a dispute for the professorship was carried on between the rival bards, upon the qualifications necessary for an Ollamh. This dispute is handed down to us, under the title of " Ꞁᵹᴀllᴀ́ṁ ᴀ́ṅ ᴅᴀ ſᵳᴀⱱ," " Dialogue of the two Sages." Two very ancient copies of this tract are in the Library of Trinity College, and a correct transcript on paper is in the collection of John Mac Namara, of Sandymount, Esq. a member of this Society, and another in the collection of the Assistant Secretary.

The language of this tract is the *Bearla Feni*, or Fenian dialect of the Irish, and appears to be of the period to which it is ascribed. The account of the work which precedes it, is mixed with fable, but it is still valuable, and the publication of it would, probably, prove a fact, more to the literary credit of ancient Alba, than all that the Highland Society have been able to produce on the subject of the poems of OISIN, or *Ossian*, as he is called by English writers.

A. M. 3982.

XIV. At this period flourished LUGHAR, the poet of Olioll and Meidhbh, king and queen of Conaught. He wrote a poem of 156 verses on the descendants of Fergus, son of Roigh, beginning " Clᴀɴᴅ ſhᴇᵳᵹuſᴀ clᴀɴɴ óſ cᴀ́ċ," " The family of Fergus, a tribe superior to all." The poet informs us, in the last rann but one of his poem, who he is, and for what purpose he composed his verses. His words are

" Iſ me Luᵹᴀᵳ ſıle ſᴇɩᵹ. Oᵳᴀoı Meıⱱⱱe ıſ Oılıll ſᴇɩl,
Do ċum ɴᴀ ᵳᴀɩ̃ɴſ co beċⱱ, ᴅ'ſᵳ̃ɩl Roɩᵹ ᴀ ccᵳuᴀ́ċᴀɩɴ Coɴᴀ́ċᴛ."

" I am Lughar, an acute poet, Druid of Meidhbh and generous Olioll; I made these *ranns* correctly, for the blood of Roigh in Crochan Conacht."

A copy of this poem is in possession of the Assistant Secretary.

A. D. 90.

xv. MORAN, Chief Judge to Feradhach Fionnfachtnach, Monarch of Ireland, wrote some laws which are now only known by quotations from them, in the works of some more modern writers. His testamentary precepts to his King Feradhach, are preserved in very ancient manuscripts. They begin " Aսpae ծօ comla a mó Nepe nuall ȝnaíծ. Nótaíծ buaíծ " nȝaɩpe. Ƨᵴ ɩn ᴄeᴄ ap a pollmaɩȝᴄep papac; pop bep pɩp pɪ̃naծ, bpanaɩծ mo " bpēᴄa no mo bpɪaᴄpa pe mbáp." " Arise, proceed, my Nere of noble " deeds. Observe this brief address. Short is the way in which the wise " are directed. Bear hence these words of truth, let my dying words " be perpetuated."

This tract is valuable, as it shews the opinions of the ancient Irish upon the qualifications necessary for a just and good prince. The language is nearly the same as that of the laws, and it may be presumed is really of the period assigned to it.

A fine copy of this tract, accompanied with an interlined gloss, is in the manuscript collection belonging to the Assistant Secretary of this Society.

A. D. 95.

xvi. FERADACH *fionfachtnach*, Monarch of Ireland, promulgated those laws which obtained for him the glorious title *Fionfachtnach, i. e.* Fair and Just.

A. D. 177.

xvii. MODAN, son of Tulban, lived in the reign of Conn of the Hundred Battles. He wrote a book for the unlearned, called Ⴟeɩll bpeᴄa, or Just decision.

xviii. Cotemporary with Modan was CIOTHRUADH the poet. He was the messenger sent by Conn of the Hundred Battles to Mac Neid, with proposals for peace, and upon this occasion composed his poem beginning " ᴀ́ meic ᴅeᴀnᴀiᴅ ꝼiᴄ ꝛe ᴍᴀc Ꝛeiᴅ," " My son, make peace with Mac Neid." This poem is given in the *Leabhar Muimhneach*, or Munster Book, a copy of which is in the collection of the Assistant Secretary.

A. D. 180.

xix. FINGIN, son of Luchta, lived in the time that Conn of the Hundred Battles governed Ireland. He wrote a poem, beginning " ᴮuᴀiᴅ Cꝛ̄nᴅ ꝛiᵹ ꝛoiᴅ ꝛo ᵹᴀiᴅe," upon the five famous roads, said to be made to Tarah, on the night of Conn's birth. This poem is given in the *Dinn Seanchas*, in the book of Leacan, folio 239, column 3, as authority for the origin of the name of *Slighe Dala*, or Dala's way.

A. D. 200.

xx. OLIOLL OLUM, king of Munster, was son-in-law of Conn of the Hundred Battles. He died, according to the " Four Masters," in the year 234. But the annals of Inisfallen represent him as living in the year 254. O'Flaherty differs from both these authorities, and says he died A. D. 237. It is said he was the author of some poems, and particularly one beginning " ᴀ́ mᴀcᴀ́in nᴀ nᴀ ci ciᴀ ꝼo," is ascribed to him. It is addressed to his grandson Fiach, whose father and five other sons of Olioll were killed at the battle of Mucruimhe, A. D. 195. But although this composition is certainly ancient, there are some allusions in it that would lead one to think it was not the work of a Pagan author. The poem beginning " ᴮeiꝛ mo ꝛciᴀᴄ," is also attributed to this prince.

XXI. About the same period in which Olioll lived, flourished FACHTNA, son of Sencha, a compiler of laws, sometimes referred to by later writers upon that subject.

A. D. 250.

XXII. CORMAC, son of Art, monarch of Ireland, lived at this period. He caused the Psalter of Tarah to be compiled, as the depository of the records of the nation. This was long considered as lost, but is now said, perhaps not truly, to be extant in the British Museum. He wrote some laws, an imperfect copy of which is to be found in the Seabright collection in the library of Trinity College. One tract, beginning "Cɩᵧ lɩᵧ ꝼoɜla eꞇɜɪö," treats of the privileges and punishments of different ranks of persons, and draws a line of distinction between undesigned injuries, such as those suffered by unavoidable accident, and those happening by neglect. The commentator on this law, makes some observations on the number *four*, and assigns reasons why that number should be preferred to others. Cormac also wrote instructions for his son Cairbre Liffeachar, who succeeded him on the throne of Ireland. These instructions are called Ceaɜaᵧɜ ᵼɪoɜöa, or royal precepts. A copy of the precepts of Cormac is preserved in the book of Leacan, another in an ancient and very valuable vellum MS. the property of Sir William Betham, another copy or two may be found in the library of Trinity College, and others in the collections of different members of the Iberno-Celtic Society. The copy belonging to the Assistant Secretary begins "ᴀ ᵼa Cᵧⁿö, a Coᵼbmaɩc, ol Caɩᵼbᵼe, cɪo ɪᵧ öeaꞇ öo Rɪ? Nɪn. Ol Coᵼmac. Iᵧ öeꞇ öo aɩⁿmⁿe cɩⁿ öebaɪö; ꝼoᵧöaö cɩⁿ ꝼeᵼɜ; ᵧo-aɜallma ceⁿ moᵼöaꞇ; öeɪꞇɪöe ᵧeⁿcuᵧa; ꝼⁿɪꞇꝼola ꝼⁿa; ꝼɪⁿ coⁿꝼⁿɪllɪoöh; ꞇᵼocaɪᵼe caⁿölᵾꞇaɪɜeö; ᵧɪꞇ öo ꞇᵾaꞇꞇaɪö; ᵼaꞇa ecᵧaⁿla; bᵼeꞇa ꝼɪⁿa; ɜeɪll ɪⁿɜlaᵧaɪö; ᵧloɜaɪö ꝼⁿa öeꞇbeᵼe; ꞇᵼoᵧcaö ꝼoᵼ coɪɜcᵼɪoꞇaɪö; moᵼaö ɜaꞇ ⁿeɪⁿe; aɪⁿmɪöe ꝼɪle; aöᵼaö öe mᵹ," ꞇc. "O descendant of Conn! O Cormac, said Cairbre, what is good for a king? That is plain, said Cormac. It is good for him to have patience without debate; firmness without anger; easy address without haughtiness; attention to the precepts of the elders, (laws); just covenants and agreements to strictly observe; mercy in the execution of the laws; peace with his districts; boundless in rewards; just in decisions; observant of his promises; hosting with justice; protecting his boundaries; honoring each noble; respecting the poets; adoring the great God," &c. This tract, occupying six folio pages, closely written, is carried on by way of dialogue between Cairbre and Cormac, in which the former asks the opinion of the latter upon different subjects, relative to government and general conduct, and Cormac, in his replies, gives precepts that would do honor to a Christian divine.

It may not, perhaps, be improper to observe that Cormac was the father-in-law of the famous FIONN MAC CUBHAIL, General of the *Fianna Eirionn,* and father of Oisin the poet; and, consequently, if the genuine poems of Oisin were extant, their language would be the same as that of Cormac's works, which are nearly unintelligible to the generality of Irish readers, and completely so to the vulgar. The language of those poems which the Highland Society have given to the world as the originals of Oisin, is the living language of the Highlanders of the present day, and if properly spelled and read by an Irish scholar, would be intelligible to the most illiterate peasant in Ireland. A comparison of the languages of Cormac and the *Scotch* Oisin, might probably go far towards ascertaining the period in which the Highland Bard was born.

XXIII. FITHIL, Chief Judge to Cormac, wrote some laws, fragments of which are to be found in the old vellum MSS. in the library of Trinity College.

A. D. 270.

XXIV. FERGUS *finbel,* son of Fionn Mac Cubhail, and brother of Oisin, flourished at this period; he wrote a poem, beginning " ϹɪႦɼɑ ɼᴇnᴣɑɼmnɑ ꝼoɼnɑɼ," which is given in full in the *Dinn Senchas,* as authority for the account there given of the origin of the name of the fountain of *Sengarmna.* See *Dinn Seanchas* under the year 550, preserved in the book of Leacan.

and in a valuable vellum manuscript in the library of Sir William Betham, and in the collection of the Assistant Secretary.

A. D. 280.

xxv. Flaithri, son of Fithil, wrote a poem, beginning " ᏅᎥᎪᏅ ᏟoꝛᏏᏏᎷᎪᎥᏟ ᏟᎥᎶᎬ ᏟᎬᎪᎷᎮᎪ," " The desire of Cormac, of the house of Tarah," upon the qualifications required by Cormac in different persons and things. Copies of this poem are common; a very ancient copy is in the collection of the Assistant Secretary.

A. D. 283.

xxvi. Fionn Mac Cubhail was killed this year, at Ath Breagh on the Boyne, not far from Tarah. He is said to have assisted in the formation of some laws, in the time of Cormac Mac Art. There are some prophecies ascribed to him, which are undoubtedly the forgeries of some Christian writer.

In the Dinn Seanchas contained in the book of Leacan, folio 231, col. 4, is given, as authority for the name of Dun Fornocht, a poem, attributed to Fionn. This poem consists of twenty-eight verses, beginning " Ꝼoꝛ-ᏁoᎬᏟ Ꮟo ᏏᏛᏁ Ꭺ OꝛᏛᎷ ᏏᎬᎪᏁ," " Fornocht to the fort of Druim Dean."

A. D. 284.

xxvii. Oisin, the son of Fionn Mac Cubhail, so much celebrated for his poetic genius, survived the battle of *Gabhra Aichle* near Tarah, fought this year, in which his son Oscar and the principal part of the Fenian heroes lost their lives. Many beautiful poems are extant that bear the name of Oisin, but there are no good reasons to suppose that they are the genuine compositions of that bard. If ever they were composed by Oisin, they have since suffered a wonderful change in their language, and have been interpolated, so as to make the poet and Saint Patrick cotemporaries, though the latter did not commence his apostolic labours in Ireland until the middle of the fifth century, when, by the course of nature, Oisin must have lain in his grave about one hundred and fifty years. There is a prophecy attributed to Oisin, preserved in an ancient vellum MS. the property of William Monck Mason, Esq. a member of this Society; but the first line of the poem being addressed to Oisin himself, shows it to be a forgery. The poem begins "A Oisīn, anraiḋ rīn," "O Oisin, melodious poet."

A. D. 405.

XXVIII. TORNA *Eigeas* (the learned) poet and instructor to our monarch Niall of the nine Hostages, flourished at this time. There are four poems, said to be the productions of this author, handed down to us. The first begins "Gaḃ mo ṫegasg a Néill náir," "Receive my precepts, noble Niall."—The second, "Dáil caṫa ittir Corc is Niall:" "The meeting of battle between Corc and Niall."—The third, "Mo ḋá daltáin nírsaid lisg," "My two foster-children were not indolent." In the first poem Torna gives instructions to his ward Niall; in the second, he appears as a mediator between Niall and Corc, king of Cashel, who is also represented as a ward of Torna's, and who had quarrelled with his foster-brother; and in the third the poet describes his manner of living alternately between these illustrious personages, and laments that he has survived them.

That these Poems were the productions of Torna Eigeas, there are some strong reasons to doubt. O'Flaherty, in Ogygia, gives presumptive proofs that they were not; and unless we admit that Christianity had made a great progress in Ireland before the mission of Saint Patrick, and that Torna was a Christian, as Colgan asserts, the poems carry internal evidence that they were not written by him. Some Irish antiquaries are of opinion that they were written by Torna O'Maolconaire, who lived several ages after Torna Eigeas. Be this as it may, the poems deserve preservation, as they give some interesting notices of the ancient History of Ireland, and were the cause of the literary contest carried on between the Bards of *Leath Chuinn* and *Leath Mhogha* (Conn's half and Mogha's half, or the north and south divisions of Ireland), for the honour and precedence of their respective Chiefs, in the reign of James the First of England.

The fourth poem ascribed to Torna, is upon the burial place of the pagan kings of Ireland, at Relig na Riogh, near Cruachan, in county Roscommon. It consists of twenty-eight verses, beginning " Ꝁꞇꞩ ꝼꞟꞇꝝꝗ ꞃꞟꝝ ꝼꞟꞥ ꝼꝗꞟꝇ," " There is under thee a king of beauteous Fail."

A copy of this poem is to be found in the Book of Leacan ; another copy is in the collection of the Assistant Secretary ; and another given in the History of Ireland, by Doctor Keating.

xxix. At this period also flourished the Son of Torna Eigeas. A small poem by this author is preserved in the Book of Invasions of the O'Clery's. It begins " Ꝁꝇꞟ ꞇꝗꞟ ꝺꞡ ꞇꝏꝋꝡꞟꞃ ꝺꝡꞟ ꝺꝗꞟꝇ," " When we went to the conflict," and is the lamentation of the poet for the death of his king, and foster-brother, Niall, who fell on the Banks of the Loire, in Armorica, A. D. 406.

A. D. 433.

xxx. Dubhthach *Mac ui Lughair,* was the Poet and Druid of Laoghaire, monarch of Ireland, at the commencement of Saint Patrick's mission, and was converted to Christianity by that Apostle. He was one of the famous Committee of Nine, who were appointed to revise the ancient Records of the Nation, and from them compiled that body of Records afterwards called the *Seanchas mor.* After his conversion, he applied his poetic talents to the praise of his Maker and Redeemer, and an elegant hymn of his on that subject is preserved in the *Felire Aenguis*, or Account of the Festivals of the Church, written by Angus *Ceile-De*, in the latter end of the eighth century; a copy of which work is inserted in the *Leabhar Breac*, or speckled Book of the Mac Egan's, in the Library of the Royal Irish Academy, and another more ancient copy is in the collection of the Assistant Secretary to this Society.

In the year 1797, the late General Vallancey published a paper, addressed to the President and Members of the Royal Irish Academy, in vindication of the ancient History of Ireland, in which he introduces what he calls a translation of the hymn above mentioned. But the learned General fell into a great error in supposing the contraction CR. in the original, to mean *Creas*, the Sun, and he therefore denominates this hymn, " A hymn to *Creas*, or the Sun." A knowledge of the original, and a little attention to its general contents, would be sufficient to convince that the hymn was addressed, not to the Sun, but to the Almighty God, who created the Sun and all that exists.

The Hymn begins——" Seŋ ɑ Cρiγꝛ mo lɑбρɑ,
" Ɑ comбiu ɼeꝛ ŋime!
" Ro mbeρꝛ mbrɑiö leρi,
" Ɑ ρi ꝣρeiŋe ꝣile!"

Literally——" Bless, O Christ, my words,
" Thou Godhead of the seven Heavens!
" Who gavest the gift of Religion,
" O King of the resplendent Sun!"

The word Comбiu, or Cóiṁбē, as it would be written in modern Irish, which I translate the Godhead, strictly means the *joint God*, or the united persons of the Blessed Trinity, and is, and always was, used in that sense, and in no other. This, and the mention of the seven Heavens, is sufficient to show that the author was a Christian, and who, therefore, would not deify a creature.

In the leɑбɑρ ŋɑ cceɑρꝛ, or Book of Rights, is preserved a very old poem ascribed to Dubhthach. It begins, " Ɲi óliꝣ cuꝣꝛ ŋo ceŋбɑiꝣeꝛ, ꝝ iŋ ꝼiliꝣ ꝼiρeolɑċ," " There is no right of visitation or headship (superiority) over the truly learned Poet." This poem is on the privileges of the Bardic Order. There is also preserved in the same Book another poem, of three hundred and ninety-two verses, ascribed to Dubhthach, beginning " Τεαιᵹ τεᷓ αmbi mαc Cᵹno:" " Tarah, house in which dwell the descendants of Conn."—This poem is on the privileges of Tarah, the rights and revenues of the Irish monarchs, and the subsidies paid by them to the provincial princes and heads of tribes. Some doubts may be reasonably entertained that this latter poem is the production of Dubhthach.

A. D. 468.

XXXI. Saint BEININ died on the ninth of November, in this year. He was the son of Sescnen, a man of great power in Meath, who entertained St. Patrick on his way to Tarah, and was, with all his family, converted by him. Benin received Holy orders from the hands of our apostle, and was also consecrated a bishop by him. In the year 455, St. Patrick placed Benin in the Archiepiscopal Chair of Armagh, which See he governed for ten years; but in 465 he resigned his bishoprick, and lived in retirement for three years, when he died A. D. 468.

The *Leabhar na Cceart*, or Book of Rights, is said to be written by St. Benin, but of this some doubts may be reasonably entertained. Its language, and some internal evidences in the composition, show it to be at least enlarged and altered in a period nearer to our own times. It is, however, a very ancient composition, and throws great light on the early history of our country. It gives an account of the revenues and rights of the monarchs of Ireland, payable by the provincial kings, and by the chiefs of inferior districts; the subsidies paid by the monarchs to the provincial kings and inferior chiefs for their services; and also an account of the revenues of each of the provincial kings, payable to them from the chiefs of districts, or tribes, in their respective provinces, and the subsidies paid by the provincial kings to those petty dynasts.—

These accounts are first delivered in prose, and the same are afterwards recorded in verse.

Ancient copies of this book, on vellum, are in the libraries of Trinity College and the Royal Irish Academy; and in the collections of Sir William Betham, and the Assistant Secretary of this Society.

The title prefixed to this work, runs thus: " Incipit do lebg na cceapt, " meopay do ċiraiḃ ⁊ do tuġaydalaiḃ Eṗeno, aṁail do opoaiġ beṅēn mac Seṛcṅēn ṛailmceolac Pattṛaicc, mg ao ṛett lebaṗ ġliṅoe oa loċa." " The " beginning of the Book of Rights, which relates to the revenues and " the subsidies of Ireland, as ordered by Benin, son of Sescnen, psalmist " of Patrick, as is related in the Book of Glendaloch."—The work itself begins with " Do oliġeadaiḃ ċṗt ċairil, acay oia ċíraiḃ, acay oia " ċanaiḃ, ino acay ayy, ano ro ryy, acay oo tṛgayoálaiḃ ṗi Muṁan acay " ṗiġte heṗeno ⁊ ċeana o ṗiġ Cairil in tan oa ṛallna ṛlaitiy ino," " Of " the just (lawful) rights of Cashel, and of its revenues and dues, in " and out, here follow; and of the subsidies of the kings of Munster, " and of the kings of Ireland from the king of Cashel, when he has " the government of the kingdom." Then follows, in prose, a list of the articles paid by the king of Cashel as subsidies to other princes, and of his rights of entertainment, &c. from them; this is followed by the same account, in a poem of 88 verses, beginning " Oliġeaö caċ ṗiġ o ṗi " Cairil," " The dues of each king from the king of Cashel." Then is given an account, in verse and prose, of the revenues of the king of Cashel, from the princes of Muscrey, Uaithne, Ara, Corcoluidheach, Corcoduibne, Ciarruidhe-Luachra, Corcobaiscin, and Borrin. The poem of this part is of 52 verses, and begins " Ceṗt Cairil cen cṗaö," " The " rights of Cashel without vexation." By this account it appears that the king of Cashel received annually from the above districts 2,300 oxen; five thousand five hundred cows; four thousand four hundred swine; one hundred vessels of strong drink; one thousand rams; two hundred wethers; and one hundred garments. A further account of the rights, &c. of the king of Cashel is then given, which says, that when he was not monarch of all Ireland, that division of it called *Leath Mogha* was under his controul, and contributed to his revenues. The tributes paid by the king of Leinster and the remainder of the states of Munster to the king of

Cashel, are then recited in prose, and supported by four poems. The first begins, " ᛒenén benꝺᴀċꞇ ꝼoꞃ ɯ ᵹen," " Benin, blessing on the birth." 2d. " Cıꞃ Cᴀıꝼıl ᴀn cᴜᴀlᴀбᴀꞃ," " The rents of Cashell have you heard." 3d. " Ꝕl eolᴀıᵹ ꟺᴜıɯᴀn moıꞃı," " O ye learned of great Munster." 4th. " Ꝕꞇᴀ " ꞃᴜnꝺ ꞃenċᴜꞃ ꝼꞃᵹc ꞃꞃeᴀċ," " Here is the history of unoppressive tax- " ation." Then follows an account of the royal mansions of Cashel, supported by a poem of 44 verses, beginning " Ꝕꞃᴀ ꝼeᴀꞃᴀꝺᵹ nᵹoıꞃ."

After Cashel follows an account of the rights, revenues, and privileges of the king of Conaught, and the subsidies paid by him to the petty chiefs of his province. This part begins, " Cıꞃᴀ ᴀcᴀꞃ ꞇᴜᴀꞃᴀꞃꝺᴀıl Con- " ꝺᴀċꞇ, .ı. ɯoꞃ ċıꞃ Conꝺᴀċꞇ ıꞇeꞃ бıᴀꞇᴀꝺ ᴀcᴀꞃ coıɯбeᴀċꞇ. Ceꝺᴀɯᴜꞃ co cꞃᴜᴀ- ċᴀn;" " The revenues and subsidies of Conaght, i. e. the great rents of " Conaght, both food (or entertainment) and attendance. First to Cru- " achan." An account is then given of the rights and privileges of the Conaght kings. The poem begins " Cıꞃꞇıᵹ ꞃe ꞃeᴀnċᴀꞃ nᴀċ ꞃᴀıll," " Hear ye a story not contemptible." This is followed by an account of the subsidies paid by the king of Conaght to the subordinate chiefs of his province. The poem here begins, " Cᴜᴀꞃᴀꞃꞇᴀl cꞃeıꝺ Conꝺᴀċꞇ," " The wages of the province of Conaght."

In this province, as in that of Munster, there were some tribes free from regal taxation, and who had other extraordinary privileges, above the other clanns of the province. In Conaght these were the Ibh Briuin; the Siol Muireadhaigh; the Ibh Fiachra; and the Cenel Aodha.

The account of Conaght is succeeded by that of *Ailigh (Oileach,* the residence of the northern Ibh Neill) or Ulster. The rights and dues of the king of Ailigh is first given, the poem of which contains fifty-six verses, and begins " Ceꞃꞇ ꞃı ᴀılıᵹ eꞇꞃıꝺ;" " The right of the king of Ailigh hear ye." Then follows the subsidies paid by that prince to his inferior chieftains; and also the subsidies received by him from the monarch of Ireland, whenever the king of Ailigh was not monarch himself. The metrical account of this consists of eighty verses, begin- ning, " Ꝕ ꝼıꞃ ꝺᴀ noᵹċᴀꞃ ꝼo ꞇꞃᴀıꝺ;" " Oh man, if thou goest north- " ward."

The rights and privileges of OIRGIALLA follow next in order. The verses are sixty-four in number, beginning " Eircig cain clrnebg," " Listen to the tribute you have heard." The subsidies received by the prince of Oirgialla, from the monarch of Ireland, and also the subsidies paid by him to his chiefs, are then set forth. The poem here consists of eighty verses, begins " In ceirc rea ro clornd Colla," " This inquiry on the descendants of Colla."

Next follows an account of the subsidies received by the king of *Uladh*, (Down, Armagh, &c. at present) from the monarch of Ireland, when he was not monarch himself, and also the subsidies paid by him to his chiefs of districts. The verses here are eighty, and begin " Alca rund roeg Ulad," " Here are the emoluments of Uladh." This is followed by an account of the provisions and revenues of Uladh. The verses are forty-four in number, of an uncommon measure, beginning " Oligid rig Eamna acar Ulad ;" " Dues of the king of Emania and Uladh."

The rights of the king of Tarah are next set down, and the subsidies paid by him to the subordinate chiefs of Meath. This section informs us, that, when the king of Tarah was not monarch of Ireland, he received as a subsidy from the monarch, one hundred swords, one hundred shields, one hundred horses, one hundred coloured garments, and one hundred suits of armour. The poem belonging to this part, consists of fifty-six verses, beginning " Oligid ri Teampa crrim," " The rights of Tarah's king I here rehearse." This is followed by an account of the revenues of the kings of Meath. The metrical account is in fifty-two verses, beginning " Cir cuaic Mid mor in rcel ;" " Tax of the district of Meath, great the report."

Then follows the will of CATHAOIR mor, king of Leinster, and monarch of Ireland, A. D. 122, by which his kingdom and his property are divided among his sons. This is followed by a poem of eighty verses, attributed to Benen, showing the subsidies the king of Leinster was to receive from the monarch of Ireland, when he did not fill that high office himself. It also gives an account of the subsidies paid by the king of Leinster to the subordinate chiefs of his province. The poem begins " Cerc rig Laigen ro luad benen," " The rights of the king of Leinster, Benen relates." This poem alone is sufficient to prove what I have said in the beginning, that this work, in its present form, is not the work of Benen.

The next article is an account of the contributions to which each of the district chiefs of Leinster was subject, for support of the king of that province. The metrical account here consists of sixty-eight verses, beginning " Coirτιὄ, a laiξmu na laoὀ," " Listen, oh Leinster of heroes."

This is succeeded by a poem of seventy-two verses, giving an account of the GALLS of Dublin, at the coming of Saint Patrick!!! The poem begins " 2lτα runὄ renὀαr ruξc renξ," " Here is a pleasant agreeable history."

The privileges of the poets and their rewards are then recited ; the prose account is supported by a poetical account, ascribed to *Dubhthach mac ui Lughair*, beginning " m ὄliξ cuξτ no cenὄαιξeὀτ, αn in rιliξ rin eolac," " There is no visitation nor superiority over the truly learned poet."

The Book of Rights closes with an account of the rights of the king of Tarah, and of the privileges and subsidies that all the princes of Ireland had a right to receive from him when he was monarch of Ireland. This account is in a poem of three hundred and ninety-two verses, ascribed to *Dubhthach mac ui Lughair*, beginning " Ceamὄ τeὀ a mbi mic Cuinὄ," " Tarah house, in which are the descendants of Conn."—See Dubhthach mac ui Lughair, under A. D. 433.

A. D. 499.

XXXII. Saint CAILIN, first bishop of Down, wrote some prophecies in Irish verse, but we cannot be sure that those now extant ascribed to him are genuine. That beginning " Eire, oll oilen," " Eire, noble island," said to be written by this author, gives, by way of prophecy, a catalogue of Irish kings, and counts two hundred and twenty-seven years from the battle of Clontarf. It may therefore be presumed that it was not written before the middle of the thirteenth century.

A. D. 500.

xxxiii. Saint Fiech, the first bishop of Sletty, was a disciple of Saint Patrick, and flourished for some years after the death of his master. He wrote a hymn in Irish, consisting of one hundred and thirty-six verses, in praise of our apostle, in which he recites his parentage, and shows that the place of his nativity was Tours, in France. It begins " Ɀeнᵹ Ρᚊᚊᚔᚐιcc ᚔ ᚅeṁ Ꚋᚱᚔᚱ," "Patrick was born in holy Tours." A very ancient copy of this poem, finely written on vellum, is in the library of Trinity College. It has been printed different times; first in Colgan's "*Acta Sanctorum*," with a Latin translation; next in the first edition of Vallancey's Irish Grammar, with a faulty English translation; again in the year 1792, by a Mr. Richard Plunkett, a neglected genius of the county of Meath, who, in pages opposite to the original text, gave a version into modern Irish; and lastly, by the late Mr. Patrick Lynch, in his " Life of Saint Patrick," with a correct English translation.

xxxiv. Cotemporary with Saint Fiech was Saint Cianan, first Bishop of Duleek, in Meath. He wrote a life of Saint Patrick, in Irish; but those lives of our Apostle, which we have seen ascribed to St. Cianan, were certainly written at a much later period.

A. D. 523 or 525.

xxxv. On the first of February, in either of these years, died Saint Bridget, Patroness and first Abbess of Kildare. She wrote a Rule for her Nuns in her native language, which is said to be extant, but we are not able to point out where it can be found.

A. D. 526.

xxxvi. Holy Brogan died in this year. He wrote a hymn in praise of Saint Bridget, which Colgan published, with a Latin translation, in in his Life of that virgin. It was again published in 1792, with a version in modern Irish, by Mr. Richard Plunkett, of the county of Meath, already mentioned.

Manuscript copies of this poem are in the library of Trinity College. It begins " Ni ċʒ bpiccrc buaʊaċ biċ," " Bridget glorious, loved not the world."

According to O'Flaherty, Brogan wrote the poem beginning " 2l coiʒioʊ caın cʒppe cpɾ̇aıʊ ;" but, for an account of this poem, see Giolla na naomh O'Dunn, under the year 1160.

A. D. 527, according to Tigernach, but 541 according to the Four Masters.

xxxvii. In either of the above years died Saint Ailbe, first Bishop of Emly. He wrote a Rule for Monks, in Irish verse, ancient copies of which are in possession of different members of the Society, and the language is a strong proof that the work is genuine. It begins " 2lppaıp ʊam ꝼpı mac Sapaın, ıɼ cpom an caıpı ʒaıbeɼ; baʊ lép, baʊ ꝼeıʒ a ċubaıɼ, cın ʒaı 'nuabʒ cın ꝼeıle," " Say from me to the son of Sarain, weighty is the charge he takes; be his conscience clear, without falsehood, without pride, without fraud."

A. D. 533.

xxxviii. Holy Cairneach was a priest, and cotemporary with Muircertagh mac Earc, monarch of Ireland, who died A. D. 533, and whose death Cairneach foretold, as is asserted. Some poems, and prophecies in metre, attributed to him, are given in the " Oıʊeaʊ Ꟁpꝑċeʒcaıʒ meıc Eapca," or " Death of Murkertagh, son of Earc," a very ancient historical tale, in prose and verse, in possession of the Assistant Secretary.

He is quoted in the Book of Invasions, by the O'Clery's, page 182, in possession of the Assistant Secretary.

***

A. D. 540.

xxxix. About this time died Saint IARLATH, first Bishop of Tuam. Some prophecies, in Irish verse, ascribed to him, are extant, a copy of which is in the collection of the Assistant Secretary to this Society; but some reasonable doubts may be entertained of their genuineness.

***

A. D. 544.

xl. On the 12th of October, in this year, died Saint BEARCHAN, of Glasnaidhin, on the North Bank of the River Liffey. In the *Felire Aonguis,* or Festivals of the Church, written by Angus *Céile Dé,* at the latter end of the eighth century, under the festival of Saint Bridget, on the first of February, a small poem of Berchan's, in praise of that Saint, is given. It begins " ɪn ban a liɼe na leiꝛᵹ," " The woman, O Liffey of plains." There are some Irish prophecies ascribed to him, which others, with more propriety perhaps, attribute to St. Braccan.

See under BRACAN, at A. D. 650.

***

A. D. 549.

xli. St. CIARAN, of Cluain-mac-Nois, died on the 9th of September this year. He wrote a Rule for Monks, in Irish metre, said to be amongst the MSS. of Trinity College library; but in the present imperfect state of the catalogue of MSS. in that library, we have not been able to discover it.

A. D. 550.

XLII. At this time died BEG MAC DE. Some prophecies attributed to him are still extant. In a very ancient vellum MS. in the collection of William Monck Mason, Esq. is to be found one of those prophecies, beginning " ꞃi bɪꝺ cꞃꝺbꝺ ꝺ ccellꝺɪƀ," " There will be no devotion in churches ;" and a copy of the same prophecy, and another, beginning " Olc bɪꞇ ꝺ upꞇꝺ," " Evil the practice of sorcery," are to be found in an ancient MS. in possession of the Assistant Secretary. In an ancient and very valuable vellum MS. the property of Sir William Betham, is to be found a poem of two hundred and eighty-eight verses, ascribed to *Beg mac Dé*, beginning " Ꞇꞃeɪꝺe ꞃꝺc ꝼꞃlꞃꝉeꝺꞃꝺ ꞃɪꝉ ꞃeɪl," " Three things a lawful king suffers not." In this Poem the author foretels the evils and destruction that were to fall upon several places and things in Ireland. This writer was descended from Cormac Cas, through Conall *Eachluaith (of the swift horses)* king of Munster, A. D. 366.

Tigernach, the Annalist, who died in A. D. 1088, mentions the death of Beg mac Dé, under the year 551, in these words, " bꝺꞃ becc mꝺc ꝺē ꝺꞃ ꝼꝺɪꝺ," " The death of Beg mac Dé the Prophet."

The " Four Masters" say his death happened in the year 557, and relate that event in these words, " S. becc mꝺc ꝺē, ꝼꝺɪꝺ oɪꞃꝺeꝺꞃc ꝺēcc," " St. Beg mac Dé, a noble Prophet, died."

XLIII. Cotemporary with the last-mentioned writer was AMERGIN MAC AMALGAID, chief poet to the monarch Dermod, son of *Fergus Ceirbheoil,* who ascended the throne of Ireland, A. D. 544, and after a reign of twenty-one years, died in A. D. 565. This poet was the original author of the *Dinn Seanchas*, or History of noted places in Ireland; a work which has been enlarged by other writers who lived some ages after the time of Amergin. Indeed some of it must have been written after the year 1024, in which year Cuan O'Lochain was killed; for some poems of that writer are given in full in this work, and extracts from some others.

The work accounts for the origin of the names of several mountains, hills, raths, plains, glenns, rivers, &c. in Ireland; and, although much blended with fable, is extremely curious, and may be considered valuable, for some authentic anecdotes contained in it, of several of the most remarkable characters in ancient Irish history. The account of each mountain, plain, river, &c. is first given in prose, and supported by poems, or extracts from poems of some of our early writers, as Finin mac Luchna, a poet of the second century; Fionn mac Cubhail; Fergus Finnbel, younger brother of Oisin, who lived in the third century; and some others.

This Amergin must not be confounded with an other Amergin mac Amalgaidh, who flourished in the latter end of the seventh century, and wrote some law tracts still extant, a copy of which is to be found in the Seabright MSS. in the library of Trinity College.

A very fine copy of the Dinn Seanchas is preserved in a vellum MS. the property of Sir William Betham. There is an imperfect copy in the Book of Leacan, and another in the collection of the Assistant Secretary.

A. D. 576.

XLIV. Saint Breandan, or Breannan, first bishop of Cluainfert, died on Sunday, the 16th of May, in this year, according to the annals of the Four Masters, or in 577, according to the annals of Inisfallen. He wrote a Rule for Monks, and some prophecies in Irish verse, and some other poems. Two copies of verses by this author, are in the collection of the Assistant Secretary, one of which begins " ᵻη ᴅᴀ ᴀleᴅ mo ᴅᴀ ċᴀᴘᴅᴀᴅ," " The two Aodhs, my two friends," upon the meeting of Aodh *caomh (mild)* son of Conall, son of Eochaidh Ball-dearg, a descendant of Cormac Cas, who was the first Christian king of Cashel, and ancestor of the

Marquis of Thomond, one of the Vice Presidents of this Society, and Aodh *dubh, (black)* son of Criomhthan, monarch of Ireland, and father of Finghin and Failbhe Flann, of the tribe of Eogan more, afterwards kings of Desmond. This meeting took place between these princes at *Carn an Righ,* (the *king's heap*) on Magh Feimhin, (the plain of Feimhin) between Cashel and Clonmel; and the cause of their meeting was to agree upon the right of succession to the sovereignty of Cashel, according to the will of their great ancestor Olioll Olum, king of Munster. Aodh caomh was then the representative of the Dalcassian race, and by the rule of alternate succession, directed by the will of Olioll between the descendants of his two sons, Cormac Cas and Eogan more, had a right to the throne of Cashel, but Aodh dubh, the representative of the Eugenian tribe, disputed this right, and would not consent that Aodh caomh should be invested with the regal power, until his own succession would be secured to him, if he should survive the present claimant. This was agreed to on both sides, and St. Breandan and his disciple Mac Leinin the poet, afterwards called Colman, and first bishop of Cloyne, were given to Aodh dubh as hostages for the performance. The second poem begins " beañáċ ın cómbē ċumaċċaıġ," " Blessings of the powerful God," and is the benediction given by Breannan to Aodh caomh and his descendants. These poems, and others of Breannan's composition, were preserved in the Psalter of Cashel, and the book of Munster in the book of Ballimote.

A. D. 592.

xlv. Saint Columb *Cille,* or Columb of Cells, or churches, died on Whit-Sunday night, the 9th of June, in this year, according to the annals of the Four Masters. He wrote several pieces both in Irish and Latin. Upwards of thirty poems in the Irish language, ascribed to him, have come down to our times, copies of which are in possession of the Assistant Secretary, a particular description of which we at present avoid. The subjects are miscellaneous, but the chief part are religious. The prophecies ascribed to this Saint, if ever they were written by him, have been interpolated and corrupted by modern writers.

A. D. 596.

XLVI. About this period flourished EOCHAIDH *Eigeas, (the wise)* or EOCHAIDH *Dallan,* or DALLAN *Forgaill,* by which latter name he is generally called. He was a disciple of St. Columb Cille, and attended him at the great assembly of Dromceat, convened by Aodh, son of Ainmireach, monarch of Ireland, A. D. 588. Dallan wrote a life of his master, and the Amhra Colum Chille, or elegiac verses in praise of St. Columb, by which it appears he survived that Saint, who, we are told, died on Whit-Sunday, the 9th of June, A. D. 592, according to the Four Masters, or A. D. 597, according to Tigernach. Several imperfect copies of the Amhra, written on vellum, are in various hands. One copy is in Marsh's library, another in the library of Trinity College, another in the collection of William Monck Mason, Esq. and another, written in 1313, is in the collection of the Assistant Secretary, who has also a perfect copy, written on paper, which was once the property of Cucoigcriche O'Clery, one of the persons employed in the compilation of the annals of the Four Masters. The Ꞃéiṁꞃcél, or preliminary discourse, prefixed to this tract, shews the time and place in which it was written. It begins " loᴄᴄ ꝺoɴ elꝺiꝺeɴꞃi ꝺꞃꞃꞧmm-chꞇꝺ hi ꞇuꝺiꞇ i ᴄiꝺɴꝺèꞇꝺ ᵹliṁ ᵹlimiɴ, ꝺ iꞃ ꝺ̃ ꝺo ꞃoɴꝺꝺ̈ iɴ móꞃꝺꞃil ꝺꞃumo ᴄeꞇꞇo· lꞃ ꝺimꞃeꞃ, imoꞃꞃo .i. ꝺimꞃeꞃ Áꝺo mꝺᴄ Ꝉiɴmꞃeꞃꝺ̇ ꞃi hƐꞃeɴ̃· iɴꝺeꞃɴꝺꝺ̈ iɴ móꞃꝺꝺ̈il. Ꞃo bꝺ̈ꞇuꞃ ꞇꞃꝺ ꞇꞃi ꞃiᵹꝺ ꝺéc iɴ hƐiꞃiɴ̃ iɴ ꞇꝺɴ ꞃiɴ, oᴄuꞃ Áꝺo ꞃóꞃ cꝺ̈ᴄ̇ ꞃi ꝺib. Uꞇ ꝺiᴄꞇ iɴ ꝼiliꝺ; " Áꝺo mꝺᴄ ꝺiɴ̃miꞃiᵹ ɴꝺ ɴeꝺll," 7c. " The place of this tract is Dromceat in the north, in Cianachta of Glenn Geimhin, for it was there the great assembly of Dromceat was held. Its time, moreover, was the time of Aodh, son of Ainmhereach, monarch of Ireland, who held this assembly. There were also thirteen kings in Ireland at this time, and Aodh was the name of each of them, as said the poet."

" Aodh, son of Ainmhereach, of battles," &c.

The Amhra begins " Ꝺiꝺ ꝺiꝺ ꝺo ꞃuᵹꝺꞃ ꞃe ꞇiꝺꞃ iɴꝺ ᵹɴꞃiꞃ."

He also wrote the *Amhra Sionain,* or Elegy on the death of Saint Seanan, beginning " Seɴꝺɴ ꞃoeꞃ, ꞃiꝺ ꝺᴄoiꞃ," " Noble Seanan, peaceful father." A copy of this poem is in the collection of the Assistant Secretary, and it and the *Amhra Coluim Cille* are in the Bearla Feni, or Fenian dialect of the Irish, accompanied by a gloss. There is a copy of another poem of Dallan Forgaills, in the Seabright collection of MSS. in the library of Trinity College, beginning " Oṅb ʒilla ᴅub aiꝱm naiꝛe." Upon the arms of Duach dubh, king of Oirgailla. From this it appears that the shaft of Duach's spear was made of the eo Roꝛꝛa, or yew of Ross. It is probable many more of the works of Dallan are extant, although they have not come within our knowledge.

A. D. 598.

XLVII. Saint CAINEACH, or Canice, Abbot of *Achadh bo,* or field of oxen, died on the 11th of October, ḥis year. He wrote a life of Saint Patrick in Irish, which, it is probable, may be still extant.

A. D. 599.

XLVIII. Saint BAOITHIN succeeded St. Columb Cille in the abbacy of Hy, and died on the 9th of January, this year. He wrote a life of Saint Columb in Irish verse, and some prophecies, which are in the manuscript collection of the Assistant Secretary.

A. D. 600.

XLIX. St. COMHGHALL, founder and first abbot of the great monastery of Bangor, in the Ardes in Ulster, died this year. He wrote a Rule for Monks, in Irish metre, and some other poems and prose works in the same language. His rule begins " Coma ꝛiʒail an Chóimᴅē," " Support the regulations of the Godhead." There is preserved in the *Felire Anguis*, a poem of Comhghall's, consisting of sixty verses, beginning " ᐃᲫᲐᲝᲚᲣᲚᲐᲘ ᎥᎷᎷᲐᲫᲣᲪᲚᲐᲘ," in praise of solitude.

These works are in the MS. collection of the Assistant Secretary.

L. St. Murus lived at this time. He wrote the Acts of St. Columb Cille, in Irish verse.

A. D. 605.

LI. Saint Molua, otherwise called Lughaidh, first Abbot of Clonfert Molua, died this year. He wrote a Rule for Monks, in Irish verse, afterwards translated into Latin; and, being carried to Rome, received the approbation of Gregory, the first Pope of that name. This Rule is said to be still extant in the Irish language, but we have not met with it.

A. D. 610.

LII. Maolcobha, Monarch of Ireland, was killed, this year, according to the Four Masters, at the battle of Slieve Toadh, by Suibhne Meann, who succeeded him on the throne, or in A. D. 615, according to the Annals of Tigernach : but the Book of Invasions states, that after his defeat at Slieve Toadh, he retired from the world, and " *took upon him the yoke of religion*," in his patrimonial lands, at a place called *Drum Diolar*, on the bank of Caoluisce, where he remained in retirement, secluded from the world, until he was expelled from his retreat by his own brother Donald, who succeeded Suibhne Meann in the monarchy, A. D. 624. The Annals of Innisfallen say that he was bishop of Clogher. Maolchobha himself relates the story of his being driven from Druim Diolar, in a poem of ninety-two verses, beginning " ᎠᲠᲝᲜᲒ ᲢᲐᲘᲐᲪ ᎠᲠᲝᲛᲐ

Ðiolᵹ," " Suffering family of Drum Diolar." In this poem the author laments the expulsion of himself and his clergy, in very pathetic terms, and severely censures Mor, surnamed *Mumhan* (of *Munster*), the wife of his brother, as the cause of their sufferings. Upon the same subject, and the number of clergy in the religious house of Drum Diolar, and the benefits conferred on different classes of people by them, he wrote a poem of twenty-four verses, beginning "Τιοmᴅᴢ ᴢo léiᴘ na lioḃᴘa," " Prudently collect the books." He also wrote the poem, beginning " Ionṁoin áᴘaᴘ ainᴢlióe aᴘ ᴅ cᴘᴘeaó ᴏÐaolcaḃa," " Pleasant the angelical habitation from which is driven Maolchobha."

These poems are all preserved in the Book of Invasions, by the O'Clery's, in possession of the Assistant Secretary of this Society.

A. D. 617.

LIII. Saint Coemhghin, Abbot and Bishop of Glendalogh, died on the 3d of June this year. He wrote a Rule for Monks in Irish verse. The *Leabhar Breathnach*, or Book of the Britons, contained in the Book of Glendalogh, and a book on the origin of the Milesians, are attributed to him. The book of Glendalogh is in the library of Trinity College.

A. D. 624.

LIV. St. Maodhog, or Edan, as he is otherwise called, first Bishop of Ferns, died on the 31st of January this year. He was a native of East Breifne (now called the County Cavan) and descended in the tenth degree from Colla Uais, who was monarch of Ireland, A. D. 327. This Saint is much celebrated for his piety and miracles ; and in an ancient MS. life of him, in the collection of the Assistant Secretary, there are preserved some poems said to be written by him. One of these is his will, by which he divides his property between three churches, founded by him, viz. Ferns, in Leinster; Drum Leathan, in Cavan; and Ross Inver, now in the county of Leitrim. This poem begins " ᏸᎥᏁᎧ ᗩᎷ ᏓᎥᎧᎷᏁᎪ ᏒᎪᎥᎧᎧᎬᏒ ᏣᎷ," " Intention of the will set forth by us." Another of these poems begins " ᎷᎪᎷ ᏒᎾᎬᎧᎧᎪᏒ ᎷᎧ ᎧᎥᏣᏣ ᎧᎪᎥᎧ," " Woe to those who pollute my noble church." In this poem woes are denounced against all that injure his churches; and such a description is given of the author, as would give cause to suspect that the verses were not the genuine productions of Maodhog.

A. D. 636.

LV. Saint CARTHAG, otherwise called MOCHUDA, first Bishop of Lismore, died on the 14th of May this year. He wrote a metrical Rule for Monks, beginning " ᏂᎥᏒᎬ ᎪᏒᏁᎪᎷ ᏁᎪ ᏑᏣᎪᎧᎪ," " It is the way of the Lord." This poem is in the collection of Irish MSS. belonging to the Assistant Secretary to this Society.

A. D. 647.

LVI. SEANCHAN TORPEST lived in the time that GUAIRE the Generous was king of Conaght. He wrote a poem of twenty-eight verses, beginning " ᎡᎧ ᏑᎥᏣ ᏑᎬᏒᎾᏌᏒ ᏑᎥᏣᎥᏣ ᎧᎪᏣᎪ," " Fergus fought twenty battles." This poem is historical, and gives an account of the battles of Fergus, son of Rossa, and grandson of Roderick, monarch of Ireland, from A. M. 3845, until A. M. 3862, according to O'Flaherty's computation. A copy of this poem is preserved in the Book of Leacan, fol. 17, col. 2d, and another copy is in possession of the Assistant Secretary. Its language and measure are strong proofs of its antiquity.

A. D. 650.

LVII. Saint BRACCAN, from whom Ardbrackan, near Navan, in the county of Meath, derives its name, is stated to have lived in this year, by Ware, in his account of Irish writers. The time of his death is not mentioned either in the Annals of Tigernach, Inisfallen, or the Four Masters, but it is probable that he died before this period, as he was the predecessor of St. ULTAN, who, at the advanced age of one hundred and eighty years, died A. D. 656, according to the Four Masters, or 657, as Tigernach relates. Several prophecies in Irish verse, ascribed to Braccan, are still existing in this country, some of which are in the possession of the Assistant Secretary.—Ware says, that the prophecies of Braccan were collected and published by Walter de Islip, in the year 1317.

A. D. 651.

LVIII. SEGINE, Abbot of Hy, or Iona, died this year. He wrote a Rule for Monks, in Irish verse, which is said to be extant, but we cannot say where it is to be found.

A. D. 653.

LIX. Saint FURSEY, founder of the Abbey of Cnobersburgh, or Burgh Castle, in Suffolkshire, England, and of the Abbey of Laigny, in the diocese of Paris, died at Peronne, in France, this year, according to the Annals of Boyle, or in A. D. 654, according to Tigernach, who relates his death in these words, " ꝼꝛꝛꝩᵹ ᴅᴇᵹ ᴀ ꝼꝼꝛᴀꞑᴄᴄᴀꞇᵬ," " Fursey died in France," and gives the following quotation to shew who were his parents:

> "Aṫair Fursa raḋ glan gleo,
> Loċinḋ do ḋail nAraiḋe
> Isi ra maṫair don ġeilġeis
> Inġean riġ Ċonaċt."

Fursey wrote some prophecies, hymns, and other poems, copies of which are in several hands, particularly in an ancient vellum MS. the property of William Monck Mason, Esq. Of these poems, being mostly on religious subjects and not illustrative of the History of Ireland, we forbear giving a particular account. The festival of this Saint is observed on the 16th of January.

A. D. 656.

LX. Saint ULTAN, the successor of Braccan in the Abbey of Ardbracken, and from whom the place was sometimes called Tobar Ultain, or Ultan's Well, died this year. He wrote a life of Saint Patrick, and some metrical prophecies in the Irish language. The copy of the Life of our Apostle that we have seen attributed to Ultan, is certainly the production of a more modern pen. Copies of the prophecies are in the collection of the Assistant Secretary.

A. D. 661.

LXI. COLMAN O'CLUASAITH, the tutor of Cuman *fada* (the tall) lived at the time of Cuman's death, which happened in the year 661. A quotation from a poem of Colman's, upon the death of his disciple Cuman, is given by the Four Masters, under that year. We cannot point out where any of his entire pieces are now to be found.

A. D. 664.

LXII. MANCHEN of Leith, died this year, according to the Four Masters, but the Annals of Ulster say he died A. D. 655. He wrote some poems of a religious kind, still extant in the Irish language. He also wrote a book intituled " The Wonders of Scripture," extant in the third volume of St. Augustine's works, and falsely ascribed to that Saint. O'Flaherty quotes a poem of Manchen's, beginning, " ᵓoᵓᵃᵼ o ᵱo hᵭᵹeᵒᵱom," " Since Idols were expelled."

A. D. 673.

LXIII. BEG BOIRCHE, King of Ulster, according to the Annalists, took the Cross, and went on a pilgrimage this year. A quotation from a poem of his on the death of Mongan, son of Feachna, is given by the Four Masters, under the year 620, and by Tigernach at 626.

A. D. 678.

LXIV. CINNFAELADH *Fodhlumtha (learned)*, or CINNFAELADH, *son of Olioll*, died this year, according to the Annals of Ulster, and the Four Masters, or A. D. 679, according to Tigernach. He is also surnamed *Eigeas*, or *wise*. He wrote many poems and prose works, some of which have descended entire to our times, and others of them are quoted by the Four Masters, under the years 499 and 507. His poem on the situation of the house of *Miodhcuarta*, or middle court of the royal palace of Tara, beginning Sᵼᵹᵼᵒ ᵼᵹe ᗰᵼoᵒᵼᵱᵹᵼᵃ, is to be found in an ancient vellum MS. the property of William Monck Mason, Esq. and another old copy is in possession of the Assistant Secretary. His poem of fifty-six verses, beginning " Ɖo lɼᵹ Ɠolaṁ aɼɩɼ Scɩᴄɩa," " Golamh departed from Scythia," upon the travels and adventures of Golamh (Milesius) from his departure from Scythia until his arrival in Spain, and afterwards in Ireland, is preserved in the Book of Invasions contained in the Book of Leacan, and also in the Book of Invasions by the O'Clery's. There are other copies of this poem in various hands, the most valuable of which is one in possession of the Assistant Secretary, collated with three very ancient copies, and the various reading given in the margin. Cinnfaeladh improved the *Uraicepht*, or as it is sometimes written, the *Uraicecht*, of Ferceirtne.

We have already shewn, under A. M. 3950, that Ferceirtne, and not Forchern, as stated by O'Flaherty and O'Connor, was the original author of the Uraicepht; but so many different copies of a book bearing that title, and author's name, now in existence, and all varying from each other, in some things, show that it has gone through various editions, with additions and alterations. The principal editor or emendator of the Uraicepht, was Cinfaeladh, but it is impossible to say what parts were written by Ferceirtne, or by this editor, although it is no difficult task to point out parts certainly written long after the time of the original author, if not subsequent to Cinnfaeladh himself.

This Book is generally preceded by the Book of *Oghams*, as in the copy preserved in the Book of Ballymote, the copy in the library of Trinity College, Dublin, class H. 54, and the copy in the possession of the Assistant Secretary; but each of these copies wants something, more or less, towards the end. The copy in Sir William Betham's book, begins " Caᴄ é loc acaɼ áɩṁɼeɼ acaɼ péɼɼa acaɼ ᴄucaɩᴄ ɼcɼɩbaɩno ɩno aɼaɩcɩucᴄa? nɩn. loc oó Emaɩn Ɱacha, acaɼ ɩɩ áɩṁɼeɼ Concobᵹ mac Neɼa aɼɩcᴄ a oenaṁ. Ꞇuᵹaɩᴄ oan a oénṁa .ɩ. oo bɼeɩᴄ aeɼa faɩno foɼ feɼ. feɼceɼᴄne fɩlɩ ooɼ ɼɩᵹnɩ. Cenofaelao mac Ʒɩlella ɼo naᴄhnuᵹeɼᴄᵹ ɩ noᵹe luɼaɩn ɩɼ áɩṁɼeɼ ſɛoa mac Ʒɩnmɩɼeᴄ ɩmaɩlle la hɩɼ móɩɼ ɩɩ beɼlaɩ," " What is the time, and the place, and the person, and the cause of writing of the *Uraicecht*? Not difficult. The place of it Eaman of Macha, and in the time of Conor, son of Nessa, it was done. The cause of doing it, *i. e.* to bring ignorant people to knowledge. Ferceirtne, the poet, performed it. Cinnfaeladh, son of Olioll, revised it in Daire Lurain, in the time of Aodh, son of Ainmireach, along with much more of the language."

The copy in the Assistant Secretary's collection, begins "Caζζe ιοcc acuγ áιmγeρ acuγ ρēργa acuγ ζuccoιζ γeριßm anaιρecacζo? nín. ιοcc δο Θaṁṇṇ ṁaċο acuγ a náιmγeρ Concoßaιρ meιc Ṇeγο aριċζ. Ḟeρceρζṇι Ḟιιι δο ριcċṇι .:. δο βρℓιζ οℓγu Ḟaιn Ḟορ Ḟℓιγ. Cℓṇṇρoeιaδ mác Oιℓιοι ρο aζṇuaδhaδh 1 ṇδoιρe ιuρaιn maιιιe ρe heρṁόρ ṇa γcρeρζρa," "What is the place, and the time, and person, and cause of writing the Uraicecht? Not difficult. The place of it Eamain of Macha, and in the time of Conor, son of Nesa, it was done. Ferceirtne the poet made it, *i. e.* to bring ignorant people to knowledge. Cinnfaeladh, son of Olioll, renewed it in Derry Lurain, with many other writings."

In addition to the works already mentioned, Cinnfaeladh revised the laws of Cormac mac Art, monarch of Ireland, A. D. 254.

* * *

A. D. 685.

LXV. FLANN *fionn* was a name given by the Irish to ALDFRED, king of the Northumbrian Saxons, who, during his exile in Ireland, passed his time in study, as we are assured by venerable Bede, in his life of St. Cuthbert. He wrote a poem in the Irish language, consisting of ninety-six verses, on Ireland, and the things he found there. This poem begins, " Ro δeaζ ιn ιnιγ Ḟṁ Ḟaιι, 1 ṇ Θρṁ ρe ιmaρßaιδ," " I found in the pleasant island of Fail, in Ireland by exile." A copy of this poem is preserved in a very old and valuable vellum MS. in the library of William Monck Mason, Esq. and another ancient copy is in the collection of the Assistant Secretary.

* * *

A. D. 696.

LXVI. We have shewn, under the year 550, that a person of the name of AMERGIN mac Amalgaidh was poet to Dermod, son of Fergus Ceirbheoil, monarch of Ireland, and was the reputed author of the *Dinn Seanchais.* By an old vellum MS. of the Seabright collection, in the library of Trinity College, it appears that another writer of that name lived in the time of Finghin, son of Cu-gan-mhathair, king of Munster. The latter AMERGIN, of whom we here treat, was author of a law tract on the privileges and punishments of persons of different ranks in society, beginning " loc ꝺon lirbaꝛꝛa ꝼꝛꞇꝛime coꝛconꝺé, acaꝛ áimꝛiꝛ ꝺo áimꝼiꝛ ꝼino-ᵹaine mic cae cin maꞇaiꝛ, no mic con cen maꞇaiꝛ, acaꝛ peꝛꝛa ꝺo ᷨlmaiꝛᵹin mac ᷨlmalᵹaiꝺ mic Ɯail ꝛuain," " The place of this book Fuitrime Corconach, and its time the time of Finghin, son of Cu-cin-mathair, or Con-cen-mathair, and its person Amergin, son of Amalgaidh, son of Maolruana."

From the similarity of names in these authors, and those of the fathers and grandfathers of each, one would be led to suppose them the same person. But the first, it appears, was the poet of Dermod, son of Fergus Ceirbheoil, monarch of Ireland, who died A. D. 566, or, as the Four Masters have it, in 558, and the latter wrote the Law tract just now mentioned in the time of Finghin, son of Cu-cen-mathair, king of Munster. The Annals of Innisfallen place the death of Cu-cen-mathair in A. D. 662, and that of Finghin in A. D. 696, full 130 years after the death of Dermod, at the lowest computation of Tigernach. Hence we may fairly infer, that the present Amergin was a different person from the Amergin who is said to have been the original author of the *Dinn Senachas.*

A. D. 697.

LXVII. Saint MOLAING, from whom *Teach Mholing,* or Timolin, in the county Kildare, is called, died on the 17th of June this year. Some prophecies ascribed to him are in the hands of the Assistant Secretary; but if they were written by him, their language has been much modernized by some later writers.

A. D. 704.

LXVIII. ADAMNAN, or Adamnanus, Abbot of **Hy,** or *J. Coluim Cille,* died on the 23d of September this year, in the seventy-seventh year of his age, and twenty-fifth year of his abbotship. In the month of June, in the year 683, the Saxons having made a predatory landing in Ireland, laid waste and plundered **Magh Breagh,** sparing neither ecclesiastical nor lay property, and carried off with them, along with the spoils, a great number of the inhabitants. In the following year, Adamnan went into England, and by prayers and intreaties, and, as the Four Masters relate, by the working of many miracles, he obtained for himself great honours from king Alfred, and for the people, that had been carried off, their liberty, and the restitution of their property. He wrote many works both in Irish and Latin. Of his Irish works but few have remained to our times. An imperfect copy of his Vision is in the hands of John M'Namara, Esq. a member of this Society, and another in the collection of the Assistant Secretary, and also a copy of his poem, of fifty-two verses, beginning " ꞁ oꞁu ce cꞁꞃꞡlaꞇ cuacca," upon the remission of the Boromean tribute to the people of Leinster, by Fionnachta *fleadhach (festive)* at the intercession of Saint Moling.

The Vision of Adamnan is in prose, partly Latin and part Irish. The Irish part begins " ꞁ eaꞇ ꞁꞁ ꞁo ꞇꞃa ꞁoꞃuꞁ acaꞁ ꞁlꞁꞡeaꞇ aꞁꞁmcaꞁꞁꞇeaꞃa ꞁeaꞃ ꞁeꞃꞁꞁꞇ ꞁꞃꞁa leꞃuꞡaꞇ a ccoꞃꞁ acaꞁ a ꞁaꞁmaꞁꞇ, ꞁꞃꞁa hꞁꞁꞇaꞃꞁaꞇ ꞁlaꞁꞡ acaꞁ ꞡeꞁꞇe acaꞁ ꞇꞃmꞁaꞇ ꞁꞁ, aꞁꞃꞁl ꞃo ꞁoꞁllꞃꞁꞡeaꞇ ꞇo Aꞇamꞁaꞁ .h. ꞇꞁe, a comꞣlꞁ ꞇe acaꞁ Paꞇꞇꞃuꞁcc." " Here is set down laws and regulations of spiritual friendship for the men of Ireland, for the correction of their bodies and souls, for expelling from them plagues and infidels, and manslaughter, as it was revealed to Adamnan, the descendant of Tine, in the counsel of God and Patrick."

———

A. D. 722.

LXIX. NUADHA ILOMHTUR flourished at this time. Tigernach, in his Annals, under this year, gives a quotation of twelve verses from Nuadha, in praise of the prowess and courage of Morogh, son of Bran, king of Leinster, who defeated and killed Fergal, son of Maelduin, monarch of Ireland, in the battle of Almhuin or Allen, fought this year.

LXX. At the same period flourished CUBERTAN MAC CONGUSA, who, like Nuadha, recorded in verse the bloody battle of Allen. Tigernach, in his Annals, speaking of this battle under the year 722, gives a quotation from Cubertan upon that subject.

We have not seen any entire pieces the production of either of these last-mentioned writers.

It may be necessary to observe, that the Four Masters, and Doctor Keating, in his History of Ireland, say that the battle of *Almhuin*, or *Allen*, was fought in the year 718, but O'Flaherty, in Ogygia, agrees with Tigernach in assigning it to the year 722.

A. D. 730.

LXXI. AODH Allain, monarch of Ireland, commenced his reign this year, according to the Four Masters; or 734, according to Tigernach and O'Flaherty. Some verses of Aodh Allain's composition, are preserved in the O'Clery's Book of Invasions, and other verses of his writing are quoted by the Four Masters, under the year 734.

A. D. 734.

LXXII. On the 19th of December, in this year, died Saint SAMHTHAND, Virgin. A prophecy in verse, said to be delivered by her, is quoted in the Annals of Tigernach, under the year 738. It is given more fully in the O'Clery's Book of Invasions, in the MS. collection of the Assistant Secretary.

A. D. 742.

LXXIII. In the time of Cathal, son of Finghin, king of Munster, who died A. D. 742, flourished the three O'BURCHANS, brothers, named Farann, Boethgal, and Maoltuile; the first a bishop, the second a judge, and the third a poet. They wrote some laws, fragments of which may be found in the Seabright collection in the library of Trinity College, Dublin.

LXXIV. Cotemporary with the last-mentioned writers was CEARMNADH *file*, or the poet. In the Seabright MSS. in the College library, class H, No. 54, is preserved a law tract, written by this author, as appears by a memorandum prefixed in the same hand-writing as that in which the law itself is written. It begins "Ciꝺ iſ locc acaſ iſ aimſeſ acaſ aſ peſſa, acaſ ꞇuccaiꞇ ſcſíbiñ ꝺoꞅa conꝺib fſꝣill? Ñín. locc ꝺóib Callaiꞅ o luꝣꝺ hi Ceampaiꝣ, acaſ aimſeſ ꝺóib aimſeſ Caꞇail, meic fiñꝣ⁊ne, acaſ peſſa ꝺóib Cepmꞅa file, acaſ ꞇuccaiꞇ a ꞅꝺēꞅma ꝺo fubꞇaꝺ boſb acaſ aiꞅeolaċ, acaſ ꝺo bſeiꞇ aeſ afaiñ foſꞇ feſ ꝺliꝣe," "What is the place, and the time, and the person, and the cause of writing of the ways to judgment? Not difficult. The place of them Callain of Lughair, in Tarah; and the time of them the time of Cathal, son of Fingaine; and the person of them Cearmna, the poet; and the cause of their being done, to suppress violence and ignorance, and to bring unlearned people to a knowledge of law."

A. D. 747.

LXXV. RUANAN, son of Colba, a great poet, died this year, according to Tigernach. We have not yet discovered where his works are deposited. Probably they may be in the library of Trinity College, but for the discovery of the Irish MSS. in that library, their present catalogue is of but little use.

A. D. 778.

LXXVI. The Four Masters record the death of CIARAN of Bealach-dun, this year. He wrote a life of St. Patrick, in Irish, but it has not come into our hands.

A. D. 800.

LXXVII. ANGUS *Céile Dé* flourished in the latter end of the eighth century, and died early in the ninth. He wrote a *Felire*, or Hierology, in Irish verse, giving an account of the festivals observed in the church in his time. The *reimsceul*, or preliminary discourse, prefixed to this performance, gives the pedigree of the author, through several generations, by which it appears he was descended from Caelbach, king of Ulster, who defeated and killed Muireadhach Tireach, monarch of Ireland, at the battle of Port Righ, and succeeded him on the throne. The *Reimsceul* gives the time and place in which the author wrote this poem. It commences " Cecapóa conóagap óo cać elaóaın .ı. locc acar áımyep, acar pepra, acar cucaıc ycpıbınó. locc éım óon elaóaınyı cecamuy Cúl beñćġ, amyġ pechec ıcpıè .h. fálże, acar ınaıc ı támlaċcaıh ınóépnaó óın; no ın óı ı cluaın eıóneć a ćınóycecal acar a Cúl beñóćġ a fopbaó, acar ıyın aıc ı támlaċcaın.— Æñguy ımuppo mac, 7c," " There are four co-necessaries in every learned treatise, i. e. place, time, person, and cause of writing. Therefore, the place of this piece was first Cúl Banaghar, in the plain of Rechet, in the country of *I Failge*, or O'Faiy, and its revisal in Tamhlacht; (now Tallagh near Dublin) or else in Cluain Eidhnach it was begun, and in Cúl Banagher it was finished, and revised in Tallacht.—Ængus, moreover, was son of Oiblein, son of Fidrai, son of Dermod, son of Ainmirech, son of Cellair, son of Aenluaigh, son of Caelbaidh, son of Cruinba-draoi, son of Eochaidh Coba, son of Lughdhach, son of Fiacha Airidh, from whom are the Dal-Araidhe named. It is, moreover, the time of its writing the time of Conor, son of Aodh Oirdnighe, son of Niall *frasaigh*, for it was he who took the government of Ireland after Donogh, son of Donail of Meath, king of Meath; for Angus, in the preface to the Felire, mentions the death of Donogh."

The Felire is written in that kind of verse called by the Irish poets *rinn aird*, in which every verse ends with a word of two syllables, contains six syllables in the verse, and the entire *rann* twenty-four. It begins

> " Re ꝼil ꝺálaċ ꝺaíneꝺ
> Caiꝺeꝺ in ꝛí ꞃemain,
> Lꞃꝺ ꝛo ꞃeċt nꝺ náꝛᴜɪl,
> Cꞃiꞃc hi Caleñ Enaiꝛ."

Literal translation :

> " In the congregation of the seed of man,
> Went the king before us,
> Submitted to the noble law
> Christ, on the Calends of January."

Aengus also wrote the *Psalter na rann*, which is an abridged history of the descendants of Abraham, from the birth of Isaac, until after the death of Moses.

A copy of the *Felire*, beautifully written on vellum, is in the collection of the Assistant Secretary. From its orthography, and other internal marks of antiquity, it may be concluded that this MS. was written at least as early as the eleventh century, and is, perhaps, the oldest copy of that work now in existence. There is an entire copy in the *Leabhar breac mac Aedhagain*, or Speckled Book of Mac Egan, in the library of the Royal Irish Academy, and an imperfect copy on vellum in the same library.

The Psalter na Rann is preserved in a large MS. the property of Sir William Betham. It is written in a fine strong hand, and occupies upwards of six folio pages, closely written on the largest size vellum.

A. D. 850.

LXXVIII. About this time flourished FINGIN, son of FLANN *dalta Dubh-dartaigh*. He was author of a hymn, consisting of two hundred and eighty verses, in praise of the Holy Trinity, beginning " Ⰰl mo comⰱiu ⱀell," " Oh my exalted Divinity."

Copy in the library of Trinity College, Dublin, class H. 54. page 35, and in the collection of the Assistant Secretary.

A. D. 876.

LXXIX. At this time flourished FOTHADH *na Canni*, poet to Aodh Finnliaith, monarch of Ireland, who died on the 16th of the calends of December, A. D. 876, according to this poet, or 879, according to O'Flaherty's computation from the Annals of Tigernach. We have met with but two poems of this author's writing, one of which is an ode addressed to Aodh finnliaith, on his coronation, and the other is on his death. The first consists of two hundred and forty verses, beginning " Ceⱃⱅ ceċ ⱃⰰʒ co ⱃeⰱll, " Right of every king lawfully." In this ode the poet says, " rights are lawfully due to the descendants of Niall, except from the abbot of Ardmagh, the king of Cashel, and the king of Tarah." He gives instructions to his prince for his general conduct, as a private man and as a king. He advises him to make no peace with his enemies without receiving hostages; to honour the ministers of religion; to treat his chieftains with kindness and respect; to curb villany and licentiousness by the rigor of the law; to do justice to every man, &c.

The second poem consists of only twelve verses, in which the author records the death of his king, and mentions in the first rann the number of years that elapsed from the creation of the world to that time; in the second rann he gives the number of years that had expired since the birth of Christ; and, in the last rann, mentions the particular day on which the king died.

Copies of these poems are preserved in two ancient vellum manuscripts, in the library of William Monck Mason, Esq. and in the collection of the Assistant Secretary.

LXXX. At this period also flourished FLANNAGAN, *son of Ceallach.* He was author of a poem, consisting of twenty-four verses, on the death of Aodh finnliaith, monarch of Ireland, in which he praises the piety, generosity, magnanimity, &c. of that hero.

Copies in the library of William Monck Mason, Esq. and in the collection of the Assistant Secretary.

A. D. 880.

LXXXI. LAITHEOG *Laidheach (the Poetic)* flourished at this time. She was the daughter of Laignechan, of the race of Conall Gulban, and mother of Flann mac Lonain, who held the office of Chief Poet of Ireland, from the commencement of the reign of Flann Sionna, A. D. 879, until his death, which happened in the year 891, according to the Four Masters, or 896, according to the Annals of Inisfallen. The poem beginning " benɒáєᴄ opᴄ a ꝼláṁ aıꝺne," " Blessing on thee, Oh Flann of Aidne," addressed to Flann mac Lonan, is said to be the work of this poetess.

A. D. 884.

LXXXII. The Four Masters, in their annals under the year 884, record the death of MAOLMURA of Fathan, in these words, " Ɱaolmupa an ꝼıle ꝼoıpᴄᴄᴇ ꝼıoᴘ-eolaċ, Ᵹᴄapaıꝺe ᵹpᵹna an beᴘla Sᴄóıᴄᴇᵹóa ꝺécc," " Maolmura, a well-taught skilful poet, and intelligent historian, died." This author is sometimes called Maolmuire Othna. He wrote some historical poems that still survive. One of these is quoted by O'Flaherty, in Ogygia, part 3d, chap. 72. It consists of two hundred and forty-eight verses, and begins "Canam bunúdar na nҀaeidil," "Let us sing the origin of the Gadelians." In this poem the author derives the origin of the Milesians from Japhet, son of Noah, and gives an account of the peregrinations of their ancestors, from the dispersion at Babel to their arrival in Ireland.

A very fine copy of this poem is in the collection of the Assistant Secretary.

2d, A poem of two hundred and sixty-eight verses, beginning

> " Τρıaċ oᵧ τριaċaıḃ Tuaċal τéċṁaᵧ,
> Teċᵱa aᵱ τᵧle;
> leoṁan aᵱ neᵱτ, naċaıᵱ neıṁe,
> ᵱaċaın ᵱᵧle."

> " Lord over Lords, Tuathal legal,
> A flowing ocean;
> A lion in strength, a wily serpent,
> A wounding warrior."

This poem is preserved in the Book of Invasions, by the O'Clerys, in possession of the Assistant Secretary. It gives an account of the great actions of Tuathal *Teachtmhur* (*legitimate*), monarch of Ireland, from A. D. 130, to A. D. 160. It recites the battles fought by that prince against Eochaidh, king of Leinster, who was his son-in-law; and against the *Athach Tuatha*, or Plebeians (improperly called Attacots, by some writers on Irish Antiquities) who had risen in arms against their legal sovereigns, but who were completely subdued by Tuathal. In this poem the poet endeavours, by a recital of the glorious deeds of this prince, to stimulate Flann Sionna, his own sovereign, to imitate so illustrious an example.

3d, A poem of seventy-six verses, beginning

> " ᵱlaῆ ᵱoᵱ Eᵱıῆ hı τı̇ᵹ τoᵹaıḃı,
> Tuáċaıl τeċṁaᵱ

Do nac foncnaió fonba niaónaip,
Zo neanc goill."

" Flann *reigns* over Erin in the chosen house
  Of Tuathal the legitimate,
To whom belonged not excessive contribution of a noble hero,
  With mighty valour."

In this poem Maolmura gives a catalogue of the monarchs of Ireland, from Tuathal Teachtmhar to Flan Sionna.

In the Book of Lecan, and in an ancient MS. in possession of the Assistant Secretary, these two latter poems are blended together, so as to make but one entire piece, which begins with the *rann* here given, as the commencement of the third poem; and the *rann* that we give as beginning the second poem, and the two *ranns* immediately following it, and some others, are omitted. There are also some variations in the readings, and two or three *ranns* are added that do not appear in either of these poems; one of which states, that six hundred and fifty years had elapsed between the death of Tuathal and the commencement of the reign of Flann; which must be an error, as Tuathal died, according to the Four Masters, A. D. 106, or as O'Flaherty asserts, perhaps with more truth, A. D. 160, and Flann Sionna began to reign A. D. 879; so that instead of six hundred and fifty years having elapsed, according to the Book of Lecan, seven hundred and nineteen years at least must have expired.

The death of Maolmura is related in the Book of Invasions in these words, " *Maelmrpae an file foipccce fineolaé, fcapaióe eapzna an bepla Scoicccóa, óo écc ipin occmaó bliaóam óo flaic floincc cpioña. 884.*" " Maolmura the skilful, a truly learned poet, an intelligent historian in the Scottish language, died in the eighth year of the reign of Flann Sionna, 884."

———

A. D. 891.

LXXXIII. Cotemporary with Maolmura Othna was FLANN MAC LONAN, a native of Conaght, and chief poet of Ireland, in the early part of the reign of Flann Sionna, whose government began **A. D. 879.** The Annals of Inisfallen place the death of Flann mac Lonan under the year 896. " ꝼlañ mac Lonaın aꝛꝺ ollaṁ Ᵹaoıꝺıl ꝺo ṁaꝛbaꝺ ꝺo ꞃꝺb Ccuꝛbꝛꝭꝺe .ı. o hꞃꝺb ꝼoꞇa aıᵹ loc ꝺa ċaoċ a nꝺeıꞃıꝺ Cꝺuṁan," " Flann, son of Lonan, chief poet of the Gathelians, was killed by the descendants of Curbruidhe, i. e. of the Hy Fotha, at *Lough-da-chaoch*, in the Desies of Munster." The Four Masters, by some strange mistake, record the death of this poet twice in the same words; first under the year 891, and again A. D. 918. " ꝼlañ mac Lonaın, Uıꞃᵹıꞇ ꝼıl Scoꞇa, pꞃımꝼıle Ᵹaoıꝺeal ꞃꝉle, ꝼıle aꞃ ꝺeaċ baı ı nⱸꝛıñ ına ꝺꝭmꞃıꞃ ꝺo maꝛbaꝺ la macꞃꝺb Ccꞃꝛꝛbꝛꝺe (ꝺo ꞃꝺb ꝼoꞇaıꝺ ıaꞇꝛen) hı noꞃꞅne ꞇaıꝺe hıc loc ꝺa ċaoċ ı nꝺeıꞃıꝺ Cꝺuṁan," " Flann, son of Lonan, Virgil of the race of Scota, chief *Ollamh* of all the Gaedhals, the best poet that was in Ireland in his time, was murdered by the sons of Currbuidhe (they were of the Hy Fotha) in Dun-Taidhe, at *Lough-da-chaoch*, in the Desies of Munster."

From the character given of Flann, it is to be presumed that his works were numerous, or at least remarkable for superior style and sweetness of number; but the few poems of his writing that have come under the observation of the writer of this account of Irish authors, are not possessed of any extraordinary beauties.

Copies of three poems written by Flann, are to be found in the account of the spreading branches of Heber, son of Milesius, in the *Leabhar Muimhneach*, or Munster Book, in possession of the Assistant Secretary of this Society.

1st, A poem of eighty-eight verses, beginning " Loꝛcán loċa ꝺeıꞃᵹ ꝺeıꞃc," " Lorcan of Lough Deirg dheirc." Upon the defeat of Flann Sionna, by Lorcan, king of Munster, and grandfather of Brian Boroimhe.

2d, A poem of forty-eight verses, beginning " Loꝛcán léıꞃ ꞇaꞃ ꝼıꞃ ꝼoꝺla," " Lorcan, wise beyond the men of Fodhla, *(Ireland)*." In praise of the actions of Lorcan, king of Munster.

3d, A poem of forty verses, beginning " Ceañ-Coꝛaꝺ ꝺún na ꞇꞇᵹla," " Ceann-Coradh, inclosure of harvest stores." Upon the fortress of Ceann-Coradh in the days of Cinneide, son of Lorcan, and father of Brian Boroimhe, king of Munster and monarch of Ireland.

To these are added the following:

4th, A poem of two hundred and thirty-two verses, beginning " Conall cṙinġıḋ cloıṁe Néıll," "Conall, hero of the race of Niall," by some persons attributed to this author; by others to Flann, of the monastery of Bute; and by others again, with more probability, to Giolla Brighide Mac Coinmhide. See under the year 1350.

5th, The poem, beginning " Conġal cṁ Oġaẋaıṙ maıṫ ṙı," in praise of Congal, who was monarch of Ireland seven years, from the year 704, is also attributed to this writer.

A. D. 908.

lxxxiv. Cormac Mac Cuillionan, king of Munster, and archbishop of Cashel, was killed this year, in the battle of Bealach Mughna, fought by him against Flann Sionna, the monarch of Ireland, Cearbhall, king of Leinster, and Cathal, son of Conor, king of Conaght. He wrote many tracts, both prose and verse, some of which have come down to our times, and others were extant in the days of our fathers; the most remarkable of those now extant are the following :—

1. A glossary, explaining the difficult words in his native language.

This glossary is, by some antiquarians, supposed to be written by Cormac mac Art, monarch of Ireland, in the middle of the third century after our Lord Jesus Christ; but the number of words in this tract, explained by, or derived from, the Latin, Greek, and Hebrew languages, are presumptive proofs that the work could not have been written by the last-mentioned author, unless we admit, that learning had arrived to a much higher pitch in Ireland at this early period, than some persons are willing to allow.

2. The Psalter of Cashel. This was a collection of Irish Records, in prose and verse, transcribed from more ancient documents, such as the Psalter of Tarah, &c. It contained also many original pieces, some of them written by Cormac himself. This book was extant in Limerick, in the year 1712, as appears by a large folio MS. in the Irish language, preserved in the library of Cashel, written in Limerick in that year, and partly transcribed from the original Psalter of Cashel. The writer of this

account was indulged with a perusal of the Cashel MS. by his Grace the present Archbishop. The original Psalter of Cashel was long supposed to be lost, but it is now said to be deposited in the British Museum.

Several poems ascribed to Cormac Mac Cuillionan are preserved in the libraries of Trinity College, and of William Monck Mason, Esq. and in the collection of the Assistant Secretary. Some of these poems are historical, and some are on religious subjects. One of them contains his will. We forbear giving a particular account of each poem, as they are not illustrative of the history or antiquities of our country.

LXXXV. At the same time with Cormac Mac Cuillionan, lived SEALB-HACH, the Secretary of that prince. He wrote a poem, reciting the names of the Saints of Ireland, and distinguishing the tribes to which each Saint belonged. It begins " Naoṁ ṡeancaṡ naoṁ ınṡe ṡaıl," " The sacred pedigree of the Saints of Ireland."

This poem is by some writers ascribed to Cormac, but is more generally attributed to Sealbhach.

Copies of it are in the library of Trinity College, Dublin ; in the collections of William Monck Mason, Esq. and in that of the Assistant Secretary to this Society.

A. D. 941.

LXXXVI. CORBMACAN EIGEAS flourished in the time that Donogh, son of Flann Sionna, governed Ireland, and Muirceartach, son of Niall *glundubh* (black-kneed) ruled the province of Ulster. He was chief poet of Ulster, the friend and counsellor of Muirceartach, and his companion in all his expeditions against the Danes, who then tyrannized over Ireland. The Book of Invasions, by the O'Clerys, relates that Muirceartach, after triumphing over the Danes in his own province, and at Dublin in conjunction with the monarch, made a selection of his best troops, and with them made a circuit of Ireland, in which the kings of the other provinces, and the chiefs of districts, paid him tribute, and delivered him hostages. Upon his return to Oileach, his own people of Cineal

Eoghan advised him to go to Tarah, and demand hostages from Donogh, the monarch. This he not only refused, but sent the hostages that were given to him in his circuit, to Donogh, as the supreme governor of the entire kingdom. The monarch, highly gratified by this proof of loyalty in Muirceartach, returned the hostages to him, as the most proper person to keep what had been delivered into his hands. To commemorate this circuit, and the mighty deeds of his prince, Corbmacan wrote his poem of two hundred and fifty-six verses, beginning " Ꙃ Ɱ꜀рꚉеꚇрꚇꙇꚗ ꙇꙍеꙇꚏ ꙎᴇꙇꙆꙆ Ꙍꙇꙍ, ꙍꙍ ꙃꙇꙋꙇꙍ ꙃꙇꙇꙆꙆꙋ Ꙇꙍꙍꙍ ꙍꙇꙆ," " Oh Muirceartach, son of worthy Niall, thou who hast received hostages from Falia's Isle."

In this poem the poet extols the noble actions of his king, and declares him superior to Cuchullin, Fergus mac Roigh, Curaoi mac Daire, and other heroes of antiquity. From the extraordinary merit of this poem, we cannot but regret that more of this author's works have not come into our hands.

A copy of this poem is preserved in the O'Clerys' Book of Conquests, and in the pedigree of the once royal family of O'Neill, in the hands of the Assistant Secretary.

———

A. D. 958.

LXXXVII. FINNSNEACHTA O'CUILL, chief poet of Munster, died this year, according to the Annals of the Four Masters. Of the number and nature of his works, or where they are now to be found, we can at present say nothing. Perhaps some of them may be in the library of Trinity College, amongst the great heap of Irish manuscripts that are not described in the catalogue.

———

A. D. 975.

LXXXVIII. CINAETH O'HARTIGAN, a famous Irish poet, died this year. Tigernach, the Annalist, relates his death in these words: " Ꙇꙇꙍꙇꚇ .h. ꙗꙇꙗꚇꙋꙗꙇꙍ ꙗꙇꙇꙅ ᴇꙇꚏꚏꙒ Ꙇᴇꙇꚇ Ꙇꙗꙗꙍ ꙅꙍꙇꚇꙋꙗ," " Cinaeth O'Hartagan, chief of the learned of Leath Chuinn, *(Conn's half, or Northern division of Ireland)* dies."

Some entire poems, the works of this author, have come down to our times, and many quotations from others are preserved in ancient MSS. of great celebrity. His poem of one hundred and eight verses, beginning "Ɔoṁáṅ, ouċaṁ álaɪnɔe," "World, transitory beautiful," gives a description of the beauty of the hill, and splendour of the palace of Tarah, in the days of Cormac mac Art, otherwise called Cormac *ulfada, (long-beard),* and although only seven hundred and twenty-one years had elapsed, from the ascension of Cormac, A. D. 254, until the death of Cinnaeth, A. D. 975, it appears, that in his days the palace no longer existed, and the hill had become a desert, overgrown with grass and weeds. This gave occasion for the moral reflection with which the author commences his work.

This poem is preserved in the O'Clerys' Book of Invasions.

2. A poem of ninety-six verses, beginning "Suɴɔ ɔ'eɪɾɪɔ ɔa ṁɲ̄ṅeáṅṁáɾ," "Here of the Easa's if we explain." This gives the popular account of the origin of the name of Rath Easa, in Meath.

3. A poem of seventy-six verses, beginning "Ꝏcaɪll ɼoɾ áɪce Ceáṁáɾ," "Acaill, near to Tarah," upon the origin of the name of Dumha Earc, near Tarah, in Meath.

4. A poem of fifty-two verses, beginning "Ꝏṅ ɼɪṅ a bɼɲ̄ż ṁɪc Ꝏṅoɪż," "There is the palace of the son of Anoig." This poem gives the origin of the names of the palace of the son of Anoig, Inbher Colpa, &c.

5. A poem of seventy-two verses, beginning "Ɔa beɪɾ máɪɾɪ ɔoṅá ṁṅáɪɓ," "If bloom be given to women," upon several remarkable women of antiquity, and places called after them.

These poems are all inserted in the Dinn Seanchas; a perfect copy of which is in the possession of Sir William Betham, and an imperfect copy in the Book of Leacan, and another in possession of the Assistant Secretary.

6. A poem, beginning "Ɔo lɲ̄ɔ Olɪoll ɪɼɪṅ caɪllɪɔ," "Olioll fell in the wood." This poem gives the names of places where several of the Irish kings and heroes died. A copy of it is preserved in a vellum MS. belonging to William Monck Mason, Esq. written in the year 1487, and another copy is in the collection of the Assistant Secretary.

A. D. 980.

LXXXIX. MAC GIOLLA CAOIMH, a poet, flourished in the time of Brian Boroimhe and of Cian, son of Maolmhuaidh, chief of the Eugenians of Cashel, king of south Munster, and son-in-law of Brian. This poet lived for some years after the battle of Clontarf, fought on Good Friday, in the year 1014. We have met with but two poems ascribed to this author.

1st. A poem of forty-four verses, beginning "Uaṫmaṛ an oiḋċe anoċt," "Dreadful the night, this night." It is the lamentation of the poet after Cian, Brian, and his son Morogh.

2d. A poem of one hundred and eight verses, beginning "Raiṫ Raiṫlean Cṛṛc iṛ Cian," "Raithlean's Rath of Corc and Cian," upon the deserted state of Rath Raithlean and other Palaces, after the death of Corc, Cian and other Momonian princes.

These poems are preserved in the Pedigrees of the spreading Branches of the Stock of Heber, in the Munster Book, in possession of the Assistant Secretary.

A. D. 984.

XC. EOCHAIDH O'FLOINN, a celebrated poet and historian, died this year. He wrote several poems in his native language, which are preserved in ancient MSS. of great respectability, particularly the Books of Glendaloch, Ballimote, and Leacan, the Dinn Seanchas, Book of Invasions, Keating's History of Ireland, &c. &c. &c.

The following are the most remarkable and best known of this author's works:

1. A poem of two hundred and twenty-four verses, interlined with a Gloss, upon the Invasion of Ireland, by Partholan, giving an account of the place from which he first set out for Ireland; the places he stopped

at in his passage ; the period at which he arrived in Ireland ; the chief persons that accompanied him in his expedition ; the invasion of the Fomorians ; the number of their ships and people ; and the battle of Magh Ith, fought between them and Partholan's people. This poem begins " Paptolan, Canay taimcc," " Partholan, from whence came he." It is inserted in the O'Clerys' Book of Invasions, in possession of the Assistant Secretary.

2. A poem, interlined with a gloss, one hundred and four verses, on the colonization of Ireland, first by Ceassar, and again by Partholan, giving an account of the times in which both these colonies arrived in Ireland, the number and names of loughs and rivers discovered in Ireland in the time of Partholan, and the death of the entire colony. This poem begins " 2l coema clg Cṅnò coeinṛeing," " Oh ye learned of the plain of mild and generous Conn." It is to be found in the O'Clerys' Book of Invasions already mentioned in different places of this ac- count.

3. A poem of twenty-eight verses, upon the division of Ireland betweeen the four sons of Partholan, marking the places where the boundaries of each met.

This poem begins " Ceaṫpaṗ maċ ba gṅibòa, glop," " Four sons, who were fierce, clamorous." It may be found in the first volume of Doctor Keating's History of Ireland, published by Barlow, in its original lan- guage, with a literal translation by the late Mr. William Haliday, a young gentleman of extraordinary talent, whose early death is an irre- parable loss to Irish literature.

4. A poem of sixty-eight verses, giving the names of the Druids, Artists, &c. that accompanied Partholan to Ireland.

This poem begins " Ro bo maiṫ an ṁṅṅtip ṁoip," " Good were the great family." It is in the collection of the Assistant Secretary.

5. A poem of fifty-six verses upon the destruction of Conaing's tower, and the battles fought between the Fomorians and Nemethians.

This poem begins " Togail tṅp Conuing co ngoil," " Destruction of the tower of Conaing by valour." It is inserted in the O'Clerys' Book of Invasions.

6. A poem of one hundred and ninety-six verses, interlined with a gloss. In this poem Eochaidh mentions the creation of Adam, and the time that elapsed from that era to the time that Ceassar is said to have landed in Ireland; the number of years that expired between the universal deluge and the colonization of Ireland by Partholan; and the interval between the destruction of the Partholanian colony, by the plague, and the arrival of Nemeth. He then gives an account of the Nemethian colony, of their coming from Scythia, and their passage to Ireland; and recounts the number of their ships, and the names of their leaders. The transactions of the Nemethians after their landing in Ireland are then related; such as the clearing of several plains, by cutting down the timber with which the country was overgrown; the discovery of lakes and rivers; the hardships and oppression they suffered from the Fomorians; the battles they fought with them, and the destruction of Conaing's tower; the return of part of the colony to Greece, and the emigration of another part into Britain, under Britan, the bald, from whom that country is said to derive its name.

This poem begins " Eιρe oll oιρòηιc ʒáoιòιl," " Erin grand, where rule the Gaels." It is preserved in the Book of Invasions, by the O'Clerys, and in other MSS. in possession of the Assistant Secretary.

7. A poem, with an interlined gloss, beginning " ḃEρe co ηuáιll co ηιoò-ηáιḃ," " Eire, by excellence and force of arms." A copy of this poem, containing seventy-two verses, without a gloss, is in the Book of Invasions, inserted in the Book of Leacan, fol. 11, column 2. There is another copy in the O'Clerys' Book of Invasions, accompanied by a gloss inter-lined, but in this copy there are only sixty verses.

8. A poem of sixty-eight verses, giving the names of the principal leaders that came with the sons of Melisius to Ireland, and also the names of the places where several of them died.

This poem begins " Coιρícch ηá loιηʒρι òáρ leρ," " Chiefs of this fleet across the sea." An entire copy of this poem is preserved in the Book of Leacan, fol. 12, col. 2, and ascribed to Eochaidh O'Floinn. In the Book of Invasions, by the O'Clerys, an extract is given from this poem, which they attribute to Flann of Bute.

9. A poem of seventy-two verses, with an interlined gloss, upon the accession of Sobhairce and Cearmna *Fionn* to the throne of Ireland, A. M. 3045, the partition of the island between them, and upon the raths or forts erected by them, or that were called after them; particularly those of Dún Sobhairce, now called Carrickfergus, in the North, and Dún Cearmna, now Kinsale, in the South of Ireland.

This poem begins " Ďún Soḃairce, ⱱiaɲ ſluaᵹ liⁿ," " Sobhairce's Fort, shield of a numerous host." It is preserved in the Book of Invasions by the O'Clerys, and in the Book of Leacan, fol. 15, col. 3. In the first of these MSS. the text is accompanied by a copious gloss, without which it could not be easily understood. In the last-mentioned MS. the text alone is given.

10. A poem of three hundred and twenty-eight verses, with an interlined gloss, upon the Invasion of Ireland by the sons of Golamh, or Milesius, and the kings of his race, who governed Ireland from the first landing of the Milesian colony, A. M. 2935, to the time of Aengus, (*Ollmhuchach*, or *Ollbhuadhach* (*All-extinguishing*, or All-conquering), in A. M. 3150). The name of each king is recited, an account given of the plains cleared by them, of the lakes that sprung up, and the rivers that began to flow in their times, and of the battles in which they were engaged.

A copy of this poem is given by the O'Clerys in their Book of Invasions. It commences " ⱸᴛᵹⱱ oeſ eccɲa aⱱⱱinⱱ," " Hearken ye people of delightful wisdom." There is another copy in the Book of Leacan, fol. 14. col. 2. but this copy wants the Gloss, and contains only three hundred and twelve verses.

11. A poem of one hundred and eighty-eight verses, with an interlined gloss, giving an account of the building of the palace of Emania, in Ulster, (now Ardmagh) by Cimbaeth, king of that province, A. M. 3596; the kings that ruled there, from the time of Cimbaeth to the reign of Conor Mac Nessa, cotemporary with our Lord Jesus Christ, and from the death of Conor, to the destruction of Emania by the three Collas, immediately after the battle of Achadh-leith-dearg, in which they defeated and slew Fergus fogha, king of Ulster, A. D. 331. It also gives the names of the provincial kings of Ulster, who became monarchs of Ireland.

This poem is given by the O'Clerys in their Book of Invasions, and in the Book of Leacan, fol. 16. col. 1. This last copy has no Gloss. The poem begins " Eaṁṛn ioḋnac aiḃinḋ," " Well armed, delightful Emania."

12. A poem of fifty-six verses, giving the names of the twenty-five sons of Ugaine Mor, or Hugony the Great, monarch of Ireland; an account of the partition of the country between them, and the districts that fell to the share of each son.

This poem begins " Uᵹoine, uallaċ, aṁṛa," " Hugony, learned, illustrious." It is to be found in the Book of Leacan, fol. 16, col. 4, and in the O'Clerys' Book of Invasions.

13. A poem of seventy-two verses, which gives the names of the fifteen kings that reigned over the province of Ulster, from the time of Cimbaeth to that of Conor, son of Nessa, and the number of years that each king reigned; speaks of the building of Emania, and the number of kings that reigned there from the time of Conor, son of Nessa, to the destruction of that palace by the three Collas, sons of Eochaidh Doimhlein, and grandsons of Cairbre Liffeachar, monarch of Ireland.

This poem begins " Cimbaeċ, cleiċe noc n Emna," " Cimbaeth, protector of the poets of Emania." It is preserved in the Book of Invasions, inserted in the Book of Leacan, fol. 16. col. 3.

14. A poem of two hundred and thirty-two verses, on the creation of the world; the names and ages of the Patriarchs who lived before the general deluge; the building and dimensions of Noah's ark; the deaths of Noah and his sons; the building of the Tower of Babel; the confusion of languages, and the settlement of NIULL, son of FENIUS *farsaidh*, in Egypt.

This poem begins " Aⱦaiṛ caiċ coiṁṛiḋ niṁe," " Father of all who measurest the heavens." A very ancient copy of this poem is to be found in a vellum MS. the property of Sir William Betham, and another copy on vellum, written in the 13th century, is in the collection of the Assistant Secretary.

There is another poem that by some persons is attributed to this author, beginning " Riᵹ na loc in locṛa ⱦeaṛ," " King of lakes, this southern lake;" but it is by others, perhaps more properly, ascribed to Flann of Bute. It is to be found in the Dinn Seanchas.

A. D. 990.

xci. Tighernach the Annalist, under the year 990, records the death of Urard Mac Coise, in these words, " Upapò mac Coiρe pρim écceρ Ʒaoiòil ò'ecc iaρ mbuaiò aiċρiʒemoiρe a ccluaiη meic noiρ," " Urard Mac Coisi, the first learned of the Gathelians, died, after great penance, in Cluain-macnois." He wrote

1. A poem beginning " Woelρeclaiη fiŋρeaρ Ʒaoiòil," " Maolseachlainn, elder of the Gael, or Gathelians."

2. A poem of eighty-eight verses, upon the death of Sean Fergal O'Ruairc, king of Conaght, who was killed A. D. 964, by Congalach, lord of Breagh and Cnoghba in Meath.

This poem begins " bρóηaċ ollam òeiρ ã ρi," " Sorrowful the poet after his king." It is to be found in the collection of the Assistant Secretary.

3. A poem, beginning " Waρċaiη òρċ a loρaiρò feil," " May you live, Oh generous Iorard," is ascribed to this author; but as it is addressed to himself, it is more likely it was written by some of his cotemporaries.

The Four Masters, under the year 1023, record the death of an Erard Mac Coisi; but from the poem on the death of Fergal O'Ruairc, above-mentioned, written immediately after the fall of that king in 964, when the writer must have been a man of full age, it would appear the Erard of the Four Masters, and the Urard of Tighernach, were two distinct persons. The Erard who died in Anno 1023, is said to have been the Secretary of Maolseachlainn, and was perhaps the author of the poem beginning " Waoilρeċlaiη fiŋρioρ Ʒaoiòil," which we have above given to the Mac Coisi of whom we are now speaking.

A. D. 1008.

xcii. The Four Masters, under this year, record the death of CLOTHNA, son of Angus, chief poet of Ireland in his time. Some poems attributed to him are in the library of Trinity College.

A. D. 1009.

xciii. MAL SUTHAIN O'CARROLL, lord of the Eoganachts of Lough Lein, one of the people (Monks) of Inisfallen, the most learned of the western world, died this year, according to the Four Masters. He is said to be the first writer of the annals of Inisfallen.

A. D. 1015.

xciv. MAC LIAG, Secretary to Brian Boroimhe, monarch of Ireland, died this year, according to the annals of the Four Masters, who record his death in these words, " Ɱac liacc, .i. Ɱu͘ɼceaɼτaɕ, ɱac Conceaɼτaiɕ, aɼ óllaṁ eɼeaɼ an τan ɼin ꝺecc," " Mac Liag, i. e. Muirkeartagh, son of Conkeartach, at that time chief doctor (professor) of Ireland, died." He was author of the following works :

1. " leaꝺaɼ oiɼiɼ aɼaɼ aɼala aɼ ɕoɼτaiꝺ aɼaɼ aɼ ɕaτaiꝺ Eiɼionꝺ," " A book of Chronology and Annals on the wars and battles of Ireland." This book, notwithstanding its title, is confined to an account of the battles of Munster, during the time of Brian Boroimhe. A fine copy, written in 1710, by John Mac Solly, a celebrated scribe, and native of Ꞇiɼ callain, or Stickallen, near Slane, in the county Meath, is in the collection of the Assistant Secretary.

2. A Life of Brian Boroimhe. An extract from this work was given by the late General Valancey, in the first edition of his Irish Grammar.

3. A poem of one hundred and sixty verses, beginning "Ꝺá ṁac ꝺéaᵹ ꝺo ċiñ o Chaᵹ," "Twelve sons descended from Cas," upon the descendants of Cas, son of Conall *Each luath*, king of Munster, A. D. 366.

4. A poem of thirty-two verses, beginning "Ꝺá ṁac ꝺéaᵹ Chiñeiꝺiᵹ ċaiꝺ," "Twelve sons of chaste Cinneide," giving an account of the twelve sons of Kennedy, father of Brian Boroimhe.

These poems are in the collection of the Assistant Secretary, in the hand-writing of John Mac Solly, mentioned above.

5. A poem of forty-four verses, beginning "Ꙇ Chiñ-copaꝺ caiꝺi ḃpian," "Oh Cinn-coradh, where is Brian," upon Cinn-coradh, the palace of Brian Boroimhe.

This beautiful and pathetic poem was written by Mac Liag, after the death of Brian, in which the author laments the loss of that hero, and other illustrious chiefs that used to resort to his hospitable mansion. It is preserved in the library of John Mac Namara, Esq. in a volume of very valuable poems, collected in the Netherlands in the year 1650, by Nicholas, alias Fergal O'Gara, a friar of the order of Saint Augustine, who, after finishing his studies in Spain, returned to Ireland, where he was highly respected, and in the days of Cromwell left his native land, with many others, and retired to Lisle. Another copy is in the collection of the Assistant Secretary.

6. A poem, beginning "Ꙇniap ꞇainicc ꞇꞧꞇim ḃpiain," "Westward came the fall of Brian."

7. A poem of twenty verses, beginning "faꝺa ḃeiꞇ ᵹán aiḃneꝼ," "Long to be without delight." This short poem was written by the author when he had retired to iñꝼe ᵹall, (the Hebrides) after the death of Brian Boroimhe; and in it he bitterly laments his absence from Ceann-coradh, and his want of the pleasures he was there accustomed to enjoy.

The two last-mentioned poems are in the collection of the Assistant Secretary, in the hand-writing of John Mac Solly.

The Four Masters, in recording the death of this writer, give two ranns, which they say were the first and the last that were written by him.

First Rann:

" Ořꞃꝺelꞃꞇaċ becc mac mail ceaꞃꞇaċ. bai ac ꞇoꞃᵹaꞃe na mbó
Ꝺꞁꞇe aꞃ ꞇꞃóꞃaꞇc naċ aꞃ ꞇꞝmlaꞇꞇ. Ꞇabᵹ ꞃᵹeanaꞝ ꞇꞝꞃꞃaꞃ꞊p óó."

Last Rann:

" Ꝺ ċlꞃ̨cc aꞇa 1 cꞝꞝ maꝺaꞃꞃꞇ. ꝺo ꞇꞃꞃ ꞇꞇ ꞇeccaꞇꞇ cáꞃaꞇꞇ
Ᵹo ꝺoꞃe ꞇa ꝺo ꝺꞝꞃᵹ ꝺaꞃᵹ. aꞃ óꞇꞇ ꞃꞝꞃꞇeaꞃ an ꞃalaꞃ̃."

A. D. 1020.

xcv. About this time DONOGH, son of Brian Boroihme, carried on a dispute with Iorard, or Erard Mac Coise, Secretary to the monarch Maolseachloinn, in which Donogh endeavours to shew that his father and the Munster troops were superior to Maolseachloinn and his followers. A poem, of one hundred and ninety-two verses, upon this subject, ascribed to Donogh, has come down to our times, a copy of which is in the collection of the writer of this account. It begins " Ꞃꞃeᵹoꞃꞃ meꞃꞃꞃ, ꝺ ꞆꞀꞡc Coꞃꞃꞁ!" " Answer me, Oh Mac Coisi."

A. D. 1023.

xcvi. The Four Masters, under this year record the death of ERARD MAC COISI, the chief historian of Ireland, in these words, " Єꞃaꞃꝺ Ꞁꝺac Coꞃꞃe aꞃꝺċꞃꞝꞃꞃcꞃꝺ na nᵹaoꞝꝺeal ꝺ'ecc hꞃ Ccꞡꞝaꞃꞃ mac Ꞁꞝꞃꞃ ꞃꝺ nꝺeꞃᵹ beaꞇa." " Erard Mac Coisi, Chief Chronicler of the Gaels, died in Cluain-mac-Nois, after a good life."

From the similarity of names between this author and the Urard Mac Coisi, mentioned under the year 990, and Cluain-mac-Nois being mentioned as the place where both died, some antiquarians have supposed them to be the same person. But this is improbable, though not impossible.

Urard Mac Coisi, who, Tighernach says, died in the year 990, was poet to Ferghal O'Ruairc, king of Conaght, who was killed A. D. 964. Urard should be therefore near one hundred years old, if he lived to the year 1023, when Erard Mac Coisi died, according to the Four Masters, and consequently, would be unable to carry on a literary contest with Donogh, son of Brian Boroimhe, which we are assured Erard Mac Coisi, Secretary to Maolseachlainn, did. These circumstances considered, it may be fair to conclude that they were two distinct persons, and that Erard who died in 1023, was the real author of the poem beginning " Ɯɑoıʃeɑċloɯ̃ ʃɪñʃeɑʃ ʒɑoıƀeɑl," attributed to Urard Mac Coise, who died A. D. 990.

See A. D. 990.

A. D. 1024.

CXVII. CUAN O'LOCHAIN, the most learned and celebrated antiquarian and historian of Ireland, in his time, was killed in Teathbha this year, according to the concurrent testimonies of the annals of Tighernach, Inisfallen, and the Four Masters. His talents and his virtues were so highly appreciated by his countrymen, that he was made joint regent of Ireland with Corcran *Cleireach*, (a clergyman) after the death of Maolseachlainn. He was author of the following much esteemed pieces:

1. A poem of one hundred and eighty-eight verses, beginning " Ceɑmɑıʃ ċoʒɑ nɑ ċċulɑċ," " Tarah, choice of hills," upon the splendor of the royal palace of Tarah, in the time of Cormac Mac Art, monarch of Ireland, A. D. 250.

A copy of this poem is given in the Book of Invasions, by the O'Clerys, and other copies are in the Dinn Seanchas, in an old vellum MS. belonging to Sir William Betham, and in the Book of Leacan.

2. A poem of one hundred and forty-eight verses, beginning " ᾽Ʒfıʃ ɑın ıɑƀɑʃ ɑn ceɑċ, ıʃ me ɑn co leoċɑın lɑıƀeɑċ," " Oh praiseworthy man, who closest the house, I am the poetic O'Lochan," upon the royal rights and privileges of the monarch and provincial kings of Ireland.

Copies of this poem are preserved in the Book of Leacan, in an ancient vellum MS. the property of Sir William Betham, and in the collection of the Assistant Secretary.

3. A poem of fifty-six verses, beginning "Sꝺeꝛ ainm Sinꝺa ꝼaiᵹiꝺ uaim," "Noble name of Shanon, hear from me," upon the origin of the name of the river Shanon.

This poem is to be found in the copies of the Dinn Seanchas, in the Book of Leacan, fol. 188, col. 2, in Sir William Betham's large vellum MS. and in the Assistant Secretary's collection.

A. D. 1030.

XCVIII. Cumara, son of Mac Liag, chief poet of Ireland, died this year. We are not able to say where any of his works are now to be found.

A. D. 1041.

XCIX. Tighernach, the annalist, records the death of the son of Ainmhire, a judge, this year, in these words: "Oⱦac Ꝉinmiꝛe Ꝉꝛobꝛeicioṁ Ꝉꝛoamaꝺa, acaꝼ ꞇꝛle eolaiꝼ Eꝛioñ ꝺꝛcc," "The son of Ainmhire, chief judge of Ardmagh, and flood of knowledge, or science, of Ireland, died."

We cannot, at present, point out where any of this author's works are to be found.

A. D. 1048.

c. Cennfaoladh O'Cuill, ollamh (professor) of Munster, died this year. He wrote a poem of one hundred and sixty verses, beginning "Ceaⱦ ꝼuan na hoꝛⱦꝛa a naꝛꝺ ⱦiaꝛ," "House of rest, of sorrow in the west," on the death of Eogan *(Owen)* grand nephew of Brian Boroimhe, who was killed in a battle fought in Ossory, in the year 1027.

Copy in the library of John Mac Namara, Esq.

A. D. 1050.

ci. COLEMAN O'SEASNAN flourished about this time. He was author of, 1st. a poem of three hundred and twenty-eight verses, beginning " Clanꝺ ollaman ꞃaιꞅle Eaṁna," " Children of poets, the nobles of Emania," on the palace of Emania, and the Christian kings and nobles of Ulster. 2d. A poem, beginning " Eaṁꞃn alaιnꝺ aꞃuꞅ Ulaꝺ," " Beautiful Emania, mansion of Ulster," gives an account of thirty-four Ulster kings that reigned in Emania, from the time of its foundation by Cimbaeth to the time of its final destruction. Copies in the Book of Ballimote in the library of the Royal Irish Academy.

A. D. 1056.

cii. FLANN MAINISTREACH, or Flann, Abbot of the monastery of Bute, died in the month of December this year. He was author of several poems, of which the following are the most remarkable :

1. A poem of one hundred and sixty verses, beginning " Eιꞅτιꝺ, a eolca cen on," " Attend, oh ye learned without reproach," on the deaths of the most remarkable of the Tuatha-de-dannans, and the places where they died.

This poem is preserved in the Book of Leacan, fol. 28, col. 1. and in the Book of Invasions by the O'Clerys.

2. A poem of one hundred and forty-eight verses, with an interlined gloss, beginning " Rιᵹ Ceaṁꞃa ꝺιa τeꞅbanꝺ τnu," " Kings of Tarah, who were active in life," gives the names of the monarchs of Ireland from

Eochaidh Feilioch, who began to reign A. M. 3922, to the death of Dathy, at the foot of the Alps, A. D. 428, and also an account of their deaths.

Copies of this poem are to be found in the Book of Leacan, fol. 24, col. 4, and in the O'Clerys' Book of Invasions. The Leacan copy has no gloss.

3. A poem of two hundred and eight verses, beginning " Ríg Teámpa ταοbαιδε ιαp τταιη," " Kings of Tara afterwards joined," giving an account of the names and deaths of the Christian Monarchs of Ireland, from Laogaire, whose reign began A. D. 429, to the death of Maolseachlainn the 2d, A. D. 1022.

Copies of this poem are preserved in the Book of Leacan, fol. 25, col. 1, and the O'Clerys' Book of Invasions.

4. A poem of one hundred and thirty verses, beginning " Oṅṅτίρ Pατρραιce na pραιττεαρ," " Family of Patrick of the prayers," gives an account of Saint Patrick's household, and the names of the persons who filled different offices under him.

A copy of this poem is in the collection of the Assistant Secretary, in the hand-writing of John Mac Solly.

5. A poem of one thousand two hundred and twenty verses, beginning " Reιδιg δαṁ α δhe δο ṁṁ," " Prepare for me, oh God of Heaven," on the emperors, kings, and other sovereigns of the Assyrians, Persians, Grecians, Romans, &c. from the days of Ninus, to the time of the emperor Theodosius.

Copies of this poem are preserved in the Book of Leacan, fol. 20, col. 2.; in Sir William Betham's large vellum MS. and in the collection of the Assistant Secretary.

6. A poem of seventy-two verses, beginning " Ατα ρυηδ ρεηċυρ naċ ρuαιll," " Here is a history not mean," on the taxes or tributes payable to the princes of Tirconnell, and the subsidies paid by them to their subordinate chiefs.

An ancient copy of this poem is in the collection of John M'Namara, of Sandymount, Esq. and another in that of the Assistant Secretary.

7. A poem of seventy-two verses, beginning " A lırbαιρ ατα αιρ δο lαρ," " Oh book, there is on thy page," on the rights and privileges of the kings of Oiligh and Cineal Conaill, the O'Neills and O'Donells.

Copies of this poem are in the collections of the Rev. Doctor O'Brien, professor of Irish in the Royal College of Maynooth; John M'Namara, of Sandymount, Esq. and the Assistant Secretary of this Society.

8 A poem of two hundred and thirty-two verses, beginning " Conall cηηзιδ cloinδe Neill," " Conall, hero of the race of Niall," in praise of Conall Gulban, son of Niall of the nine hostages, who conquered a settlement in Ulster for himself and three of his brothers, Owen, Cairbre, and Eanna. From this hero, the district called Tir-Conel, or Conall's country, is named, which anciently comprehended the present counties of Donegall and Londonderry. The bounds of Tirconnel are set out in the poem, and fifty battles fought by Conall in different parts of Ireland, are enumerated. This poem is by some writers attributed to Flann Mac Lonain.

Another poem on the same subject, and beginning with the same words, written by Giolla Brighide Mac Coinmhidhe, appears in the account of that author's works, under the year 1350.

A fine copy of this poem is in the manuscript collection of the Rev. Doctor O'Brien, Irish professor in the Royal College of Maynooth.

9. A poem of one hundred and twenty-four verses, beginning " 2ἱ eolἐα Conaill ἐeolaἳ," " Oh ye learned of musical Conall," on Dalach, Chief of Tirconall, from whose grandson Donald, the noble family of O'Donell derive their name, as they are also called Clann Dalaigh, or sons of Dalach, from himself. From this poem it appears that Dalach was the youngest of the five sons of Muircheartach, prince of Tirconell, the tenth in descent from Conall Gulban, son of Niall, of the nine hostages. It is shown that Dalach was a man of great wealth, and purchased the chiefry of his tribe from his elder brothers.

Copies of this poem are in the manuscript collections of the Rev. Doctor O'Brien, and of the Assistant Secretary.

10. A poem of forty-eight verses, beginning " Caιρρε, ἐocchan, Enδa eἰń," " Cairbre, Owen, active Enna," on the territories or portions of land possessed by four of the sons of Conall Gulban, son of Niall of the nine hostages. The boundaries of each son's land is set out, and the names of their several districts given. This poem is also attributed to Giolla Brighde Mac Coinmhidhe.

Copies in possession of the Rev. Doctor O'Brien, and of the Assistant Secretary.

11. A poem of one hundred and eighty verses, beginning " Eña, ɞalτa Caɲppɲe cɲuaɪɞ," " Enna, ward of valiant Cairbre," on the descendants of Fergus, and Earc, the daughter of Loarn, king of Scotland. This is by some ascribed to Loughlin, son of Teige og O'Daly.

Copies in the collections of Doctor O'Brien, and of the Assistant Secretary.

12. A poem of eighty-eight verses, beginning " Eɪʄτɪᵹ ɲe Conall calma," " Attend ye to valorous Conall," on the dispute between Owen, ancestor of the O'Neills, and Conall, founder of the O'Donell family.

Copies of this poem are in the collections of Doctor O'Brien and the Assistant Secretary.

13. A poem, beginning " 2ιτa ʄɲnɞ ɲɲɪɪaɞ na ɲɪoᵹ," " Here is a catalogue of the kings."

14. A poem of fifty-six verses, beginning " 1ɞɪɲ ᵹaċ oɞaɪɲ ɲᵹɲɪoɞaɲ, an manaċ 1oɲelɪnuɲ," " Between every work that the monk Joceline writes." This poem is on the family of the O'Donells, whose great ancestor Conall, as Joceline tells us, in the 138th chapter of his Life of St. Patrick, received a particular blessing from our Apostle.

Copy in the manuscript collection of the Rev. Doctor O'Brien, and in that of the Assistant Secretary.

Some of these last-mentioned poems are, by some writers, ascribed to Giolla Brighide Mac Coinmhidhe, and, by others, to Fergal Mac an Bhaird, who lived long after the time of Flann.

See Mac Coinmhidhe, under the year 1350.

A. D. 1064.

CIII. The Blind O'Lonan, chief poet and historian of Munster, died this year, according to the Annals of the Four Masters. We are not, at present, able to say where any of his works are to be found.

A. D. 1065.

civ. Dubhdaleithe (Dudley), Archbishop of Ardmagh, died this year. He was a man in so high estimation, that in the year 988 he was appointed successor to St. Patrick and St. Columb Kille, by the general consent of the people of Ireland and Scotland. In the year 1050, he made a circuit of Cineal Conaill, and obtained three hundred cows from the people of that country. He wrote Annals of Ireland, to his own time, which are quoted in the Ulster Annals, under the years 962 and 1021, and by the Four Masters, under the year 978.

cv. At this period flourished Donnchuach O'Fuathghaile, a Cleric, who wrote a poem giving an account of the children of Adam and Eve, of Noah and his sons, and of the tribes or nations sprung from each. The poem consists of three hundred and ninety-two verses, beginning " Reıᵭıᵹ ᵭam a Ɗe ᵭo nıṁ," " Prepare for me, oh God of Heaven."

Copy in the Books of Leacan and Ballimote, and in the collection of the Assistant Secretary.

A. D. 1067.

cvi. Tigernach, in his Annals under this year, records the death of Morogh O'Cairthe, a writer of Conaght, in these words, " ⱮoƩcha ᵳa Caıƥƈı aƥᵭ Ɗƥaeı aᵹaƴ aƥᵭ ollaṁ Coñaȼƈ ᵭo bȼaᵭ a loȼ calᵹaıᵭ," " Morogh O'Cairthe, Arch Druid, and Chief Professor of Conaght, was drowned in Lough Calgaidh." The word Ɗƥaı in this passage, deserves the attention of those who assert that Druidism was the established religion of Ireland, before the introduction of Christianity. A fact which others deny, and which cannot be proved from the use of the word Ɗƥaı, or Ɗƥaoıᵭ, which means only a Sage, a Wise Man, a Philosopher, a Magician or Sorcerer.

A. D. 1072.

cvii. GIOLLA CAOIMHGHIN, a celebrated poet and historian, died this year. He was author of the following poems:

1. A poem of one hundred and seventy-two verses, beginning " Ʒaeóal ʒlaʏ o cáıɓ Ʒaeıóıl," " Gaodal green, from whom Gathelians sprung."

This poem gives the names of the ancestors of the chief line of the Gaels, from the dispersion at Babel until their arrival in Spain. Copies of it are to be found in the Books of Ballimote and Leacan, in the library of the Royal Irish Academy, and in the Book of Invasions, and other ancient MSS. in possession of the Assistant Secretary. One of these is collated with some other copies, and the various readings marked in the margin.

2. A chronological poem of six hundred and thirty-two verses, beginning " Eıʏıu aıʏɓ mıʏ na ʏıʒ," " Noble Eire, Island of Kings."

This poem commences with an account of the first colonization of Ireland, and gives the names of the monarchs, and the number of years that each reigned until the coming of Saint Patrick, in the reign of Laoghaire, A. D. 432. This was one of the principal documents on which O'Flaherty founded his technical Chronology.

Six copies of this work are in possession of the Assistant Secretary. One of them is on vellum, transcribed by Adam O'Cianan, a famous scribe, in the year 1450; and another, collated with other copies, and the various readings noted, with a view to publication. Copies are also in the Books of Ballimote and Leacan.

3. A poem of one hundred and fifty-two verses, beginning " Ʒlca ʏunɓ ʏoʏba ʏeaʏa," " Here is the finishing of information," on the Christian kings of Ireland.

This poem is ascribed to Conaing O Maolconaire, by O'Flaherty, and others.—See Conaing O'Maolconaire.

4. A poem of one hundred and ninety-two verses, beginning " Ʒl eolca Eıʏean aıʏɓe," " O ye learned of illustrious Erin," gives the names and number of Milesian monarchs that reigned in Ireland, shewing from which of the sons of Golamh each king was descended, and which of

them reigned alone, or were joined with others in the government. It also gives the names of the kings who ruled in Ireland, of the Fir Bolg and Tuatha-de-Danan race.

Copies of this poem are in the hands of almost every Irish scholar. There are six copies in the collection of the Assistant Secretary, some of them written on vellum, and of great antiquity.

5. A chronological poem of two hundred and twenty verses, beginning " ᴀᴎᴅᴀlᴀʙ ᴀᴎᴀll ᴦle," " All the annals down."

The time of this poem commences with the creation, and is carried down to the year 1072, when the author wrote. The poet divides his chronology into different æras, and gives the names of several memorable persons who lived in each period.

There is a fine copy of this poem preserved in an ancient vellum MS. in possession of Sir William Betham, and another old copy in the collection of the Assistant Secretary.

———

A. D. 1088.

cviii. Tigernach, Abbot of Cluain-mac-nois, died this year. He wrote annals of Ireland, from the reign of Cimbaeth, king of Ulster and monarch of Ireland, A. M. 3596, to his own time. These annals are partly in Latin and partly Irish, and were continued by Augustin M'Grath to the year of Christ, 1405, at which time he died. A copy of the Annals, and the continuation, are in the library of Trinity College, Dublin. Another copy, with the continuation to the year 1163, is in the manuscript collection of John M'Namara, of Sandymount, Esq.

———

A. D. 1100.

cix. About this period flourished Maol Iosa, a Divine, who devoted his pen to the service of religion. Two poems only of this author's works have come under our observation. The first consists of fifty-two verses, beginning "Ⰰ mo cóimⱊⰋⱃ ⱀⰰm coⰊⰿⰐⰄ," "O my God, who art my protector."—In this poem the author begs of God to keep him from sin. The second poem is an exhortation to keep the fasts prescribed by the Church. It begins, "ⰃⰊⰰ ⱈⰰeⰐⰊⰰ ⱀⰊ ⰎoⱀⰳⱘⰄ," "No feasting on Fridays."

These poems are preserved in a fine vellum manuscript in the library of William Monck Mason, Esq. and copies are also in the collection of the Assistant Secretary.

cx. About this time also lived MAELMUIRE O'MOIRIN. A hymn, composed by him in his last sickness, is preserved in a beautiful vellum manuscript, written in the year 1561, in the library of William Monck Mason, Esq. It consists of forty-eight verses of an uncommon measure, beginning "ⰀⰎⰊⰎⰊⰿ mo ⰄⱈⰊⰰ," "I beseech my God."

cxi. Cotemporary with the two last-mentioned authors was William O'Hanley, who, like them, employed his time and talents in the service of God and religion. A hymn, consisting of fifty-two verses, in the same measure as that of Maelmuire O'Moirin, is preserved in the library of William Monck Mason, Esq. and also in the collection of the Assistant Secretary. It begins "ⰀⰎⰊⰎⰊⰿ Ⰺⱀ ⰑⱃⰊⱃⱂ," "I beseech the Trinity."

A. D. 1136.

cxii. TANAIDHE O'MULCONAIRE, a celebrated historian and poet, died this year. He was author of the two poems following :

1. A poem of forty-eight verses, beginning "ⱇⰊⱃⰲoⰎⰳ ⰲⰰⱌⰰⱃ ⱃⱃⱀⰄⰰ ⱃeⰰⰎ," "The Firbolg they were here a while."

This poem treats of the Firbolg, who possessed Ireland before the arrival of the Tuatha de Danan, and whose posterity remained in possession of a great part of the island, until after the introduction of Christianity. It gives the names of their kings, the number of years that each king reigned, and the places where they died.

2. A poem of forty-four verses, beginning " ᚊuᚐᚈᚐ ᚅᚓ Oᚐᚅᚐᚋ ᚱᚑ ᚅᚔᚐ-
ᚋᚐᚔᚱ," " The Tuatha de Danan were obscure."

This poem gives the names of the seven kings of the Tuatha de Danan
race, who ruled Ireland for a period of one hundred and ninety-seven
years. It also mentions the arrival of the Milesians in A. M. 2935.

Copies of both these poems are to be found in the Book of Invasions,
by the O'Clerys, in possession of the Assistant Secretary, and a copy of the
latter poem is in the Book of Conquests, or Invasions, preserved in the
Book of Leacan, fol. 11, col. 3, in the library of the Royal Irish
Academy.

In the Book of Ballimote, fol. 18, a. col. 2, this writer is called
Tanaidhe O'Dubhsailech.

CXIII. NEIDE O'MAOLCONAIRE, another historian, of the same family as the
foregoing writer, died this year, according to Tigernach's continuator.
We have not met with any of his works.

A. D. 1138.

CXIV. CUCHONACHT O'DALY, of Meath, said by the Annalists to have
been the best poet of Ireland in his time, died this year. We are unable
to say where any of this author's works are to be found.

CXV. In this year also died Auliffe mor M'Firbis, Ollamh of Hy Fiachra. This author was of the family of M'Firbis of Lecan, and probably
one of the original compilers of the Record now known by the name of
the Book of Leacan.

A. D. 1143.

CXVI. GIOLLA MODHUDA O'CASSIDY, otherwise called DALL CLAIRINEACH,
Abbot of Ardbraccan, in Meath, died this year. He was a very learned

man, a well-informed historian, and a famous poet. Of the works of this author three poems only have come down to our times, all of which are on the history of Ireland.

1. A poem, beginning " Eιριu oǵ, mιy na naoṁ," " Sacred Erin, Isle of Saints," gives a catalogue of the Christian monarchs of Ireland, from the reign of Looghaire, A. D. 428, to the death of Maoilseachlainn the Second, A. D. 1022. It also gives the number of years that each king reigned.

Four copies of this poem, some of them of great antiquity, are in the MS. collection of the Assistant Secretary. They vary in the number of their verses from three hundred and fifty-two, to three hundred and sixty-eight. The concluding rann of one of these copies shews that the number of verses of which it was originally composed, was three hundred and sixty.

" Deιċ roιnd oċtṁoǵad uaιm,
Do randaιḃ ιyιn ríoǵ ḃuaιm,
Aιyṁιm cen ɼoycyaḃ cen ɼell
Do toyċyaḃ tyén Eyend."

" Ten ranns*, and eighty from me
Of the ranns in the poem of Kings,
I number without excess, without falsehood,
That fell the mighty of Erin."

2. A poem of two hundred and four verses, containing a catalogue of the monarchs of Ireland, shewing how many kings of each name governed the country. It begins " Cyḃdear coṁanmand na yιǵ," " Becoming the synonima of the kings."

An ancient copy of this poem, on vellum, is in the collection of Sir William Betham; and another, transcribed in the year 1610, is in the collection of the Assistant Secretary.

3. A poem consisting of three hundred and seventy-four ranns of irregular verses, beginning " Aḃam den aċaιy na nḃaeme," " Adam only

---

* Each rann consists of four verses.

father of men," is to be found in the Book of Leacan, fol. 198, a. col. 1. The last rann but six, gives the year 1147 as the time in which the poem was written; and the last rann but one says it was written by Giolla Modhuda of Ardbracken. The general opinion is, that Giolla Modhuda died in 1143, and if so, the date mentioned in this copy must be erroneous. There is a copy of this poem in a very ancient vellum manuscript in possession of the Assistant Secretary, but as it wants a few ranns in the latter end, the date cannot be ascertained by it.

This poem gives the names of the wives and mothers of the kings and chiefs of Ireland of the Milesian race.

———————

A. D. 1160.

CXVII. GIOLLA NA NAOMH O'DUNN, died on the 18th of December in this year. He was chief bard to the king of Leinster, and wrote many poems, of which the following have come to our hands:

1. A poem of three hundred and ninety-two verses, beginning " Aibino ꞇin a Einiu áino," " Pleasant that, oh noble Erin," upon the tribes that sprung from the sons of Milesius, and from Lughaidh, son of Ith, and the districts possessed by them.

Two copies of this poem are in the hands of the Assistant Secretary, one of them in a very ancient vellum MS. the other transcribed in the year 1712, by John M'Solly, a native of Stickallen, in the county of Meath.

2. A poem, beginning " Coigeaꝺ laigean na leaꝿꞇ níog," " Leinster, province of the tombs of kings," two hundred and eighty verses, gives a catalogue of the Christian kings of Leinster, and the number of years each king reigned.

Copies of this poem are preserved in the books of Leacan and Ballimote.

3. A poem of one hundred and twenty-eight verses, beginning " Aiꞃgialla a hEamam Maꞇa," " Oirgiallans, from Eamhain of Macha," giving

an account of the chief tribes descended from the three Collas, sons of Cairbre Liffeachair, monarch of Ireland, who was killed at the battle of Gabhra Aichle, a small distance to the N. E. of Tara, in Meath, A. D. 296, after a reign of seventeen years.

A copy of this poem, in the hand-writing of James Maguire, A. D. 1708, is in the collection of the Assistant Secretary.

4. A poem of two hundred and ninety-six verses, beginning " Fíoñac ſeanċaiðe ꝼꝼeſ ꝼꝼail," " The historians of the men of Fail (Ireland) testify," gives a catalogue of the Christian kings of Conaght.

5. A poem beginning " A coiʒeað́ cáin Caiſſſe cſuaið," " O beautiful province of hardy Carby."

This poem is by some ascribed to Brogan, who flourished A. D. 526.

6. A poem beginning " Cſuaċa Coñáċ ſaċ co ſaiċ," " Cruachan of Conaght, a fortress with prosperity," two hundred and ninety-six verses, on the Christian kings of Conaght. It was written in A. D. 1150.

This poem is by some, perhaps more properly, ascribed to Torna O'Mulconaire, who flourished A. D. 1310.

Copy in the Book of Ballimote, fol. 37, b. col. 1.

cxviii. About this period also, flourished Aodh Ollabhar O'Carthach, chief poet of Conaght. He was author of a poem, consisting of sixty-four verses, beginning " Aċa ſuñð ſoċáſ ꞃa ſíʒ," " Here are the privileges of the kings," on the rights and immunities of the M'Dermotts, princes of Moy-Luirg.

Copy in possession of the Assistant Secretary.

A. D. 1170.

cxix. Maurice O'Regan, a native of Leinster, was employed by Dermod Mc. Morogh, king of that province, as his ambassador to Strongbow, Robert Fitz-Stephen, and others of the English nobles, to solicit their aid in the recovery of his kingdom, from which he had been expelled by Roderick O'Conor, king of Conaght, and other Irish chiefs, for having forcibly carried off Dervorgilla, the wife of Tighernan O'Rourke, and daughter of Maolseaghlainn, king of Meath. He wrote, in his native language, a history of the Anglo-Norman invasion of Ireland, from the year 1168, to the siege of Limerick, in 1171. This was translated into French verse by a gentleman, his cotemporary, from which a version was made into English by Sir George Carew, in the reign of Queen Elizabeth. This latter translation is the first tract in Harris's Hibernica, published in Dublin, 1770.

A. D. 1197.

cxx. The Annals of Munster record the death of Giolla Patrick O'Huidhir, or O'Heidhir, a famous poet, on the 16th of December, this year. He was superior of the convent of Inisfallen, and founder of many religious houses. We are not at present able to say where any of his works are to be found.

A. D. 1220.

cxxi. About this period flourished Conor O'Kelly. He was author of a metrical History, or Pedigree, of his own Tribe, the O'Kelly's, chiefs of Hy-Maine, an ancient district now comprehended in the present counties of Galway and Roscommon. Rev. Charles O'Conor, in his catalogue of Irish MSS. in the Marquis of Buckingham's library at Stowe, mentions a copy of this poem preserved in No. 16, fol. 62, of that collection.

A. D. 1240.

CXXII. EOGHAN, or OWEN M'CRAITH, son of *Donogh mhaoil (the Bald),* flourished at this time. He was author of the following pieces:

1. A poem of forty-four verses, in answer to the poem No. 14 of Donogh mor O'Daly's works, beginning " Sᵹᵼᵽ ᴅoᴅ ᴅɪoᵹᴜᵽ ᴀ ᴏᵹᵽᴇ." M'Craith's poem begins " Cᵽᴇᴀb ᵽoᴄ ᴀ ᴘɪᵽ ᴀ ʜᴜᴀɪʟʟᴇ," " **Plough** before thee, oh man of pride."

2. A poem in dispraise of the flesh, consisting of fifty-two verses, beginning " Oɪʟᵽɪᴀᵹᴄ ᵹᴀɴ ᴄᴇɪʟʟ ᴀɴ ᴄoʟᴀɴ," " A beast without understanding is the flesh."

Fine copies of these poems are in the collection of the Assistant Secretary.

A. D. 1244.

CXXIII. DONOGH MOR O'DALY, Abbot of Boyle, a famous poet, who, for the sweetness of his verses, was called the Ovid of Ireland, died this year. He was author of many poems, of which the following have come within our notice :

1. A poem of forty-eight verses, in praise of the Blessed Virgin Mary, beginning " bᵽᵹᴍᴇ ᴄᵽɪᵹᵽ ᴍᴀᴄᴀɪᵽ ᴍɪᴄ ᴅē," " Nurse of three, mother of the son of God."

2. A hymn addressed to the Blessed Virgin, beginning " ᴀ ɴᴀoᴍ ᴍʜᵽᵽᴇ ᴀ ᴍᴀᴄᴀɪᵽ ᴅē," " O Holy Mary, O mother of God." Sixty verses.

3. A hymn of one hundred and eighty-four verses, addressed to the Cross of our Lord Jesus Christ, beginning " ᴍᴀᵽᴄᴀɪɴ ᵹᵽᴄ ᴀ ᴄᵽoɪᴄ ᴀɴ Choɪᴍᴅē," " Hail to you, Oh Cross of the Godhead."

4. A poem of seventy-six verses, on the vanity and instability of human life, beginning " Oᵽᴄ ᴅo ᵽᴇᴀᵽᴀᵽ ᴀ ᵽᴀoᵹᴀʟ," " On thee I relied, O world."

5. A poem of one hundred and forty-four verses, on the goodness of God, and the merits of our Redeemer, beginning "Ɗιɑ ɗom ꝼειɔeaṁ aιꝛ ꝼꝛeaꝛᵹ nɗé," "God be my defence against the wrath of God."

6. A poem of one hundred and forty-four verses, on the neglect of Religion, the punishment that attends the irreligious, and the necessity of Penance, begins "Ϲɑιnιc ceo ɔaꝛ an cꝛeιɔeaṁ," "A cloud has come over the Faith."

7. A poem of one hundred and twenty verses on the death of a person of the name of Aongus, shewing that he was only lent for a while from God to the world. It begins "Ɑιꝛ ιaꝛaċɔ ꝼuaꝛaꝩ Ɑonᵹuꝩ," "On a loan I had Angus."

8. A penitential hymn of one hundred and twenty verses, beginning "Ɑιċꝛιɓe ꝛuñ huιɔ a ɗé," "Repentance here to thee, Oh God."

9. A poem of one hundred and forty-eight verses, in praise of the Blessed Virgin Mary, beginning "Ϝꝛᵹeall beañaċɔ bꝛú Ϻꝛꝛe," "Promise of a Blessing, the womb of Mary." This is sometimes attributed to Giolla Brighide M'Coinmhidhe.

10. A prayer to the Deity, forty verses, beginning "Ϲꝛeιɔιm ɓuιɔ a ɗé nιṁe," "I believe in thee, Oh God of Heaven."

11. A poem of sixty-eight verses, on the necessity of reflecting that we must die. It begins "Ɑ ċolañ ċuᵹaɔ an baꝩ," "O body, to thee belongs death."

12. A poem of sixty-four verses, in praise of the Blessed Virgin Mary. It begins "Clú naċ caιɔeaꝛ clú Ϻꝛꝛe," "Praise not exhausted, the praise of Mary."

13. A poem of one hundred and thirty-six verses, in praise of God and the kingdom of Heaven, beginning "Ɗιɑ ɗo ċꝛuɔaιɔ ᵹꝛιanbꝛꝛᵹ nιṁe," "God, who hast created the luminous palace of Heaven."

14. An exhortation to humility and amendment of life, fifty-two verses, beginning "Sᵹꝛꝛ ɗoɗ ɗíomaꝩ a ɗꝛne," "Cease thy pride, O man."

15. A poem of twenty-four verses, in which the author declares he has found all his desires in God. It begins "ꝼuaꝛaꝩ mιañ, ón ꝼuaꝛaꝩ mιañ." "I have found my desire, Oh I have found my love." This is by some ascribed to O'Daly fionn.

16. A hymn to the Blessed Virgin Mary, forty-two verses, beginning "Oꝛ na mban baιnċeañ nιṁe," "Gold of women, Queen of Heaven."

17. On the Day of Judgment, and the signs by which it is to be preceded, one hundred and forty verses, beginning " ᵹaꞃᵬ eiꞃᵹió ióᵬna an ᵬꞃaċa," " Boisterous arise the arms of Judgment."

18. A poem addressed to our Lord and the Blessed Virgin, one hundred and eighty-four verses, beginning " Loċꞃaⁿ ꞃoillꞃe aiᵹ ꞃiól Ꙟᵭaiᵯ," " Lamp of brightness to the seed of Adam."

19. On the Day of Judgment, the merits of Christ's sufferings, and the intercession of the Blessed Virgin. This poem consists of two hundred and twenty-four verses, beginning " Iꞃ ꞃaᵭa ꞃaiꞃꞃiⁿᵹ poᵬal Óé," " Long extended are the people of God."

20. Upon our Lord Jesus Christ, two hundred and eighty-four verses, beginning " ᵹaᵬaᵯ ᵭeaċmaᵭ ꞃ nóᵭna," " Let us give tythe of our songs."

21. Upon the difference between heavenly and worldly riches, eighty verses, begins " Óo ᵹⁿᵭ ᵭꞃne Óia ᵭa ᵯaoiⁿ," " Man made a God of his riches."

22. A poem of forty-eight verses, contains a prayer, beseeching grace from God to lead a pious and holy life. It begins " Ceaᵹaiꞃᵹ meiꞃi a ᵯeic mo Óé," " Instruct me, Oh Son of my God."

23. A poem exhorting to penance, thirty-two verses, beginning " Caoin ċu ꞃéin a ᵭꞃne ᵬoiċᵭ," " Weep for thyself, Oh miserable man." This poem is by some ascribed to Mahon O'Heffernan.

24. On the death and resurrection of the Son of God, two hundred and twenty-eight verses, begins " Ciꞃció ꞃe maꞃᵭnaió ᵯic Óé," " Hark ye to the elegy of the Son of God."

25. A poem addressed to God Almighty, beseeching him for his grace, and begging his mercy, forty-eight verses, beginning " Foiꞃ m'áᵯᵹaꞃ a Óia ᵬⁿ," " Help my afflictions, Oh dear God."

26. A poem, in which the author laments the hardness of his heart, and want of tears for his sins, twenty-four verses, beginning " Cꞃuaᵹ mo ċuꞃaꞃ ᵹo Loċ Óeaꞃᵹ," " Sorrowful my pilgrimage to Lough Dearg."

27. A poem of twenty-four verses, on three that wished for his death, the devil and his imps, and the worms. This poem begins " Cꞃiuꞃ aċa aiᵹ ᵬꞃaċ aiꞃ mo ᵬáꞃ," " Three there are that expect my death:" Although the name of Donogh mor O'Daly appears on some of the copies of this poem, there is reason to suspect that he was not the author.

28. A poem of forty-eight verses, beginning " Ná tréig mo teagafg a meic," " Fly not from my instructions; Oh son!" an exhortation to Christian piety.

Copy in the library of John Mac Namara, Esq.

29. A poem of one hundred and twenty verses, beginning " Aitriõe fuñ ort a Ðhé," " Here repentance to thee, oh God!" The poet here acknowledges his sins and his unworthiness, and begs forgiveness and mercy from the Lord.

30. A poem of one hundred and sixteen verses, beginning " Cred agaib doiõig a gcein," " What have ye for a long time, oh youths!" on Rickard, son of William de Burgo. In this poem the author says that he is O'Daly of Meath.

31. A long poem of one thousand two hundred verses, in praise of the power, majesty, and goodness of God. This poem begins " Mo rìye rì mime," " My king, the King of Heaven."

Besides the above, we have seen three other poems attributed to this author, but there are strong reasons that induce us to withhold a belief that they were written by him.

The first of these is a long poem, on the last end of man, but the versification, and the kind of rhyme used in this poem, being but of modern invention, shew it to be the work of a less skilful genius than Donogh mor O'Daly.

This poem begins " A õrne crìmne do criõc deigeanac," " Oh man, remember thy last end." We have not seen any very correct copy of this piece; one of the best has been lately printed in this city.

The second of these pieces, which we suppose to be erroneously ascribed to Donogh mor, is a poem of twenty-four verses, inquiring why our Lord Jesus Christ, not being a builder, smith, or other artizan, or labourer, had received honour from some person of the name of Owen. It begins " A Ìyfa Crìoyð cred an toil, ra bþrapaiy onóiy ó Eogaм," " Oh Jesus Christ, what is the cause that thou hast received honor from Owen."

This little poem wants that gravity, dignity, and sweetness, which so eminently distinguish all the productions of Donogh.

The third is a poem of seventy-eight verses, on the three sons of Edan. It begins " Cuaine ríogna rug Eðan," " Brood of a queen Edan bore."

This piece, though possessed of much poetic merit, and written in the language of the period in which Donogh lived, is not written in that style for which he was so remarkable.

Copies of all these poems are in the collection of the Assistant Secretary.

A. D. 1293.

CXXIV. GIOLLA IOSA ROE O'REILLY, Prince of East Brefney, succeeded to the government of that principality upon the death of his brother, in the year 1293. By his valour and prudence he was enabled to extend his dominion over all the country from Drogheda to Rath Cruachan, in the present county of Roscommon. In the year 1300 he built and endowed the monastery of Cavan, for the Friars de communi vitâ. In this building he erected a chapel, and a monument of hewn marble as a place of sepulture for himself and family. In the year 1313, Edward II. king of England, wrote circular letters to the princes of Ireland, requesting their aid against the Scotch. One of these he addressed to Giolla Iosa O'Reilly, in the following style: " *Rex, &c. dilecto sibi Gilly's O'Reily, Duce Hibernicorum de Breifeny, Salutem, &c.*" In the year 1326 he resigned the government of his principality to his nephew Maoilseach-lainn, son of his eldest brother Mathew O'Reilly, and retired from the cares of the world into the monastery of Cavan, where he died, full of years, A. D. 1330, justly celebrated for wisdom and sanctity, and was interred in his own chapel.

He was author of some verses on the death of his brother Mathew, beginning " ᘔ ᚃᛁᚱ leaᵹaᚱ an leac ᵹo ᚳᚱom," " Oh man, who layest the flag heavily ;" and a poem upon the great power and extent of territory of his nephew Maolseachlainn, whom he calls his son, as being adopted by him as his successor. The poem begins " O'Ṅeill oiliᵹ ᚃa mo ṁac," " O'Neill of Ulster is subject to my son."

CXXV. Maoilire O'Maolagain (Myler O'Mulligan) flourished during the time that Giolla Iosa Roe O'Reilly governed the territory and tribes of Muintir Maolmordha (E. Breifne), and celebrated the actions of that chief, in a poem, beginning " Do ċramaᚱ aiᚱ ċᚱeiċ ᚱe Ᵹiolla Ioᚃa anaiᵹ," " We went on a hosting with Giolla Iosa the valiant."

Copies of the poems of Giolla Iosa and Maoilire, are in the registry of the House of O'Reilly, in the collection of the Assistant Secretary.

CXXVI. TADHG MOR O'HIGGIN, a poet of Conaght, and a cotemporary of the two last-mentioned authors, flourished at the time that Magnus O'Conor was king of that province. He wrote a poem in praise of that prince, consisting of one hundred and sixty-eight verses, beginning " Ʒaċ én maṛ a aóba," " Every bird according to its kind, (literally " according to its nest.")

A copy of this poem, in the handwriting of Cucoigcriche (*Peregrinus*) O'Clery, one of the Four Masters, is in the collection of the Assistant Secretary.

A. D. 1300.

CXXVII. COBHTHACH O'CARMAN, a poet of Leinster, flourished at this period. A poem of this author's production, consisting of two hundred and thirty-two verses, has made its way down to our times. It begins " Ꝺl ċaeṁa ċoiʒió laiʒean," " O ye nobles of Leinster province," and gives the names of persons by whose hands fell several of the most remarkable characters in Irish history. It also gives a catalogue of Leinster kings, who became monarchs of Ireland. An ancient copy of this poem is in the collection of the Assistant Secretary.

CXXVIII. EOGAN or OWEN M'CARITH, a Munster poet, flourished at this time. He was author of the following pieces:

1. A poem on the dissentions between the descendants of Teige Coaluisge O'Brien, and those of Brian Roe O'Brien, at the commencement of the fourteenth century. This poem consists of one hundred and fifty-six verses, beginning " Cia aṛ ʒaiṅóe oṅ ʒaḃaó Eiṛe," " Who is the shorter from whom Ireland is seized ;" in which the author endeavours to reconcile those contending relations.

2. A poem of one hundred verses, beginning " Ceaċ cáṛaió óo ċiṛ ḟolaṁ," " To see the house of a friend vacant," on the deserted mansion of Conor O'Brien.

Copies in the collection of the Assistant Secretary.

A. D. 1310.

cxxix. The Rev. Charles O'Conor, in his Catalogue of Irish MSS. in the Marquis of Buckingham's library at Stowe, gives an account of TORNA O'MAOLCONAIRE, chief poet of Conaght, who attended at the inauguration of Felim O'Conor, on the Hill of Carn Fraoich, where he delivered his poetic address to Felim, beginning " *Lrat oμt a ſheιölιme*," " On thee be activity, Oh Felim."

Doctor O'Conor says that Torna was also the author of a poem, upon the succession of Conacht kings, beginning " *Cμuàċa Coñàċt μàċ co μαιċ*," " Cruachan of Conaght fortress with prosperity."

The poem beginning " *Eιſtιö μe ſeñċuſ nàc ſuàιll*," " Hear ye a story not contemptible," is said to have been recited by Torna, at the restoration of Felim O'Conor, A. D. 1315, and from this circumstance the poem was supposed to be composed by him for this occasion. We have shewn already, under the year 468, that this poem forms a part of the Book of Rights. said to be written by Saint Beinin.

The two first-mentioned poems, attributed to this author, we have not seen, but we know that a poem beginning like the second, " *Cμuàċa Coñàċt μàċ co μαιċ*," is to be found in the Book of Ballimote, fol. 37, b, col. 1. This poem consists of one hundred and ninety-six verses, giving a catalogue of the Christian kings of Conacht, and the length of their reigns, written by Giolla na naomh O'Dunn.

See under the year 1160.

———

A. D. 1314.

cxxx. CONAING O'MAOLCONAIRE, chief poet of Conaght, died this year. He was author of many poems, of which two only have come under our observation.

1, A poem of sixteen verses, beginning " *Oċt meιc Ʒolàιm na nʒàιμe*," " Eight sons of Golamh, of the shouts," on the eight sons of Golamh, or Milesius, who led the Milesian colony from Spain to Ireland, A. M. 2935.

In this poem the birth-place of each of the sons of Golamh is pointed out. Copies of it are preserved in the Book of Leacan, and in the Book of Invasions by the O'Clerys.

2. A poem of one hundred and forty-eight verses, beginning " Ⱥⱦⱥ ꝛⱳⱨ ꝼⱷⱨⰱⱥ ꝼⰵⱥꝛⱥ," " Here is the completion of knowledge." This poem gives a catalogue of the kings of Ireland, from Laoghaire, who died A. D. 463, to Brian Boroimhe, who was killed at the battle of Clontarf, A. D. 1014.

Copy in a fine vellum manuscript in the library of Sir William Betham.

This latter poem is attributed by the O'Clerys to Giolla Kevin, who died A. D. 1072, and by other writers to a Conaing O'Mulconaire, who died A. D. 1420.

See under the years 1072 and 1420.

A. D. 1320.

cxxxi. At this time flourished CATHAN O'DUINNIN, chief poet to the *Ibh Eachach*, of Munster, (the O'Donoghoos, O'Mahonys, &c.) He was the author of the Ode delivered at the inauguration of Teige, the generous O'Donoghoo, prince of Lough Lein. This ode consists of three hundred and sixty four verses, containing the pedigree of the O'Donoghoos, with their filiations for twenty-seven generations, from Corc, son of Luigheach, king of Desmond, A. D. 380, to Teige the Generous, A. D. 1320.

This poem is contained in the Book of Munster, a copy of which is in the collection of the Assistant Secretary. It begins " Ⰵⱱⱷⱶⱱⰱ ꝛⰵ ⱪⱷⰱⱨⰵⱥ ɬꝛⱶ ⱦⱦⱥⱦ," " Hear the affinity of your tribe."

cxxxii. About this time flourished MAOLMUIRE O'LEANNAIN. He was author of a poem, consisting of one hundred and seventy-two verses, against adultery, the sins of the flesh, &c. beginning " Ⱶⰵⱦⱦⱥⰱ ⱥꝛ ꝼⱷⰱ ⱨⱥꝛ ꝼⱶⱱⱥⰲⱶⱥⱷ," " Sinful our seed in our people."

Copy in an ancient vellum manuscript, in the library of Sir William Betham.

A. D. 1348.

CXXXIII. MALACHY MAC AEDHA, Archbishop of Tuam, died on the feast of Saint Laurence the Martyr, this year. He was author of a large volume of miscellaneous matter in Irish, containing, amongst other things, a catalogue of Irish kings, from Niall Naoighiallach to Roderick O'Conor. Sir James Ware, in his account of Irish writers, says, it was extant in his time, and called the Book of Mac Aodha. We can not say where it is to be found at present.

A. D. 1350.

CXXXIV. ANGUS ROE O'DALY, a noted poet, died this year. He was author of the following poems, and most likely of others that have escaped our observation.

1. A poem of one hundred and ninety-two verses, on the erection of the castle of the hill of Carn Fraoich, by Aodh, son of Eogan O'Conor, A. D. 1309. It begins " An tu apir a pait Theampac," " Art thou again *revived*, oh fort of Tarah." A fine copy of this poem is in the library of John Mac Namara, Esq. a member of this Society.

2. A poem of one hundred and ninety-two verses, addressed to Rory, son of Aodh O'Mulloy, chief of the territory of Fearcall, a district of the ancient kingdom of Meath, and now comprehended in the baronies of Fercall, Ballyboy, and Ballycowan, in the King's county. It begins " Ceangal do riot riom a Ruaioṁ," " Confirm thy peace with me, oh Rory."

It appears from this poem, that the author was of the Tribe of O'Daly of Meath, and that he had incurred the displeasure of O'Molloy, by some words that fell from him in a state of intoxication. He beseeches that prince to pardon his offence, begs that he will imitate Fergus, son of Roigh, in forgiving those by whom he had been offended, and calls upon him to spend his wrath upon the English, the plunderers of his native country.

A fine copy of this poem is in the collection of the Assistant Secretary to this Society.

3. A poem of four hundred and forty-eight verses, beginning " Aoam, αταιη, γηυτ αη ςluaᵹ," " Adam, father, stream of our people." The first two hundred verses are on the patriarchs, to the deluge, the remaining verses treat of the first colonies that possessed Ireland before the Milesians.

This poem is sometimes ascribed to Angus Ceile De, of whom we treated under the year 800, but the language does not justify us in giving it so early an origin.

Copies of this poem are in the library of William Monck Mason, Esq. and in the manuscript collection of the Assistant Secretary.

cxxxv. Giolla Brighide Mac Coinmhide, *(Conway)* a poet of Ulster, flourished at this period. He was a retainer of the house of O'Donnell, and devoted the most of his verses to the praise of that illustrious family. The following pieces of his composition have descended to our days.

1. A poem of one hundred and twenty-eight verses, beginning " Conall cηηᵹιᵒ claṁe Ṅeill," " Conall, hero of the race of Niall," on the settlement of the Conallians in Ulster, and of Maolseachlainn, son of Donall, the brown O'Donell.

We have seen, under the year 1056, that Flann of Bute wrote a poem, beginning with the same words as this poem, treating of the same family.

Copies in the collections of the Rev. Doctor O'Brien, and of the Assistant Secretary.

2. A poem on the same subject, beginning " Roᵹa na cloṁᵒe Ṅeill," " Choice of the sons of Neill."

3. A poem of one hundred and sixty-eight verses, beginning " Roᵹa na cloṁᵒe Conaill," " Choice of the sons of Conall," in praise of Brian, son of Donald O'Donell, prince of Tir-Conell.

A fine copy of this poem is preserved in a very valuable volume of Irish historical poems, collected in the Netherlands in the year 1656, by the Rev. Nicholas, alias Fergal *dubh (the black)* O Gara, an Augustinian Friar. This volume was once the property of O'Daly of Dunsandle, but now belongs to John M'Namara, of Sandymount, Esq.

4. A poem on the birth of Donald, son of Donald O'Donell, prince of Tir-Conell, ninety-six verses, beginning "Οο ᵽιοιη Οια Cenel Conaill," "God considered the Kineal Conall (descendants of Conall) *i. e.* the O'Donells.

Copy in the library of John M'Namara, Esq.

5. A poem on Aodh O'Conor, beginning "Οεαηπαο ϧο ᵽαζϧαᵹ αιζ Ꮂοᴓ," "By forgetfulness I neglected Aodh;" one hundred verses on the hospitality of Aodh, son of Felim O'Connor. Copy in the library of John M'Namara, Esq.

Copies of the foregoing poems are also in the collection of the Assistant Secretary, in an imperfect paper copy of the Leabhar hua Congabhala.

6. A poem of ninety-six verses, beginning "Ꮂᴌα ᵹϣηϧ ᵹεαηϲϣᵹ Ꮇᴦαιη," "Here is the history of Moain," on Moain, son of Muireadhach, grandson of Niall of the nine Hostages, by his son Eoghan, or Owen. Moain was brother to Muirceartach, who was Monarch of Ireland from A. D. 513 to A. D. 533, and who from his mother Eirc, daughter of Loarn, king of the Dalriada of Alba, was called Muircheartach Mac Earca. From Moain are the *Cineal Muain* descended, one of the principal families of which were the O'Gormly's, for whose chief, Niall O'Gormly, this poem was written.

Copy of this poem is in O'Gara's collection of poems, in the library of John Mac Namara, Esq.

7. A poem of one hundred and sixteen verses, beginning "Οεαη οηπ ᴄᵹοϲαιηε α ᴢᵹιοηοιϧ," "Have mercy on me, O Trinity." In this poem, which is composed in that kind of poetry called Ꮪεαϧηα, the author begs for several particular blessings from the Holy Trinity, one of which is, that he may not be left without children.

An ancient copy of this poem is in the hands of the Assistant Secretary.

The poem beginning "Cαιηηηε, Εϧεϲϧαη, Εῆα εıπ," and some other poems on the O'Donells, which we have ascribed to Flann Mainistreach under the year 1056, are sometimes, and perhaps with more truth, attributed to this author.

cxxxvi. At this time also flourished Aodh, or Hugh O'Kelly, author of a poem, consisting of eighty-four verses, on his own tribe, beginning "Εıηıζ α ϲαᴌᴌαιηε ιη ηıζ," "Arise, Oh proclaimers of the king."

Copy of this poem is preserved in an ancient vellum manuscript, once the property of the O'Kellys, now in possession of Sir William Betham.

———

A. D. 1370.

CXXXVII. TADHG CAMCHOSACH O'DALY flourished about this period. He was author of the following poems:

1. A poem of one hundred and sixty verses, on the inauguration of Niall mor O'Neill, beginning " *bean aꞃ naιceιꞃże ℮ꞃe*," " A woman recovering is Erin."

2. A poem of one hundred and sixteen verses, on his choosing to become a friar, begins " *ꝺa żꞃaꝺ ꝺ'ꝼażbuꞃ ℮ꞃιn*," " For its love I left Erin."

Copies of these poems are in the collections of John Mac Namara, Esq. and of the Assistant Secretary.

———

A. D. 1372.

CXXXVIII. JOHN O'DUGAN, chief poet of O'Kelly of Ibh Maine, died this year. He was author of the following valuable historical and topographical pieces.

1. A poem of five hundred and sixty-four verses, beginning " *Ꞃta ꞃunꝺ ꞃeancuꞃ ꞃíoż ℮ꞃeanꝺ*," " Here is a history of the kings of Erin." This poem gives a catalogue of the kings of Ireland, from Slainge of the Fir-Bolgian race, who, conjointly with his four brothers, Gann, Geannann, Seangan, and Rudhraidhe, sons of Deala mac Loich, began to reign over Ireland, A. M. 2245, to Roderick O'Conor, son of Turlogh the great, who held the reins of government in Ireland at the Anglo-Norman invasion, A. D. 1168.

Copy in the library of Sir William Betham, and in the MSS. of the Assistant Secretary.

2. A topographical and historical poem, of eight hundred and eighty verses, beginning "Tᵹⁱⱥllⱥm cⁱmċeⱥll nⱥ ꝼoðlⱥ," "Let us go around Fodhla, (Ireland)." This poem gives the names of the principal tribes and districts in Meath, Ulster, and Conaght, and the chiefs who presided over them, at the time Henry the Second, king of England, was invited to this country by Dermod Mac Morogh, king of Leinster.

From the first line of this poem, and from the few *ranns* that this author has left us, on the districts of the province of Leinster, it would seem, that it was his intention to have given a complete account of all the districts and chief tribes in Ireland; and it would be a cause of much regret that he left unfinished so interesting a work, if it had not afterwards been taken up and completed by his cotemporary, Giolla na naomh O'Huidhrin, who died an old man, in the year 1420.

The work of O'Huidhrin has been sometimes joined to O'Dugan's poem, so as to appear but one entire piece of one thousand six hundred and sixty verses, and the merit of the whole is given to the latter, though he really wrote but thirty-eight ranns, or one hundred and fifty-two verses on Meath; three hundred and fifty-four verses on Ulster; three hundred and twenty-eight verses on Conaght; and fifty-six verses on Leinster, making in all eight hundred and eighty verses. For the account of the ancient families of Leath Mogha (Leinster and Munster) we are indebted to O'Huidhrin.

See O'Huidhrin, under the year 1420.

Copies of this poem are numerous, but few of them are perfect. The copy used by the author of *Cambrensis Eversus* must have been incomplete, or he has not translated it fully. A complete copy, in the handwriting of Cucoigcriche O'Clery, one of the *Four Masters*, is in the collection of the Assistant Secretary.

3. A poem of two hundred and twenty-four verses, beginning " Rⁱoᵹ-Ɽⱥⁱð lⱥⁱᵹeⱥn clⱥñ CⱥċⱥoⁱⱤ," "Kings of Leinster, descendants of Cathaoir," on the families descended from the thirty sons of Cathaoir mor, monarch of Ireland, from A. D. 174, to A. D. 177.

A copy of this poem is in the collection of the Assistant Secretary.

4. A poem of two hundred and ninety-six verses, beginning " CⱥⁱⱤⁱol cⱥċⱥⱤ clⱥñⱥ Ⓜhoᵹⱥ," "Cashel, seat of Mogha's sons," giving a catalogue

of the kings of Cashel, and the years that each prince reigned, from its foundation by Corc, son of Luigheach, about A. D. 380, to Torlogh O'Brien, A. D. 1367.

A fine copy of this poem is in the Book of Ballimote, fol. 36, a. col. 2, and another in the collection of the Assistant Secretary.

5. A poem of three hundred and thirty-two verses, beginning " Ceaṁᵹ na ṗioᵹ ṗaiṫ Coṗmaic," " Tara of the king's fortress of Cormac," gives an account of the battles and principal actions of Cormac mac Art, monarch of Ireland, in the middle of the third century.

A fine copy of this poem, beautifully written on vellum, is in the library of Sir William Betham.

6. A poem, beginning " bliaóain ṛo ṛoluṛ a óaṫ," " This year bright its dye," upon the festivals of the year, with practical rules for finding the moveable feasts and fasts, by the Epacts, Dominical Letters, &c.

Copies of this poem are in the hands of every Irish Scholar, and its Rules are frequently quoted by hundreds of persons who never learned a letter.

7. A poem of two hundred and ninety-two verses, beginning " ṛoṗuṛ ṛocal lṛaióteaṗ liḃ," " A knowledge of words spoken by you." This poem is a vocabulary of now obsolete words, and words which, though spelled alike, have different, and often contrary meanings; all of which are inserted in the Irish-English Dictionary lately published by the Assistant Secretary to this Society.

Copies of this poem are to be found in the library of Trinity College; in Sir William Betham's large vellum MS.; in the collection of John Mac Namara, of Sandymount, Esq. and in that of the Assistant Secretary.

A. D. 1373.

cxxxix. ADAM O'CIANAN, or KEENAN, a famous historian and canonist, died in Lisgoole this year, according to the Four Masters. We have not met any of his original works, except the pedigrees of a few Northern families; but there are in the collection of the Assistant Secretary two volumes on vellum, transcribed by him in very fine writing. These volumes contain a number of historical tracts, both verse and prose; a copy of the ancient laws relating to the clergy, poets, and artists; an Irish-Latin Grammar, &c. &c.

About this period the Annalists record the deaths of many famous historians, poets, scribes, and lawyers, with whose works we are not at present acquainted.

A. D. 1378.

CXL. JOHN O'FIALAN, Chief Poet of Henry, son of Owen O'Neill, Prince of Tirone, died this year. He was author of the Ode pronounced at the inauguration of Henry, one hundred and eighty-eight verses, beginning " ꝼꞃᵭᵫᵻꞃ ᴄᵻᵭᵽᵽᵫᵻᵬ Єᵻᵽᴇ," " Thou hast obtained thy request, oh Erin." From the two concluding ranns of this poem, it appears that Judith, the daughter of Mac Mahon, prince of Oirgialla, was the wife of Henry O'Neill.

A fine copy of this poem is to be found in O'Gara's collection, in the library of John Mac Namara, Esq. and another in that of the Assistant Secretary.

A. D. 1380.

CXLI. At this time flourished MAHON O'REILLY, Lord of Clan Mahon, and father of Thomas O'Reilly, who succeeded his uncle Philip as Prince of East Breifne, A. D. 1384. He was author of a poem in praise of the mighty actions of his son Thomas, who, in a short period, levelled eighteen castles belonging to the English of the Pale, and laid the country, from

Drogheda to Dublin, under contribution. The poem begins " ᵹrl ᵹaill-rⁱᵹ oʏ cıon̄ ᵹaıll," " The cry of an English sprite over Englishmen."

Copy in the Registry of the House of O'Reilly, in possession of the Assistant Secretary.

CXLII. About this period flourished MAC CRAITH M'GOWAN, who wrote genealogies of the Irish Saints, and of the kings and princes of Ireland.

A copy of this work is in the collection of the Assistant Secretary.

———

A. D. 1385.

CXLIII. TANAIDHE O'MAOLCONAIRE, son of Paitricin mor, son of Tanaidhe, died on the 1st of August this year. He was a poet of Conaght, and his works are much praised by some of his cotemporaries, and by subsequent writers. We are not, at present, able to say where any of them are preserved.

———

A. D. 1387.

CXLIV. GEOFFREY FIONN O'DALY, chief professor of poetry in Munster, died this year. He was author of the following pieces:—1. A poem of fifty verses, beginning " Cıon̄uʏ oıolꝼao mo luác leıᵹıʏ," " How shall I pay the price of my cure," on the benefits derived by man, from the merits of Christ. Copy with John Mac Namara, Esq.

2. A poem of two hundred and twenty-four verses, beginning " ꝼa nᵹnıoṁꝼao meaʏcaʏ mac ꝼıoᵹ," " By deeds is the son of a king valued," on Dermod, surnamed of Muskery, son of Cormac, son of Donald Mac Carthy.

3. A poem of forty-eight verses, beginning " 2l ꝼıʏ ceıo ı ccıʏ Chonaıll," " Oh man, who goest to Tir-Conell," addressed to O'Donell, Conor son of Aodh, (Hugh) son of Donald oge.

Copies of these poems are in the collection of the Assistant Secretary.

4. A poem of one hundred and forty verses, beginning " ᴍⱥⱥⱬ ⱥⱨ ⱡⱦⱬⱬ ⱥⱨⱥⱨⱨⱨⱬ ⱱⱬⱬⱬ," " Forgive the fault, Oh youthful king," addressed to Donald, son of Donald Mac Carthy, exciting him to oppose the English, and holding up as a pattern Conn Cead-Cathach, (of the Hundred Battles) who forsook his youthful sports, and flew to rescue Tarah from the yoke of Cathaoir mor, king of Leinster.

Copy in O'Gara's collection of poems, in possession of John Mac Namara, Esq. and in a very fine collection of Poems in possession of the Assistant Secretary.

A. D. 1390.

CXLV. At this period flourished ᴍᴀᴏʟᴍᴜɪʀᴇ ᴍᴀᴄ Cʀᴀɪᴛʜ, poet of Desmond, or South Munster. He was author of an Elegy on the death of Donald Mac Carthy, chief of the Clann Carthy of Carbery. This poem consists of one hundred and forty-four verses, beginning " ⱱⱦⱥⱨⱬ ⱥⱡⱨⱬⱬ ⱥⱨ ⱦⱨⱨⱨ ⱦⱬⱬ ⱨⱦⱬ," " A load of sorrow to Ireland, the death of a king."

Copy in the manuscript collection of the Assistant Secretary.

CXLVI. At this period also flourished Soʟᴀᴍʜ O'Dʀᴏᴍᴀ, or Soʟᴏᴍᴏɴ O'Dʀᴜᴍ, one of the compilers of the great Book of Ballimote, now in the library of the Royal Irish Academy.

CXLVII. At this time also lived ᴍᴀɢɴᴜs O'Dᴜɪɢᴇɴᴀɴ, whose name appears on different pages of the Book of Ballimote, particularly at fol. 248, at the end of the account of the Argonautic expedition and destruction of Troy, which, it appears, was finished by him in the house of Donald Mac Aodhagan, or Mac Egan, on Thursday before the feast of Saint Michael, but the year is not mentioned. We are unable to say whether he was the author of this piece or only the transcriber.

As the Book of Ballimote is so often mentioned in this work, and referred to by almost every writer who has treated on Irish antiquities for the last fifty or sixty years, the following account of it may be gratifying to some of our readers, or perhaps direct the attention of future writers to matters contained therein, illustrative of the history of the country and the manners and customs of the people.

The Book of Ballimote is a large folio volume, finely written on vellum of the largest size. It originally contained 550 pages, very closely written, but the first two pages are at present wanted. It was written at different times and places, and by various hands, as appears by the concluding lines of several of the tracts; but the principal part was written by Solomon O'Drum. A part of it was once the property of Manus O'Duigenan, who wrote it for his own use, but afterwards became the property of Tumaltach M'Donogh, prince of Tir-Olioll, Artagh, the two Corans, Tir-Tohill, and Clan Fernmoy, districts now comprehended in the present counties of Sligo, Roscommon, and Leitrim. Under the patronage of this chief, and in his house, were some other parts of this book written, as appears by a passage at the conclusion of the account of the O'Conor family, at folio 62, a. col. 1. " ⁊ íṡé ιn Coιn-ꝺelḃaċ oᵹ ṡιn, mac Ꝉeḋa, aṡ ṗι Conaċꞇ aᵹ ṡꞯιḃaꝺ na coꝺaċṡa ꝺon leaḃaṗ, a ꞇιᵹ Ċomalꞇaιᵹ meιc Ċaιꝺᵹ, meιc Ċomalꞇaιᵹ, meιc Ṁṗṗᵹeaṡa, meιc Ꝺoñċaꝺa, meιc Ċomalꞇaιᵹ, meιc Ċonċoḃaιṗ, meιc Ꝺιaṗmaꞇa, o ṡṗleꝺ Ṁeιcc Ꝺιaṗmaꞇa, a mḃaιle ιn muꞇa," " And it is that Torlogh og, son of Hugh, that is king of Conaght, at writing this part of the book, in the house of Tomaltagh, son of Teig, son of Tomaltagh, son of Muirgheasa, son of Donogh, son of Tomaltagh, son of Conor, son of Dermod, from whom are the Mac Dermotts, in Ballimote." Torlogh og O'Conor, began his reign over the province of Conaght in 1384, and died in 1404, so that this part of the book must be written about the year 1390. By a memorandum at folio 180, a. col. 1, written in a hand-writing different from any other part of the book, it appears that Hugh *duff*, son of Hugh *roe*, son of Niall *garbh* O'Donell, bought it in the year 1522, from M'Donogh of Coran, for one hundred and forty milch cows. Hugh duff O'Donell died A. D. 1537.

This venerable Repertory of ancient Irish Literature, although much blended with fable, contains a vast quantity of valuable and authentic historical matter, drawn from the purest sources; such as the Psalter of Cashel, the Book of Glendaloch, the Chronological Poems of Eochaidh O'Flinn, Flann of Bute, Giolla Caomhghin, Giolla Modhuda O'Cassidy,

Giolla-na-naomh O'Dunn, John O'Dugan, and other senachies of repute. Some parts of it, indeed, are of less estimation; but even the historical tales are not without their value to an antiquarian. The stories of the birth of Conor Mac Nessa, and of Cormac O'Cuinn; the adventures of Cormac in the Land of Promise; the deaths of Crimhthann, son of Fidhaidh, and of the sons of Eochaidh Moighmheodhain, Brian, Olioll, Fiachra, Fergus, and Neill, though mostly fabulous, contain some authentic historical facts, and much matter illustrative of the manners and customs of the people, and of the religious opinions of Pagan Ireland.

The law tract, commencing at folio 181, is well deserving the attention of the historian and antiquarian. It contains the Rights and Immunities, the Rewards and Punishments due to different ranks in society, ecclesiastical and civil, from the Bishop down to the Liaċṫ̇peoiṗ, or Reader in the Church; from the Ollaṁ, or Professor, to the ṗocloċ, or lowest rank amongst the poets and learned men; and from the king to the artizan, or labourer, amongst the laity.

This book was formerly in the library of Trinity College, Dublin; but when, how, or by whom it was taken from that establishment, is not now a matter easily to be decided. General Vallancey, in his *Green Book*, which was bought for the Record Commission at the price of one hundred guineas, much above its intrinsic value, gives an account of printed books and MSS. on the History of Ireland, in various languages, and amongst the rest, mentions the Books of Ballimote and Leacan. The General says, that Doctor Raymond, about thirty years ago, lent a manuscript volume out of Trinity College library, to a person of the name of Thady Naghten; that a man of the name of Egan stole it from Naghten, and gave it to Judge Marlay, whose servant he was; that it remained in the Judge's library until his death, and then was, by some means, conveyed to the Lombard College in Paris. The General was of opinion that this manuscript was the Book of Leacan, which the Superior of the Irish community in Paris presented to him in 1788, for the Royal Irish Academy, in whose library it now is. This opinion of the learned General is not supported by any authority; on the contrary, there is the testimony of Abbé M'Geoghegan, in the Introduction to his History of Ireland, to prove that the Book of Leacan was deposited in the library of the Irish College at Paris, by James II. after his abdication; and that the deposit was made in the presence of a Notary, who attended for that purpose. But though the book lent by Doctor Raymond to O'Naghten, could not have been the Book of Leacan, there is a probability that it might have been the Book of Ballimote. There is at present in the library of Trinity College, a paper copy of the Book of Ballimote, in the hand-writing of Teige or Thady O'Naghten; and this is a strong proof that he had the original in his possession. Whether the book was stolen from him, or whether it was ever in the library of Judge Marlay, is not very clear. Indeed there is reason to believe it was not in the Judge's library. There are different memorandums on several pages of the book, in the hand-writing of Mr. Thomas O'Dornin of Drogheda, a good Irish Scholar, which shew that it was in his possession in the year 1769; and that it remained in his hands until at least the year 1774, appears by a list of Mr. O'Dornin's MSS. now in possession of the writer of this account. Whether it ever made its way to Paris, where it is said the late Chevalier O'Gorman obtained it, is not now necessary to inquire, but we know that it did come into his hands, and that he presented it to the Royal Irish Academy, in the hope, as he himself told the writer of this article, that that learned body would publish some of the useful parts of its contents.

Dermod O'Connor, the translator of Doctor Keating's History of Ireland, says, in his preface, that he had the Book of Ballimore, in Co. Meath, in his possession for six months, for the safe return of which, Doctor Raymond, of Trim, had given his bond to the College for one thousand pounds. It is observable that a Book of Ballimore, in Meath, was never so much as heard of by any Irish scholar, but the Book of Ballimote in Co. Sligo, is much celebrated. The innumerable errors in O'Connor's translation of Keating, and the blunder he makes in the name of this book, prove he was unable to make any thing of its contents. His name is introduced here, merely to shew, that though the Book of Ballimote was then in Trinity College, the Book of Leacan was not: otherwise he would have taken notice of it, as he had access to the College manuscripts.

The book wants the two first pages. At folio 2, is an account of the posterity of Cain, Noah, &c. At folio 4, commences the Book of Synchronisms, in which is mentioned the names of the Patriarchs, the Assyrian, Persian, Irish, Grecian, and Roman kings and emperors who were cotemporaries. In this part is introduced Donchuach's poem, "Reiḋiġ ḋaṁ a Ḋe ḋo ṅiṁ." At the end of folio 6, col. 2, are six *ranns*, giving an account of the different ages of the world. By the last rann it appears that this small poem was written in the year 1126. At folio 6, the synchronisms of Flann commence. At folio 8, begins an account of the first inhabitants of Ireland, in which are introduced several of the poems of our earliest bards. At folio 32, b. col. 2, is an account of the monarchs of Ireland, from Laoghaire, son of Niall, to Roderick, son of Torlogh, son of Rory na soighe buidhe O'Conor, A. D. 1166. At folio 34, is an account of the Christian kings of Ulster. At folio 35, the Christian kings of Leinster. At the bottom of this page is a prayer for Manus O'Duigenan, the owner of the Book. At folio 37, the kings of Conaght, and the length of their reigns, from Amalgaidh, son of Fiachra, son of Eochaidh Moighmheodhain, to Torlogh O'Conor. At 38, the Christian kings of Munster, from Eoghan, son of Deirg, son of Deirgreineadh, to Donald, son of Torlogh, son of Dermod, son of Torlogh, son of Teige, son of Brian Boroimhe. In this account of the provincial kings, several poems of our best historical writers are introduced, a particular account of which is given under their proper dates in the course of this work.

At folio 39, b. col. 2, are the royal precepts of Cormac Mac Art to his son Cairbre Liffeachair, monarch of Ireland.

At folio 43, a. col. 1, commences an account of the descendants of Milesius, and first of the O'Neills. At folio 54, account of the Hy Briuin Heremonians, which ends at folio 62, with an account of the O'Conors. At folio 63, a. col. 1, an account of the Hy Fiachra race of Tir-Awly, according to Flann. At folio 64, the clann Colla; at 69, the Hy Maine tribes, the O'Kellys, &c. At folio 70, the Leinster tribes; at 80, the Conarian race of Ireland and Scotland.

At folio 87, commences the account of the Ultonian tribes, descendants of Ir, son of Milesius, to folio 97, where the Munster Book begins "*Eber a quo dicitur Hibernia.*" Folio 102, b. col. 1, of the Dalcassians; folio 109, b. col. 5, of the race of Lughaidh, son of Ith.

At folio 113, the Book of the Britons and Picts, from Nennius. At 116, account of the Saxons in England.

At folio 117, the mothers of the most remarkable of the Irish saints; and at folio 126, a. col. 2, begins the sacred pedigree of the saints of Ireland, " Naem ʃeançaʃ naem inʃe ʃail;" one hundred and seventy-three ranns, or six hundred and ninety-two verses.

At folio 131, an account of the Hebrew patriarchs, Moses, the Temple, &c.

At folio 136, fabulous account of Conor Mac Nessa, and the death of Daithi, the last of our Heathen monarchs. Folio 137, an account of Art Aonfhir, and on the same page, the kings and nobles of Ireland of the same names.

At folio 140, a. col. 1, the names of the Chiefs of the Athach Tuatha, who overthrew the Milesian government in the first century; and on the same folio, b. col. 1, are the wonders of Ireland. Folio 141, the marriage of Luain, and the death of Athairne the poet.

Some of these latter articles are much tinctured with fable, and more of our ancient historic tales of a similar description, are to be found on every page, to folio 147, where begins the Book of Rights, fathered on Saint Benin, of which we have given an account under the year 468.

At folio 154, begins the "baïnʃeançaʃ eʃeano," or History of the women of Ireland, giving the names of the wives and mothers of the most remarkable characters in Irish history.

At folio 157, commences the Irish Prosody, with examples of the different kinds of versification.

At folio 163, a. col. 2, account of the Ollamhs or Fileas, (the Professors or Poets) shewing the qualifications necessary for the different orders of poets.

At folio 167, b. col. 2, commences the Uraicepht and Book of Oghams, to folio 180, where, in a different hand-writing, is an account of the purchase of this book from the M'Donogh's, by Hugh *dubh* O'Donell.

At folio 181, a. col. 1, begins the *Seanchas bheg*, a law tract, on the rights, privileges, rewards and punishments of the different ranks of kings, clerics, poets, artizans, &c. At the commencement of this tract, there is the following note, in the late venerable Charles O'Connor's hand-writing: " Elements of Law, obscure to me for want of a Law Glossary. Caçal ua Conçobaiʃ." This is followed by another note, in the hand-writing of the late General Vallancey, in ungrammatical Irish, "ᴄɪᵹᴀᴍ ɪᴀᴅ ᵹᴏ ᴍᴀɪᴢ ᴍᴏ ᴄᴀᴘᴘᴀᴅ. Cᴀᴢᴀl ʀᴀ ᵬᴀllᴀɴᵧᴇɪ," "I understand them well, my friend. Charles Vallancey." Those who understand the law dialect of the Irish, and have compared with the originals the translations of the fragments published by the General, in the Collectanea de Rebus Hibernicis, are able to set a proper value on this boast.

At folio 188, a. col. 1, commences the *Dinn Seanchas,* of which we have given an account when treating of Amergin Mac Amalgaidh, under the year 550, where we have shewn that this work was enlarged after the year 1024. Perhaps the *Dinn Seanchas* in the Book of Ballimote, may be the first edition of that work, in its present form.

At folio 230, a. col. 1, account of the Argonautic Expedition and the Trojan war, to folio 248, a. col. 2, where, on the bottom margin, is a memorandum, in the hand-writing of Magnus O'Duigenan, in which he says, he finished writing the story of Troy, on Thursday, before the feast of Saint Michael, in the house of his tutor, Donald M'Aodhagan, or M'Egan, but he does not mention in what year.

At folio 249, a. col. 1, The Adventures of Æneas, &c. after the destruction of Troy, from Virgil, to folio 267, where is, in Irish characters, *Finit, Amen, Finit. Solamh O'Droma nomine scripsit.*

At folio 268, a. col. 1, commences the history of Alexander the Great, according to the Latin author Justin. It continues to folio 275, where it ends, with the conclusion of the Book of Ballimote.

A. D. 1395.

CXLVIII. At this period flourished O'Maoilciaran, a Conaght poet, author of a beautiful elegy on the death of his son. This very pathetic poem consists of one hundred and seventy-two verses, beginning "ᴄᴜᵹᴀᴅ ᴏɪᵱɴᴇ ᴇᴀᵧᵬᴀɪᴅ·ᵯᴏᵱ," "A great loss has happened to us."

Copy in the library of John M'Namara, Esq.

CXLIX. At this time also flourished Ainglioch O'Donellan, poet to the Mac Dermotts, of Moyluirg. He was author of a poem in praise of

Moyluirg and of Aodh, or Hugh, M'Dermott, chief of his tribe. This poem consists of one hundred and ninety-two verses, beginning "Ꝛoṁ leiꞇe aıꞃ Coıʒeaꝺ Choṅaꞇꞇ," "The province of Conaght is divided."

CL. Cotemporary with the two last-mentioned writers, was OWEN *an torthoir* M'CRAITH, a Munster man by birth, but attached to the House of O'Neill. He was author of the following poems:

1. On the inauguration of Niall og, son of Niall mor O'Neill, chief of Tirone, one hundred and eighty-eight verses, beginning "Ꝺa ꞃoıṅ ꞇoṁ-ꞇꞃoṁa aıꞃ Chꞃıc Ꞃeıll," "Two equal shares on mighty Niall's land."

2. In praise of Art O'Cavanagh, king of Leinster, who died at Enis-corthy, A. D. 1417, one hundred and sixteen verses, beginning "Ꞇoṁꝺa ꞃaıꞃle ꝺ ıaꞇ laıʒean," "Many chiefs on Leinster's land."

3. In praise of Cormac O'Maoilseachlainn, prince of the clann Col-man, or southern Hy Niall, whose chiefs were called kings of Meath, one hundred and fifty-six verses, beginning "Ϻıꞇıꝺ cꞃeıꝺeaṁ ꝺo ꞇloıṅ Ꞃeıll," "It is time to believe in the descendants of Niall."

4. In dispraise of the world, eighty verses, beginning "Oʒ an ꞃeanóıꞃ an ꞃaoʒal," "The world is a young senior."

The first of these poems is sometimes ascribed to Tcige og O'Higgin.

Copies of all the above poems are in possession of John M'Namara, Esq. and the Assistant Secretary.

A. D. 1400.

CLI. SIODHRUADH O'CUIRNIN, a poet of Breifne, died this year. He was author of a poem on the Life of Saint Maodhog, first Bishop of Ferns, and patron Saint of Leinster. The poem consists of one hundred and forty-four verses, beginning "Seanꞇaꞃ Ϻhaoꝺoıʒ meaꝺaıꞃ lıṅ," "The History of Maodhog let us remember."

Some copies of this poem are in the MS. collection of the Assistant Secretary.

CLII. BLADHMAC, son of Conbhreatan, son of Congasa, flourished at this time. He was a man in holy orders, but we do not know to what house or family he belonged. He was author of two poems, consisting of upwards of one thousand five hundred verses, addressed to the Blessed Virgin Mary, upon the principal actions and sufferings of her Son, our Lord Jesus Christ. The first begins "Ϲαρ ϲυϲαm α Ϻhϯϱe ϧοιϧ," "Come to me, Oh holy Mary ;" five hundred and ninety-six verses. The second begins "Ἀ Ϻháιϱe, α ϧϱιαn αϱ ϲϲϧοϊϻe!" "Oh Mary, Oh sun of our people!"

Copies of these poems, once the property of Michael O'Clery, one of the Four Masters, are in the collection of the Assistant Secretary.

A. D. 1404.

CLIII. DONOGH BAN O'MAOLCONAIRE, chief poet of the O'Conors of Conaght, died this year. He was author of a poem, consisting of one hundred and seventy-two verses, beginning " Ϲιϱοιϧ α ēιϧϱι ϧαnϧα," " Attend ye, Oh learned of Ireland." It contains a catalogue of the kings of Conaght, and the number of years that each prince ruled over that province, from Torlogh, son of Roderic the Great, to Torlogh O'Conor, who lived at the time in which this poet wrote. From a rann in this poem it appears that two hundred and thirty-eight years had elapsed from the first year of Torlogh, son of Roderick, to the time in which the poem was written: therefore it must have been composed in the year 1374. This is further confirmed by the name of O'Crede, Archbishop of Tuam, being mentioned in the last rann of the poem as being then some time dead. In Ware's History of the Bishops, the death of this prelate is said to have happened in the year 1371, but he is improperly called John O'Grada.

Copies of this poem are in the Book of Leacan, and in the Manuscript Books of the Assistant Secretary.

CLIV. In the same year with the last-mentioned author, died CARROL O'DALY, the poet of Corcamroe. Several of his poems and tales are repeated from memory by the common people of the country ; but we are not able to say where any good copies of them are to be found in manuscript.

clv. In this year also died Donald, son of Donogh O'Daly, who, from his facility in writing verses, was nick-named *bolʒ an ḋána, (A wallet of Poems)*. We cannot with certainty say where any pieces of this author's composition are now to be found.

A. D. 1405.

clvi. Augustin Magradian (Austin M'Craith), a Canon of the order of Saint Augustin, in the Isle of All Saints, in the river Shanon, died on the next Wednesday after the feast of All Saints, this year. He wrote Lives of some Irish Saints, and continued the Annals of Tigernagh to his own time. These Annals have been since continued, by another hand, to the year 1571.

A copy of the Annals is in the Library of Trinity College, Dublin, Class H.

A. D. 1408.

clvii. Coll O'Doran, a Leinster man, died this year. He wrote Annals of Ireland, which Sir James Ware says were extant in his time. We are not able to say where they are now to be found.

A. D. 1415.

clviii. Maurice O'Daly, chief poet to O'Reilly, lived A. D. 1415, in which year he, Dermod O'Daly of Meath, and many other poets, were plundered by Lord Furnival. We know of but one poem now extant ascribed to this author. It begins " Ʒúl Ʒaıllrıʒ óʏ cıoñ Ʒoıll, aʒ ʏm Ʒúl naċ caoınım," " A cry of an English hag over English men, that is a cry that I lament not." This poem is, by several writers, attributed to Mahon O'Reilly, Lord of Clann Mahon. It was occasioned by the destruction of eighteen castles of the English, bordering on Breifne, and the laying the country, from Drogheda to Dublin, under contribution, by Thomas O'Reilly, Lord of that part of Breifne called Clann Mahon by descent from his father, and prince of all the districts of East Breifne by consent of the tribes.

See under the year 1380.

A. D. 1418.

CLIX. At this time lived GIOLLA IOSA M'FIRBIS, the famous antiquary of Leacan, by whom, with the assistance of others, that valuable treasure of Irish Antiquities, called " THE BOOK OF LEACAN," was compiled. We cannot say what parts of the Book of Leacan were the original compositions of this writer; but at folio 40, b. col. 2, is given a poem of two hundred and forty verses, beginning " Ʒl éıcʏı banba na mbeanʒ," " O ye learned of Ireland, of illustrious descent;" by the last rann of which we find that Giolla Iosa M'Firbis was the author. And at the bottom of the same page the reader is requested to " pray for M'Firbis, who wrote this Book for generations that will succeed him for ever; and it was in the time of Rory O'Dowd the Book was written."

Maoil-Iosa M'Firbis, was also the author of a poem of three hundred and seventy-six verses, beginning " Reıʒıʒ ʒaṁ a Ơhé ʒo nıṁ," " Make ready to me, O God of Heaven," giving the synchronisms of the Roman Emperors with the monarchs of Ireland, from Augustus Cæsar to the Emperor Theodosius.

This poem is to be found in the Book of Leacan, folio 180, a. col. 1.

CLX. At this time also flourished ADAM O'CUIRNIN, Historiographer of Breifne. He was the writer of the Book of Conquests, or Invasions, and the Synchronisms of the Assyrian, Persian, and Grecian kings with the monarchs of Ireland, and of the monarchs with the provincial kings of Ireland, contained in the Book of Leacan, as appears by a memorandum at the end of that tract, at folio 30, b. thus, "Finit, Adam o Cuirnin do sgrib do Gilla Isa mac Firbisig .i. d'ollaim o Fhiachrach, año Doi M° cccc° *xiii*." "Finis, Adam O'Cuirnin wrote for Giolla Iosa M'Firbis, *i. e.* for the Professor of Hy Fiachra, A. D. MCCCCXIII."

Whether O'Cuirnin was the original compiler of the Book of Conquests and Synchronisms, or merely the transcriber of the work from the compilations of some other persons, we are not at present able to say. The work, however, is a very valuable document for the History of Ireland, commencing with the earliest account of time, and carried down to the period that Roderick, son of Hugh, son of Cathal *Croibhdhearg* (red-hand) O'Conor was king of Conaght, and Torlogh, son of Teige, son of Brian Boroimhe, was king of Munster. Turlogh dethroned his uncle Donogh, and took upon himself the government of Munster in A. D. 1086.

CLXI. Cotemporary with the two last-mentioned writers was MOROGH *riabhach* O'CUINDILIS, and who, like them, was concerned in the compilation of the Book of Leacan. We are not able to point out any tracts or poems of the original compositions of this writer; but at the end of the Uraicepht, or Book of Ferceirtne, at folio 162, b. col. 1, of the Book of Leacan, it appears that he was the transcriber of that tract, and that he wrote it for his friend M'Firbis, to whom he gives his blessing in addition.

The Book of Leacan has been so often referred to of late, and is, in fact, a book of such consequence to all who are desirous of an acquaintance with Irish antiquities, that it may be necessary here to give an abridged account of its contents.

The Book of Leacan consisted originally of six hundred and twenty-four pages, closely written, with a great number of contractions, on vellum of a large size. It was the work of several hands, as appears by the hand-writing, and by the account given of the three last-mentioned writers. At present the first nine folios are lost. It begins with that part of the Book of Conquests, or Invasions, that treats of the Firbolgian colony, and continues the History of Ireland down to the twelfth century. In the course of this work are given extracts from the Psalter of Cashel, the Book of Glendalough, &c. and a great number of historical poems, the compositions of our earliest and most esteemed bards. In it are also introduced the Synchronisms of the Babylonian, Assyrian, Grecian and Roman kings and emperors, with our monarchs, and the synchronisms of our monarchs with our provincial kings. This work forms the basis of O'Flaherty's Ogygia, and from it Doctor Keating extracted the materials for his History of Ireland.

At folio 58, b. col. 1, is given the pedigree of the Saints of Ireland, in verse.

At folio 64, b. col. 2, begins an account of the principal families who possessed Ireland at the time of writing the book, with the chiefs who then presided over each, and the filiations of their tribes. This subject continues to folio 148, where the *Leabhar Breathnach*, or Book of the Britons, commences. This latter book is taken from the British author Nennius.

At folio 151 begins the Uraicepht, in the hand-writing of Morogh riabhach O'Cuindilis.

At folio 163, a catalogue of Saints, and the families from whom they descended.

At folio 164, a. col. 4, a vocabulary of obscure words.

At folio 168, a. col. 1, an account of the different orders of poets.

At folio 172, a religious poem by St. Cuimin.

At folio 175, an account of Eochaidh, Feidhlioch, and Meidhbh queen of Conaght, and an account of that province. At that same folio begins an account of the Athach Tuatha, or plebeians, who overturned the established government of the Milesians, at the end of the first century after Christ.

At folio 180, Giolla Iosa M'Firbis's poem on the synchronisms of the Roman emperors with the monarchs and provincial kings of Ireland.

At folio 184, commences the Book of Rights, ascribed to St. Beinin.

At folio 193, an account of famous women of antiquity.

At folio 198, a poem of three hundred and seventy-four ranns, giving the names of the wives and mothers of the monarchs and kings of Ireland.

At folio 203, begins the ᥫᎯᎯ ᎷᏬᎥᎷᏁᎬᎯᎬ, or Munster Book, giving an account of the descendant of Heber, the eldest son of Milesius. This contains a great quantity of interesting matter relating to the history of Munster.

At folio 221, Etymology of Irish proper names, in alphabetical order.

At folio 224, Account of the kings of Conaght from the time of Olioll and Meidhbh to Brian, son of Eochaidh Moighmheodhain.

At folio 231, The ᥫᎯᎯ ᎾᎷ ᎱᎬᎯᎷᎬᎯᎥᎽ, or History of remarkable Places in Ireland, giving an account of the derivation of their names. This tract wants something in the beginning, but a perfect copy of it is in the Book of Ballimote, and another in Sir William Betham's large Irish manuscript.

At folio 264, Account of the Creation of the World, of the Patriarchs, &c. tracing the ancestors of the Milesians, from Adam to their settlement in Egypt, and afterwards through Scythia, Spain, &c. to Ireland. This continues to the end of the book, at folio 312.

This last-mentioned tract may be considered as another ᥫᎯᎯ ᎩᎯᎾᎯᎯᎯ, or Book of Conquests, and a great number of poems, from our best authors, are given as authority for the facts related therein.

The Book of Leacan was once the property of Trinity College, from the library of which it was taken, by order of James II., brought to France, and deposited by him in the archives of the Irish College at Paris, in the presence of a notary, who attended for that purpose, as we are assured by the Abbé Mac Geoghegan, in the Preface to his History of Ireland. In the year 1787, through the influence and patriotic zeal of the Chevalier O'Reilly, (who, though born in France, still felt a warm attachment to the land of his forefathers), the book, in the expectation that its contents would be translated and published, was, by the consent of the Irish seminary and the Archbishop, restored to its native country, by the superior of the Irish college at Paris, who gave it to the late General, then Colonel, Vallancey, to be lodged in the library of the Royal Irish Academy, where it now remains, and where, through the obliging indulgence of that erudite body, the writer of this account has had an opportunity of consulting it and other valuable Irish manuscripts, and noting their contents.

The learned General, who brought the book back to Ireland, in the account which he gives of it in his *Green Book*, already mentioned under the year 1390, supposes it to have been in the library of Trinity College, Dublin, long after the time in which the Abbé Mac Geoghegan says it was taken from this country.   He says it was lent by Doctor Raymond to a person of the name of Thady Naghten, from whom it was stolen by one Egan, who gave it to his master, Judge Marlay, in whose library it was at the time of his death.   He says the book was afterwards carried to Paris; but by whom, or by what means procured from the heirs of the Judge, he does not inform us.   Against the authority of Abbé Mac Geoghegan there is nothing to support the General's conjecture, unless we take the mention made of the book by the learned Edward Lhuyd, in his Archælogia Britannica, as a kind of collateral proof.   That gentleman published his book in 1707, and in it he gives a short table of the contents of the Books of Ballimote and Leacan, both of which he says he found in the library of Trinity College.   Hence it may be said, if these books were then in Trinity College, the Book of Leacan could not have been taken away by James II.   But Lhuyd does not say these books were in Trinity College at the time he was publishing his book; and it is well known that he was employed in collecting his materials for that work a great number of years before he published.   It is known that he was in Ireland for that purpose long before 1690, at which period he might have consulted the Book of Leacan, and James might have subsequently removed it to Paris.

In the account given of the Book of Ballimote, under the year 1390, we have given reasons to suppose it was that book that Doctor Raymond had lent to O'Naghten, and that the Book of Leacan was not in the College library when he procured for Dermot O'Connor, the translator of Doctor Keating's History of Ireland, a loan of the Book of Ballimote. In addition to this, the writer of this account has the authority of his venerable friend, the late Chevalier O'Gorman, to say, that he frequently consulted the Book of Leacan, in the library of the Irish College at Paris, upwards of seventy years ago.   Hence it may be safely concluded, that the Abbé Mac Geoghegan, who had the best means of obtaining information on Irish affairs about the period of the Revolution, must be correct, when he says the Book of Leacan was carried to France by James the Second.

A. D. 1420.

CLXII. GIOLLA-NA-NAOMH O'HUIDHRIN, a learned historian, died this year, according to the Annals of the Four Masters. He was author of a topographical poem, intended as a Supplement to John O'Dugan's Criallam timceall na foóla. We have seen, under the year 1372, that John O'Dugan has given an account of the chief tribes and territories of Leath Conn, (Meath, Ulster, and Conaght) at the time of the Anglo-Norman invasion. O'Huidhrin's work gives an account of the principal families of Leath Mhogha, (Leinster and Munster) and the districts occupied by them, at the same period. The poem consists of seven hundred and eighty verses, beginning "Cuille feafa af Eifin oż," "An addition of knowledge on sacred Erin."

A very valuable copy of this poem, in the hand-writing of Cucoigcriche O'Clery, is in the collection of MSS. belonging to the Assistant Secretary to this Society.

CLXIII. In this year also died ANGUS, son of CARROLL buidhe *(yellow)* O'DALY. He was author of the two following poems, of which copies are in the library of John Mac Namara, Esq. a Member of this Society.

1. A poem of one hundred and thirty-six verses, beginning Coihuf muif Cruacna aż cluain friaoic," "Dimensions of the wall of Cruachan at Fraoich's retreat." This poem is, by some, ascribed to Angus roe O'Daly, who died A. D. 1350. The subject is, the description of the castle of Carn Fraoich, erected by Aodh O'Conor, king of Conaght.

2. A poem, beginning " Aithnio an ccnéfi a clañ Neill," " Know this country, O sons of Niall!" one hundred and sixty verses, addressed to Art O'Maoilsheachlainn, exciting him to take arms against the English, and rescue his country from their tyranny. Copy in collection of John Mac Namara, Esq.

CLXIV. FERGAL, son of Teig, son of Angus roe O'DALY, chief poet of Corcamroe, also died this year. In the year 1415, this author, together with Maurice O'Daly of Breifne, Dermod O'Daly of Meath, Hugh og Mac Cuirtin, Dubthach, son of Eochaidh the learned, and several other poets, were cruelly plundered by Lord Furnival.

CLXV. In the same year with the three last-mentioned writers died CONAING O'MAOLCONAIRE, a Conaght poet. He is said, by some writers, to have been the author of the poem beginning " ᄋᆝᅳᅡ ᄼ ᄉᆝ ᄃ ᄍ ," which, on the authority of the O'Clerys, we have ascribed to Giolla Caoimhghin, or Giolla Kevin. Others, however, say that it was written by a Conaing O'Maolconaire, who died A. D. 1314.

See under the years 1072 and 1314.

CLVI. DONALD, son of Eogan O'DALY, flourished at this period. He was author of a poem on the death of Donald, son of Donald O'Sullivan, prince of Dunboy, who died in Spain. The poem consists of two hundred and four verses, beginning " San Sbáin do coiʃneaṁ Ceaṁuiʃ," " In Spain Tarah was interred."

A fine copy of this poem is in the collection of O'Gara, in the library of John Mac Namara, Esq.

A. D. 1423.

CXLVII. Under this year the Four Masters record the death of FAELAN MAC A GOBHAN, a learned historian. He was the transcriber of a great part of the Book of the O'Kellys, a valuable Irish manuscript, now in the library of Sir William Betham, and the original author of some of the tracts therein contained. At folio 103 of that book, is given a poem of two hundred and twenty-eight verses, the composition of this author. It begins " ᄋᆝᅳᄃᆞᆷ ᄋᆞʃ ᄀ ᄍᆞᆦᆢ ᄀᆝᆯe," " Adam, father of us all," and gives the names of the wives and daughters of several of the Pagan heroes and deities. This is followed, at folio 104, with an account of the wives of the patriarchs, and a synchronism of the Roman emperors with the monarchs and provincial kings of Ireland, from Julius Cæsar and Eochaidh Feidhlioch, monarch of Ireland, to the Emperor Severus, and Art the Solitary, monarch of Ireland, from A. D. 220 to 250, in which latter year he died. After this follows, to the end of folio 111, an account of the Jewish high priests and the first Christian bishops, the officers of Saint Patrick's household, and different members of his family.

We cannot say whether these latter tracts are the original productions of Faelan Mac a Gobhan or not; but by a memorandum at the bottom of folio 111, b. col. 2, it is said they were written by Faelan Mac a Gobhan *na scel (of the Histories)* for his lord and his friend Bishop Muirchear-tach O'Kelly. This prelate was Bishop of Clonfert from A. D. 1378 to A. D. 1394, at which time he was translated by Pope Boniface IX. to the See of Tuam, over which he presided as Archbishop, until his death, on the 29th September, 1407.

The large vellum manuscript of Sir William Betham has been so often mentioned in the course of this work, that it may gratify the curiosity of our readers to give them a short account of its contents. It may very properly be called the *Leabhar Hy Maine,* or the Book of the O'Kellys, as it contains sufficient proofs to shew that it was for them it was compiled, and that it remained in possession of a branch of that family until at least the year 1757. It is a very valuable document, written on vellum of the largest size, but wants some leaves in the beginning and the end. In its present state it commences at folio 24, with an account of the descendants of Nial *naoighiallach,* and gives the pedigrees and filiations of the most noted families who trace their origin to that monarch. In this part are introduced several of the valuable historical poems of Giolla Caoimhghin, Giolla Modhuda, Giolla na naomh O'Dunn, Erard M'Coise, Flann Mainistreach, Fotha ua Canni, &c. &c. of whose works we have given a particular description in the course of this work. There are also contained in this part several other ancient historical poems, with the names of whose authors we are at present unacquainted.

From folio 29 there is a chasm to folio 39, where we meet an account of the descendants of Maine, son of Niall, of which the principal were the O'Kellys, the O'Maddens, and other ancient tribes of Roscommon and Galway. At folio 40, b. col. 1, is a catalogue of the kings or princes of Hy Maine, from Ceallach, the great ancestor of the family of O'Kelly, from whom they take their name, to Donogh, son of Maoileaghlainn O'Kelly, who was killed on the 10th of October, 1427, in which year this part of the book was written. This account is in prose, supported by the authority of ancient poems, and ends at folio 46, from which to 57 there is another chasm.

At folio 57, is part of the Leinster Book, extracted from the Book of Glendalogh, giving an account of the descendants of Cathaoir mor, king of Leinster and monarch of Ireland, at the close of the second century. Another chasm occurs from folio 58 to folio 65, where we meet with an account of the men of Ulster, with pedigrees of the principal families of that province, extracted from the Book of Saul Abbey, in the county of Down, founded by Saint Patrick, in A. D. 432. In this account are comprehended the descendants of IR, third son of Milesius, who made settlements for themselves in other provinces, such as the O'Connors of Kerry and Corcamroe, the O'Loghlins of Burren, the O'Moores of Leix, the O'Farrells of Annaly, &c. &c.

At folio 80 commences the Munster Book, with " *Eber a quo dicitur Hibernia*," in Irish characters, containing a great quantity of the early history of Munster, and the pedigrees and filiations of the chief families descended from Heber, the eldest son of Milesius.

At folio 91, b. col. 2, the *leabaµ bµeaċnaċ*, or Book of the Britons, commences with *Ego Nennius*, in Irish characters, and continues to folio 94, a. col. 1. At the head of this tract there is a memorandum, which says that Nennius was the author, and that Giolla Caoimhghin translated it into SCOTIC.

At folio 94, a. col. 1, is Eochaidh O'Floinn's poem of two hundred and thirty-two verses, beginning " *Aċaµ ċaiċ coiṁµiṡ niṁe*," tracing the ancestors of the Irish through the Patriarchs, to their arrival in Egypt, under Niall, son of Fenius *Farsaigh* (*i. e.* the Persian).

At folio 95, a. col. 1, the *baiṅµeaṅċaiµ*, or History of Women, giving an account of the wives and mothers of the kings and chiefs of Ireland, first in prose, and then in a poem of three hundred and seventy-four ranns, beginning " *Aḋaṁ aeṅaċaiµ na nṡaeine*," by Giolla Modhuda O'Cassidy.

At folio 100, b. col. 2, Flann Mainistreach's poem on the synchronisms of the kings and emperors of the Assyrians, Persians, Irish, Greeks, Romans, &c.

At folio 103, a. col. 2, Faelan M'a Gobhan's productions, as above-mentioned, to folio 111.

From folio 113 to the end of folio 127, Divine Poems, Prophecies, &c. ascribed to SS. Benin, Bercan, Beg mac Dé, Diring Draoi, Geoffry O'Clery, Donogh mor O'Daly, Maolmuire O'Leanain, &c. &c.

At folio 127, a. col. 1, begins an account of the Israelites from the days of Abraham, &c. to folio 133, where is an account of the death of Dermod, son of Fergus Ceirbheoil, monarch of Ireland, from A. D. 544 to 565.

At folio 135, the Book of Rights, ascribed to St. Beinin, of which we have already given a particular account.

From folio 139 to folio 143, Historical Poems, by Giolla Caoimghin, John O'Dugan, and others of our most esteemed bards and historians.

At folio 143 commences the *Dinn Seanchas*, or History of noted Places in Ireland. We have given a full account of this production when treating of Amergin M'Amalgaidh, A. D. 550, and of the Book of Ballimote, under the year 1390.

At folio 172, John O'Dugan's poem on the wonderful things of Ireland, four hundred and eighty verses, beginning " Ειρι ιαρται calman coιριξ," " Western Erin of fruitful lands."

At folio 173 an historical poem on the building of Babylon. On the same folio Giolla Caoimhghin's poem, beginning " Anoalao anall ηle," followed by three poems on Irish Topography, &c.

At folio 174, O'Dugan's Irish Vocabulary, beginning " ροηυρ ροcal lraιoceαη lιb," followed, on the same folio, by two poems on the birth of Christ.

At folio 175, John O'Dugan's poem on the battles of Cormac O'Cuinn, beginning " Ceαίηαιη ηα ηιξ ηαιζ Coηiaιc."

At folio 176, are three anonymous historical poems.

At folio 177 commences a vocabulary of hard words, and etymology of some proper names, in alphabetical order.

At folio 184, another vocabulary, not in alphabetical order; and on the same folio, the etymology of Irish proper names.

At folio 188, the monarch Cormac's royal precepts to his son Cairbre Liffeachair.

At folio 190, account of several remarkable things in Ireland, of which there were three of each kind.

At folio 191, a. col. 2, commences the Irish Prosody; an account of the Bardic profession and qualifications necessary for the different orders of bards, the Uraiceapht, or Primer of the Bards; account of the Ogham, or secret writing, &c. to folio 201.

From folio 201, to the end of the book at folio 216, are several poems by our earliest and most esteemed Fileas. Some of these are authentic history, and others are mixed with fable. Of this latter description are the poems on the Knights or Heroes of the Red Branch; such as Cuchullen, Conall, Cearnach, Curaidh mac Daire, Fergus mac Roigh, &c. and of the Fianna Eirionn, or famous Irish militia, commanded by Fionn Mac Cubhail, (the Fingal of Macpherson), such as Goll mac Moirne, Dermod O'Duibhne, Caoilte Mac Ronan, Conan maol, Oisin the poet, Oscar, son of Oisin, &c. &c.

From the above short account it will be seen, that this book contains the chief part of the matter to be found in the Books of Ballimote and Leacan; in addition to which, are several other valuable pieces, which render it a most interesting document to the Irish historian and antiquary.

A. D. 1425.

CLXVIII. In this year died THOMAS, son of Giolla-na-naomh, MAC-A-GOBHAN, or SMITH, surnamed *Mac craith na sgel.* He was chief genealogist of O'Loghlainn of Corcomroe. It is probable he was the author or transcriber of the Irish manuscript book, mentioned by Nicholson, in his Irish historical library, as being in the library of the Duke of Chandos, under the title of " *Collectanea* Magraithi Mac Gowna, *de Genealogiis Sanctorum* Hiberniæ.

A. D. 1430.

CLXIX. About this time flourished AGNUS O'DALY FIONN, surnamed *na diadhacta*, (of the divinity). He was author of the following pieces.

1. A poem of forty verses, beginning " Cᵱeιⴷιm ⴷυιⵀ ⴰ ⴷhé heⵑⵑe," " I believe in thee, Oh God of heaven." This is a thanksgiving after Communion.

2. A poem on the benefits arising to man from the incarnation of the son of God; forty-eight verses, beginning " Cοᵱⴰⵀ ᵱιⴷe ᵱⴰⵑυᵱ Ⴏⴰⴆᵱιel," " The salutation of Gabriel is the beginning of peace."

3. A poem beseeching the intercession of Saint John the Baptist, sixty verses, beginning " Ⴏυιⴷe οᵱm, ⴰ Cοⵑⵑ ⴆⴰιᵱⵀe," " Pray for me, Oh John Baptist."

Copies of these three poems are in the MS. collection of the Assistant Secretary.

4. A poem, beginning " Sοᵱⴰιⴷ ⵀeⴷ ⴺeιle ⴰ Chⴰιᵱιl," " Farewell with thy companion, O Cashel," two hundred and eight verses on the death of Donald M'Carthy, prince of Desmond, who died, according to the Annals of the Four Masters, A. D. 1409. This chief, the poet informs us, died without issue.

Copy in O'Gara's book, in the library of J. M'Namara, Esq.

CLXX. HUGH O'DALY, chief poet of O'Reilly, prince of East Breifne, died this year. He wrote a poem on the marriage of Eoghan *na feasoige* (of the beard) O'Reilly, with Gormly, the daughter of Tiernan mor O'Rourke, prince of West Breifne, an imperfect copy of which, together with some other imperfect poems by the same author, are in the collection of the Assistant Secretary. The poem on the marriage of his patron with O'Rourke's daughter begins " Iᵱ ⴰοιⴆⵑ ⴷυιⵀ ⴰ ⴆhᵱēιᵱⵑe," " Happy is it for thee, Oh Breifne."

A. D. 1440.

CLXXI. About this time flourished GOFFREY O'CLERY, of whose productions, four poems, on religious subjects, are preserved in an ancient and valuable vellum MS. in the library of Sir William Betham.

1. Upon the respect that Christians should have for Friday above the other days of the week, one hundred and thirty-two verses, beginning " Ꞇabꞃaꞃꝺ onóꞃꞃ ꝺon aeꞃne," " Give reverence to Friday."

In this poem the author shews that on Friday our Lord Jesus Christ died for the sins of man; on Friday Saint Stephen was stoned; Saint John the Baptist beheaded; Saints Peter and Paul crucified, &c. &c.

2. Upon the gift of tongues to the Apostles, and the different nations to which each of them preached the Gospel; one hundred and forty-four verses, beginning " ꝱaꞃꞇ ꞃa comꝺmeaꝺ coꞃñeaꞃn Ꝺé," " The spouse of God well merits support."

3. Upon the instability of earthly dwellings, and the kingdom of God as the permanent abode to which man should aspire; one hundred and twenty-four verses, beginning " ꝼaꝺa ᵹo ꞇuꞃᵹꞃm mo ꞇeaċ," " Long until I go to my house."

4. A poem beginning " Ꝺꞁꞃᵹꞃꝺ ꞃaꞃaċꞇ aꞃꝺꞁeꞃacaꝺ ꞃe a Ꞇhaꞃba," " It is right to return a loan with its profit;" one hundred and twenty-eight verses.

CLXXII. At this time flourished BRIAN *roe* M'COINMHIDHE, a retainer of the houses of O'Neill and O'Donnell. He was author of the following poems:

1. On the O'Neill family, shewing that to them belonged the sovereignty of Ireland. This poem consists of one hundred and fifty-six verses, beginning " Ꞇeaꞃñaꞃꞃ ᵹaċ baꞃꞁe a mbꞃ ꞃꞃ," " Tarah is every town where a king is.'"

Copy in the library of John M'Namara, Esq.

2. On Neachtan, son of Torlogh *an fhiona* (of the wine) O'Donell, prince of Tirconell, one hundred and forty-eight verses, beginning " ꞃomꝺa ꞃꞃꞃꞃꞃm aᵹ Ullꞇaꞃᵹ," " The Ultonians have great respect."

Copies in the possession of Rev. Doctor O'Brien, and of the Assistant Secretary.

A. D. 1441.

CLXXIII. MAOILIN, son of Tanaidhe, son of Paidin O'MAOLCONAIRE, chief poet of the Siol Muireadhaigh (O'Connors of Conaght) died on the 13th of February this year, according to the Annals of the Four Masters. He was author of the poem beginning " Ɗlιʒιɓ ɲιʒ eoluɲ ɓ'ollaṁ," " The knowledge of a professor behoves a king," one hundred and sixty-four verses, upon the division of Conaght between Cathal Crobh-dhearg (red-hand) and Brian Luighneach, the two sons of Torlogh, (the great) O'Conor, king of Conaght and monarch of Ireland, who died A. D. 1156. The poet gives an account of the districts and boundaries of each son's share, and a list of the descendants of Brian who obtained the government of the entire province of Conaght, and the number of years that each prince ruled.

A copy of this poem is in the hands of the Assistant Secretary.

A. D 1446.

CLXXIV. TANAIDHE, son of Maoilin, son of Tanaidhe O'MAOLCONAIRE, died about the feast of Easter, this year, and was buried in the monastery of Ballybogan. He was author of the poem beginning " Ʒl ēιccɲιu baɲbaɓ co mɓlaιɓ," " Oh ye learned of Ireland with great renown," twelve verses, on the battle of Tenus, in Ibh-Failge, fought between Heber and Heremon, two sons of Milesius, A. M. 2935, in which the former lost his life.

Copy in the Book of Leacan, fol. 13, col. 4, and in the Book of Conquests, by the O'Clerys, in possession of the Assistant Secretary.

CLXXV. DONALD MAC AN CLASAIGH (the fat) O'COFFEY, and his two sons, were killed this year at Lough Ainnin, in West Meath, by the descendants of Art O'Maoilseachlainn, and by the sons of Fiacha Mageoghan. He was, as the Four Masters say, " a good leader of an army, and well skilled in poetry." He was author of the poem beginning " Ｔαιπε ρ\ot α \ic Ｍhuрcàóα," " Be cautious, oh son of Morogh," one hundred and sixty-eight verses, cautioning the prince of Leinster to be prepared to resist the attacks of the English.

A copy of this poem, beautifully written on paper about the year 1600, is in the collection of the Assistant Secretary.

A. D. 1448.

CLXXVI. The Annals of Conaght, and of the Four Masters, under this year, record the death of " ＴADHG or ＴEIGE OG, son of Giolla Columb O'ＨIGGIN, first preceptor of the poets of Eirin and Alba," (Ireland and Scotland). He was author of the following poems:

1. In praise of the river Shannon, forty-two verses, beginning " Ｑl Ｓioɲaιɲó Ｃrɲò cēó càtaιȝ," " O Shannon of Conn of hundred battles."

Copy with Assistant Secretary.

2. A poem beginning " Ｑtàιó τｐι coṁραιc um ｄιoñ," " They are three that contend on my account," one hundred and twenty-four verses, shewing that the world, the flesh, and the devil contend against his spiritual good. Copy in collection of John M'Namara, Esq.

3. A poem beginning " Ｏ'η αｐó τrαιt τιȝ αη ｄobαιｐ," " From the North the assistance came," one hundred and forty-four verses, on the mighty deeds of Niall og O'Neill.

Copy in the collection of John M'Namara, Esq.

4. A poem beginning " Ｑ\óｐ mo ｄｒȝò óo ｄuṁαιó Ｔhαιòȝ," " Great my share of sorrows for Teig," one hundred and ninety-two verses, on the death of Teige O'Conor, Sligo.

Copy in the collection of John M'Namara, Esq.

5. A poem, beginning " Ｑlɲoιｒ óo τuιȝｒιòe Ｔαòȝ," " Now Teige was taken," one hundred and sixty verses, on the death of Teige O'Kelly.

Copy in the collection of John M'Namara, Esq.

6. A poem beginning " Ｆuιlιɲȝιó buｐ leúη α lειt Ｃhuíñ," " Suffer your sorrows, oh Leath Chuinn," one hundred and sixty-four verses, on the death of Ulick Burke.

Copy with John M'Namara, Esq.

7. A poem beginning " ᴀᴅᴏᴄᴛ ᴦᴦᴀᴏɪʟɪᴅ ᴛᴅ ᴦᴣᴏʟᴅ," " To-night are dissolved the schools," one hundred and twelve verses, on the death of Feargal roe O'Higgin.

Copy in the collection of John M'Namara, Esq.

The poem beginning " Ôᴅ ᴦᴏɪᴨ ᴄᴏᴨᴈᴦᴏᴍᴀ ᴀɪᴦ ᴄᴦɪᴄ Ňᴇɪʟʟ," which we have on good authority given to Owen M'Craith, under 1395, is, by some writers, ascribed to this author.

———

A. D. 1450.

ᴄʟxxvɪɪ. At this time flourished John, son of Rory, M'Craith, the chief historian of the Dalcassian or North Munster tribes. He wrote, in the year 1459, the Caɪᴈᴨᴇɪᴨ Toɪᴦᴃᴇᴅʟᴃᴀɪᴣ, or Catalogue of the battles of Turlogh, containing an account of the wars of Thomond for upwards of two hundred years, from the landing of Henry II. in Ireland, to the death of Lord Robert de Clare, A. D. 1318.

ᴄʟxxvɪɪɪ. At this time also lived Teige, son of Joseph, O'Cassidy, of Coole. He was physician to the Maguires, princes of Fermanagh, and wrote a treatise on Medicine, a copy of which is in the collection of the Assistant Secretary.

———

A. D. 1460.

ᴄʟxxɪx. John O'Cludhain flourished about this period. He was author of a poem in praise of Aodh, or Hugh, son of Owen O'Conor, one hundred and eighty-eight verses, beginning " Ôᴏᴦᴨ ɪᴏɪᴦ ᴅᴀᴨ ɪᴦ ᴅᴀᴦᴀᴄᴅ," " A hand between poetry and courage."

A fine old copy of this poem is in the collection of the Assistant Secretary.

A. D. 1468.

clxxx. John Mac Coinmhidhe, or Conway, died this year. He was author of the poem, beginning " Ruᵹ an báṟ baiṗte a néiṁiᵹ," " Death carried the palm of victory," two hundred and ninety-six verses, on the death of Niall og O'Neill, prince of Tir-Eoghan (Tyrone.)

Copy in the collection of John M'Namara, Esq.

clxxxi. Cotemporary with John Mac Coinmhidhe was Donogh O'Bolg-aidh, or Boulger, a physician, who wrote some tracts on medicine, and transcribed the works of others on that subject. A large book, containing near five hundred pages, beautifully written on vellum, in O'Bolgai's handwriting, is in possession of the Assistant Secretary. By a memorandum at the end of one of the tracts contained in this book, which treats of the medicinal virtues of herbs, minerals, &c. it appears that it was first written at Mount Pelier, in France. The date of the transcript is then given in these words and characters: " Ꝋ.cccc.lx.uⁱ. in ᴄán ᴅo ċṗiċnúᵹaᴅ an leaḃaṗ ṗo, le ᵭoñċaṡ ħ. ḃollccai, aᵹaṟ aniṟᵹ la ḟéil Ḟinén, aᵹaṟ a cómaṗᴄa aquáṗiuṟ ᴅo ui in ᴄeṟca, aᵹaṟ e ᴅo ḃo líᴄeṗ ᵭoṁnaiᵹ, aᵹaṟ a ceaᴄaiṗ maṗ nᵹiṁiṗ óiṗ ᴅo ḃi in ḃliaᴅain ṗin." " M.CCCC.LX.VI. the time this book was finished by Donogh O'Bolgai (Boulger) and the day was the feast of Saint Finian, and the Moon was in the sign Aquarius, and four was the golden number of that year."

Besides the tract above mentioned, there are separate treatises upon the diseases of the head, and other members of the human body, in which many of the Arabian physicians are frequently quoted.

Towards the end of the book there is a translation of Aristotle's Treatise " On the Nature of Matter," but it does not appear whether O'Bolgai was the translator, or only a transcriber.

The last article in this book is a law tract, regulating the rewards to be paid to physicians by different ranks in society. The language of this law tract, and the matters contained in it, prove it to have been written at a much earlier period than that in which the rest of the book was written.

A. D. 1481.

CLXXXII. CONOR ROE M'COINMHIDHE died this year. He was author of a poem on the death of Brian O'Neill, eighty-four verses, beginning " ᴉᴐɴᴍᴀᴉɴ Ⲧᴀᴉꞃᴉ ᴀᴛᴀ ᴀ ɴᴏᴏᴉꞃᴇ," " Precious are the relicks that are in Derry."

Copy in the library of John M'Namara, Esq.

A. D. 1498.

CLXXXIII. CATHALD MAC MAGNUS *(Charles Maguire)* died this year, on the 10th of the calends of April. He was author of those Annals of Ireland, called "Annals of Bally M'Magnus," "Senatensian Annals," and " Annals of Ulster." They commence with the reign of Feradach Fionn-fachtnach, monarch of Ireland, A. D. 60, and are carried down to the author's own time. They were afterwards continued to the year 1504, by Roderick O'Cassidy, Archdeacon of Clogher.

The Annals of the Four Masters give the character, and relate the death of Cathald, in words, of which the following is a literal transla-tion : " Mac Magnus of Seanaigh, *i. e.* Cathal og, son of Cathal, son of Cathal, son of Giolla Patrick, son of Mathew, &c. was master of a house of general hospitality, and a public victualler in Seanaidh Mac Magnus ; Canon of the Choir in Ardmagh, and in the Bishoprick of Clogher ; Parson of Iniscaoin ; Deacon of Lough Erne ; and Deputy of the Bishop of Clogher, for fifteen years before his death. He was an encourager and protector of learning and science in his own district ; a treasured branch of the Canons ; a fountain of love and mercy to the poor and unprotected of God's people. It was he who collected and brought together many books of Annals, from which he compiled the Annals of Bally Mac Magnus, for himself. He died of the small pox on the 10th of the calends of April, on a Friday, in particular, in the sixtieth year of his age."

These Annals are partly Irish and part Latin. A copy of this work, in folio, written on vellum, is in the library of Trinity College, Dublin.

A. D. 1501.

CLXXXIV. The Annals of the Four Masters under this year, record the death of Donald O'Higgin, teacher of the schools of Ireland in poetry, after his return from a pilgrimage to the church of Saint James, in Spain. The Annals of Conaght say he died in 1502. He was a native of the county of Sligo, and author of a poem, consisting of one hundred and thirty-two verses, beginning " Ⲙⲉⲓⲣⲟⲉ ⲛⲁⲥ ⲉ́ⲁⲟⲙⲁⲣ Ⲉⲓⲣⲉ," " Woful that not jealous is Erin," in praise of John, son of Alexander M'Donald.

Copy with the Assistant Secretary.

A. D. 1504.

CLXXXV. PIERCE, son of Thomas O'Cassidy, of Coola, Maguire's professor of physic, died this year. He wrote on the nature and cure of different diseases incident to the human frame.

A copy of his work is in the collection of the Assistant Secretary.

A. D. 1508.

CLXXXVI. GEOFFREY O'DALY, *fionn*, died this year, according to the Annals of Conaght. To this author we are indebted for the following poems :

1. One hundred and eighty-four verses, beginning " Ⲙⲁⲓⲣⳉ ⲙⲉⲁⲗⲗⲁⲣ ⲙⲏⲣⲏ ⲁⲛ ⳉⲣⲁⲟⳃⲁⲓⲗ," " Woe to him whom the riches of the world deceive," upon the folly of great attachment to worldly matters.

2. A poem of two hundred verses, beginning " Ɖo τόʒbaιꝋ meιɲʒe ᴍuɲ-ċaꝋa," " The standard of Morogh was raised," in praise of Morogh O'Madden, prince of the Siol nAmchadha, or tribe of O'Maddens. The author compares the actions of his hero to those of his namesake, Morogh, son of Brian Boroimhe, at the battle of Clontarf.

3. A poem of two hundred verses, beginning " ᴍaꝋ ɲιaɲɲaιꝋeaċ buꝋ ɲeaɲaċ," " If you are inquisitive you will be knowing," upon Irish grammar. It treats of the parts of speech, and the genders of nouns.

4. A poem of two hundred and four verses, beginning " Ⱥ ʒheaɲóιττ ꝋeaɲa mo ꝋáιl," " Oh Gerald, do my bidding." This poem is addressed to Gerald, son of Maurice, Earl of Desmond, requesting his powerful protection.

Fine copies of this author's works are in the collection of the Assistant Secretary.

A. D. 1510.

CLXXXVII. OWEN ROE M'AN BHAIRD (Ward), chief poet of Tirconnel, died this year. He was author of many poems, none of which have come under our notice, except one, consisting of one hundred and thirty-six verses, on the death of Donald O'Donell. It begins " leaɲʒ an aꝋaιʒɲι aɲ eaɲ ɲuaꝋ," " Sloth this night on Eas Roe."

Copy of this poem in collection of the Assistant Secretary.

A. D. 1511.

CLXXXVIII. At this time flourished CAIRBRE O'MAOLCONAIRE, a famous scribe, who made a beautiful copy of one of our ancient Law tracts, that had been glossed or commented on by Donogh, son of Cairbre M·Aodhagain, or M'Egan. This tract was once the property of the author of the Archæologia Britannica, and afterwards of Sir John Seabright, who made a present of it, and several other valuable Irish manuscrips, to the library of Trinity College, where it now is, in class H. 54.

A. D. 1518.

CLXXXIX. CIOTHRUADH, son of Athairne O'HEOGHUSA, died this year, according to the Four Masters. He was author of a poem in praise of the O'Rourkes, beginning " *brme na ffilead frl Ruapcac,*" " Nurse of the poets is the family of O'Rourke ;" one hundred and thirty-two verses.

A fine copy of this poem is in O'Gara's collection, in the library of John Mac Namara, Esq.

A. D. 1520.

CLXC. TEIGE OG O'DALY flourished at this time. He was author of a poem, consisting of one hundred and forty verses, beginning " *Ni clram gabala grar De,*" " No deceitful prize is the grace of God," on the great advantage of living in a state of grace, and of the goodness of God.

Copy in possession of the Assistant Secretary.

CXCI. At this time also lived BRIAN CAOCH O'DALY, author of a poem on confidence in God, one hundred and forty-four verses, beginning " *Daingean conrad fa cairt rig,*" "A secure contract in the promise of God."

Copy in collection of the Assistant Secretary.

A. D. 1532.

CXCII. MANUS, son of Aodh O'DONELL, of the princely family of Tir-Conell, died this year. He was author of a Life of Saint Patrick, written in his native language, often quoted by Colgan and other writers.

About this period flourished a poet, also of the name of Manus O'Donell, but we are not able to say whether he be the same person that wrote the Life of Saint Patrick, or not. Some short poems of his composition are in possession of the Assistant Secretary.

1. A poem of twelve verses, beginning " Cροιδε lάη δο γmrαιητιξιβ," " A heart full of meditations."

2. A poem of twelve verses, beginning " Δαρ leam ιγ ξαlαρ e ιη ξραδ," " In my opinion, love is a disease."

3. A poem of twenty-four verses, beginning " Cροιδε γο δα ξοιδ uαιηe," " This is a heart that is about to be stolen from us."

4. A poem of twelve verses, beginning " Ζοιρτ αηοèτ δειρeαδ mo γξēl," " Painful to-night is the end of my tale."

5. A poem, beginning " Δαγ βραταιρ βοèτ αη βραταιρ meιτ," " If the fat brother be a poor brother," (a friar).

A. D. 1541.

CXCIII. In this year died RODERICK O'CASSIDY, Archdeacon of Clogher. He wrote a continuation of the Ulster Annals, from 1498, where they were ended by Cathal Mac Guire, to the year 1504, and added some things to the first part.

This work is in the library of Trinity College.

A. D. 1550.

CXCIV. LOGHLAINN O'DALY flourished at this period. He was author of the following pieces :

1. A poem of eighty-four verses, beginning " Uαιξηeαè α ταοι α èeαξ ηα mbραταιρ," " Solitary art thou, Oh house of the brothers," upon the expulsion of the Franciscan friars from their convents, in the reign of Henry the Eighth.

2. A poem of one hundred and thirty-two verses, beginning " Δeαllταρ mδe αη ταογ δάηα," " We, the people of song, are deceived."

3. A poem of one hundred verses, beginning " Cáiτ 'ɴaн ʒabaᴅaн ʒaoıᴅil," " Where did the Gathelians find shelter," upon the separation and dispersion of the Irish.

4. A poem, beginning " ꝼoʒuꝼ cabaın ᴅo cꞃıoċ bóıꞃne," " Assistance is near the country of Burren," upon the family of O'Loghlain of Burren, in the west of the county of Clare.

5. The poem, beginning " Eña ᴅáiτa Chaꞃbꞃe ꞃuaıᴅ," which we have given, from good authority, to Flann Mainistreach, is, by some writers, ascribed to Loghlainn O'Daly.

See Flann Mainistreach, or Flann of Bute, under the year 1056.

Copies of these poems are in the collection of the Assistant Secretary.

A. D. 1554.

cxcv. TEIGE, son of Aodh O'COFFEY, the chief teacher of poetry in Eire and Alba, (Ireland and Scotland) died this year, according to the Four Masters. He was author of the following pieces :

1. A poem of sixty-eight verses, beginning " Cꞃañ ꝼeoil ɴa cꞃuñe aɴ cꞃıoċ ɴaoṁτa," " The holy cross is the mast of the world," in praise of the cross of our Lord Jesus Christ, and of the goodness of God in sending his son to die an ignominious death for the redemption of man.

2. A poem, beginning " ꝼolaṁ Eıꞃe ᴅ'eaꞃbaıᴅ bhꞃıaıɴ," " Ireland is waste, from the absence of Brian," one hundred verses, on the death of Brian O'Connor Failge, (Faly.)

Copies of these poems are in the collection of the Assistant Secretary.

cxcvi. At this time lived a poet distinguished by the name of TEIGE *mor* O'COFFEY, author of a poem in praise of Manus, son of Aodh dubh O'Donell, who gave the writer a mare of his stud for every *rann* contained in the poem. It consists of twenty ranns, or eighty verses, beginning "Cıa ꞃe ccꞃꞃꝼñ ꝼeaᴅ ꝼꞃꞃʒe?" " Who sends the gifts of courtship?"

We know not but this and the last-mentioned writer are one and the same person.

Copy in the library of Rev. Doctor O'Brien.

A. D. 1556.

cxcvii. The annals of the Four Masters, under this year, record the murder of ANTHONY, son of WILLIAM O'COFFEY, by some persons unknown. He was author of the following pieces:

1. A poem of one hundred and fifty-six verses, beginning " ᴍó ɴᴀ ɪᴀᴘʟᴀ ᴀɪɴᴍ Shémᴀɪ𝑟," " Greater than Earl is the name of James." This was written in praise of James earl of Desmond, who survived his poet but one year.

2. A poem of one hundred and sixty verses, beginning " ꜰᴀᴅᴀ ᴀɴ ᴄ𝑟ɪᴍɴᴇ 𝑟ᴏ ᴀᴘ ᴄóɪᴘ ɴᴏé." " Long be this remembrance on the justice of God ;" in praise of our Lord Jesus Christ, and on the intercession of his mother, the Blessed Virgin Mary, in favour of sinners.

Copies of these poems are in the possession of the Assistant Secretary.

cxcviii. At this time flourished FEARFLATHA O'GNIMH, (O'GNEEVE) poet to the O'Neills of Clannaboy. He was author of the poem beginning " ᴍᴏ ċᴘᴜᴀɪᴅ ᴍᴀᴘ ᴀᴄáɪᴅ Ʒᴀᴏɪᴅɪʟ," " Alas for the state of the Gathelians," ninety-two verses, upon the miserable state of the Irish in those parts of the country where the power of the English prevailed.

An imperfect translation of this poem may be seen in O'Connor's Dissertations on the History of Ireland, at page 74, Christie's edition, Dublin, 1812. Copies of the original are in the hands of almost every Irish scholar.

A. D. 1560.

cxcix. At this period flourished FERGAL O'CIONGA, (King.) He was author of a poem upon the merits of Christ's sufferings, one hundred and fifty-two verses, beginning " ᴍᴀɪ𝑛Ʒ ᴀ𝑟 ᴜᴘᴘᴀ ᴘᴇ ħᴇáᴄᴄ ᴘɪᵹ !" " Alas! that subject to his condition is the king."

A copy of this poem is in the collection of the Assistant Secretary.

cc. At this time also lived Cᴏʀᴍᴀᴄ, son of Giolla Coluim O'Hɪɢɢɪɴ, who wrote a poem on the death of Donogh, son of Cathal O'Conor, Sligo, one hundred and eighty verses, beginning "Sɪoɳ coɪⱺceaɳ cumaɪꝺ Ᵹaoɪꝺɪl," "The sorrow of the Gathelians appears in a general shower of tears."

Copy in O'Gara's collection in the library of John Mac Namara, Esq.

A. D. 1565.

ccɪ. Dᴏɴᴀʟᴅ Mᴀᴄ Cᴀʀᴛʜʏ, created first earl of Clan-Carthy this year, was author of some poems, two only of which have reached us:

1. A small poem, of sixteen verses, beginning "Aɪꝼlɪɳᵹ ⱺꞃuaᵹ ꝺo ɱeaꞃ meɪꞃɪ," "A sorrowful vision has deceived me."

2. A poem of forty-four verses, beginning "Uc aɳ uc! a Ꝉhꞃꞃe bꞃꝺe," "Alas! alas! oh benign Mary;" a pious address to the Blessed Virgin Mary.

Copies in the collection of the Assistant Secretary.

A. D. 1566.

ccɪɪ. Jᴏʜɴ O'Mᴀᴏʟᴄᴏɴᴀɪʀᴇ, called by some of the annalists Aꞃꝺ ollaɱ Eɪꞃɪoɳ, (chief poet of Ireland) flourished at the time that Brian na murtha (of the bulwarks) O'Rourke was chosen chief of his tribe, after the death of his brother Aodh buidhe, (the yellow) A. D. 1566. He wrote a poem in praise of Brian na murtha, one hundred and thirty-six verses, beginning "ꝼuaɪꞃ bꞃeɪꝼne a ꝺɪol ꝺo ꞃaeᵹlaɳꝺ," "Breifne has obtained a prince worthy of her." This poem is written in the Bearla Feine, or Phœnician dialect of the Irish, and the poet assigns as a reason for his using that dialect, "because the beaꞃla ꞃuꞃⱺac, or dialect of plebeians, was unworthy of his hero."

A fine old copy of this poem, with an interlined gloss, is in the collection of Irish MSS. belonging to the Assistant Secretary.

A. D. 1570.

CCIII. At this time lived ANGUS O'DALY FIONN, surnamed the Divine. He was author of the following poems :

1. Forty-eight verses on our Saviour's humanity, beginning "Τ‌ṅlle‌‌ ‌ᵹan Τ‌ρaiᵹ ‌ᴅaonᴅaⅽ‌ ‌ᴅē," "A flood without ebb, is the humanity of God."

2. Forty-four verses on the Conception of the Blessed Virgin, beginning "Soiᵹeaⅽ‌ ‌balᵳaim‌ ‌bᵳu Ⅿ‌ᵐᵱ‌e," "A vessel of precious balsam is the womb of Mary."

3. Sixty-four verses in praise of God, beginning "Na cᵤᵹ‌ ‌ᵳoⅿ‌ ‌ᴅēᵹ ‌ᵳo ‌ᴅo ‌ᴅhia," "These fifteen ranns to God."

4. Forty-eight verses, in which the poet acknowledges his sins, and says it required the blood of a God to cleanse him from them. This poem begins "Ni léiᵱ ‌ᴅ'aon a aineaⅿ‌ ‌ᵱēⅿ," "The stains of a man are not visible to himself."

5. A hymn addressed to our Lord Jesus Christ, beginning "ℵl ‌loᵳa an eiᵳᴅeaᵱ ‌mo ‌ᴅáⅰ?" "Oh Jesus do you attend to my song?"

6. A penitential Address to our Saviour, eighty-eight verses, beginning "Eiᵳⅽ ‌ᵱeⅿ' ‌ⅽᵱⅰpa a ⅿeiⅽ ‌Ⅿhᵱ‌ᵱe!" "Hear my faults, Oh Son of Mary!"

7. Twenty-four verses on the Blessed Sacrament, beginning "Ꝣab ‌mo ⅽoimᵱⅽe a Chᵱᵱᵱ‌ ‌loᵳa," "Be my protection, Oh body of Jesus."

8. Fifty-two verses, beginning "Ꝣᵱⅰan‌ ‌na ‌maiᵹᴅean ‌maⅽaiᵱ‌ ‌ᴅē," "Sun of Virgins is the Mother of God."

9. Forty verses, beginning "Ⅿaⅰᵱᵹ ‌naⅽ‌ ‌molaⁿ ‌maⅽaiᵱ‌ ‌ᴅē," "Alas that I praise not the mother of God."

10. Thirty-six verses, beginning "Ⅿaiⅽ‌ ‌an ‌baᵱánⅽa ‌bean‌ ‌ᵱ‌ᵒᵹ," "Good is the authority of a queen."

11. Forty-four verses, beginning "Ꝣaⅽ‌ ‌maiᵹᴅean‌ ‌ᵹo ‌maⅽaⅰᵱ‌ ‌meiⅽ," "Each virgin to the mother of a son."

12. Thirty-two verses, beginning "ℵl ‌mbᵱēiᵹ ‌ⁿi ‌molᵱⅿ ‌Ⅿ‌ᵱᵱe," "In falsehood I praise not Mary."

13. Twenty-four verses, beginning "Ⅿiⁿⅰⅽ ‌ᴅo ‌beaᵱaᵱ ‌bean‌ ‌ᵹáoⅰl," "Often is given a fond woman."

14. Sixty verses, beginning " bean ōū mac maċaiɲ ɪoɲɑ," " A woman of two sons, the mother of Jesus.

15. Forty-eight verses, beginning " ᴍaiċ m'anacail ꝺ ꝼeiɲᵹ nꝺe," " Good is my protection against the anger of God."

The last eight poems in the above list are in praise of the Blessed Virgin Mary.

Copies of all these poems are in the collection of the Assistant Secretary.

cciv. At this time also lived John buidhe O'Daly, author of a poem in praise of Torlogh Luineach O'Neill, one hundred and seventy-six verses, beginning " Ceanꝺ na ɲíoᵹɲaiꝺe ɲiᵹ Ulaiꝺ," " Chief of kings the king of Ulster."

Copy in collection of the Assistant Secretary.

ccv. At the same time with the foregoing lived Owen O'Duffy, the friar, author of a poem, consisting of three hundred and ninety-six verses, on Miler M'Graith, and some others of the clergy, renouncing the Catholic, and embracing the Protestant religion, in the reign of Elizabeth. This poem begins " ɪeiᵹ ꝺoꝺ coṁoɲꞇuɲ ōɲ̄," " Leave thy comparison to us."

Copies in the library of John M'Namara, Esq. and of the Assistant Secretary.

ccvi. Cotemporary with the two last-mentioned writers was Donald M'Daire M'Bruaideagha, or M'Brodin, author of the two following poems :

1. One hundred and sixty verses on James Earl of Desmond, beginning " Cia iɼ ɼine caiɲꞇ aiɲ cɲíc Néill," " Which is the oldest charter of the country of Niall."

2. Two hundred and forty-eight verses on Torlogh, son of Donogh O'Brien, beginning " Cɲeaꝺ an ꞇɾamanɲa aiɲ ꝼheiṁᵹall ?" " What is this dread that is on the foreigners ?"

Copy in the collection of the Assistant Secretary.

CCVII. At this time lived a DONALL M'DAIRE, who, it is probable, was the same as the last-mentioned writer. There are two poems ascribed to him, both possessing a good deal of merit. The first consists of one hundred and sixty-eight verses, beginning " ᴀ ṁeic ᵹuⱪ meaᴅa c' aⱪma!" " Oh son! that a reproach are thy arms!" addressed to some young man that he calls " son of the Earl," but there is no clue to discover who he was.

Copy in the collection of John M'Namara, Esq.

The second poem consists of one hundred and sixteen verses, beginning " ᵹeaɫɫ ⱪe maoine móɫaᴅ ᴅē," " Pledge of reward the praise of God," in praise of our Lord Jesus Christ.

Copy in possession of Assistant Secretary.

A. D. 1580.

CCVIII. MUIRCHEARTACH O'CIONGA flourished at this time. He was author of a poem on the birth of our Lord Jesus Christ, and upon the benefits that man derives from his sufferings and death. The poem consists of one hundred and eighty-four verses, beginning " beiⱪc ċaiⱪ coᵹaᴅ ciᵹeaⱪna," " A pleasant burden is the war of a Lord."

A fine copy of this poem is in the collection of the Assistant Secretary.

CCIX. At this time flourished FLANN, son of Owen M'CRAITH (Magrath) a Munster poet, author of the following poems :

1. One hundred and eighty-four verses on Thomas Butler, tenth Earl of Ormond, or, as the poet calls him, Earl of Gowran, who succeeded to that title when but a youth, in 1564, and died in 1614. This poem begins " Coɫaċ me aiⱪ ṁeiⱪᵹe an ɫaⱪɫa," " I know the standard of the Earl."

2. One hundred and seventy-six verses on Death and Judgment, beginning " ⱪaᴅ m'raiᵹ m'ⱪeaⱪa͠n caiⱪce," " Long my grave my charter land."

Copies of these two poems in possession of the Assistant Secretary.

3. Eighty verses on the miserable state of Ireland, beginning " ᴉoṁᴅa ēaᵹnaċ aiᵹ Cⱪⱪⱪ," " Many are the woes of Erin."

Copy in collection of John M'Namara, Esq.

A. D. 1583.

ccx. On the 13th of March this year, died Fearghal og, son of Fearghal Mac an Bhaird, author of an Elegy on Hugh, son of Hugh duff O'Donell, written during the life time of Hugh, two hundred and twenty verses, beginning " Ní τρατ αιτρεαċηγ όχηl Chonꞃ̇ll," " No time of sorrow to the race of Conall."

2. An Elegy on the death of Con, son of Calbhach, son of Hugh, son of Hugh duff O'Donell, three hundred and twenty verses, beginning " ꝼill ταòaiჳ raṁ a Єꞁ̇ηe," " Turn thy face from us, Oh Erin."

Copies of these in the manuscript collections of Rev. Doctor O'Brien, and of the Assistant Secretary.

A. D. 1584.

ccxi. Rory, or *Roderick*, son of Aodh M'Craith, flourished at the time that Feagh M'Hugh O'Byrne was elected chief of his tribe. Copies of two poems written by him have come down to our time, and are in the collection of the Assistant Secretary.

1. The Inauguration Ode of Feagh Mac Hugh O'Byrne, one hundred and twenty verses, beginning " ꝼoჳꞃa cꞃꞃṁiჳτe aꞃ ċꝛú mòꞃoiṅ," " A warning to assemble the race of Brann."

The Brann here mentioned, was Brann the black, King of Leinster, who died in the year 601, from whom the O'Brainns, or O'Byrnes derive their name and lineage.

2. A poem on the family of O'Byrne, of Ranelagh, thirty-two verses, beginning " Cioṅaγ ατα aη τꞃeaḃγa aγτoiჳ," " How is this tribe within."

Copies of these poems are in the possession of the family of O'Byrne, of Cabinteely; of James Hardiman, Esq. a member of this Society; and in the collection of the Assistant Secretary.

ccxii. At this time also flourished Owen, son of Hugh O'Coffey, a poet of Leinster, and author of the following pieces:

1. A poem in praise of our Lord Jesus Christ, and of the blessed Virgin Mary, beginning " ꝼᴀᴅᴀ ᴄꞃ̃ɯ̃ꞃᵹᴄᴇᴀꞃ ᴄóıꞃ ʟᴇıɱᴃ," " Long is remembered the justice of a child."

2. A poem in praise of Rory O'More, chieftain of Leix. In the course of the poem the author mentions that twenty-five of the ancestors of his hero swayed the sceptre of Ireland. This poem consists of two hundred and four verses, beginning " ꟽᴀıꞃıᴏ ᴄᴇꞃ̃ᴇ ᴀ ᴄᴄᴇᴀʟᴀ́ᴄ̇ ᵹᴀᴏıᴃıʟ," " Fire still exists on the hearths of the Gathelians."

3. A poem in praise of Brian O'Conor, of O'Faly, beginning, " ꝼᴀıʟ-ᵹıᵹ ᴄᴏꞃɴᴀꞃ ᴄʟú ʟᴀıᵹᴇᴀɴ," " It is Faly that upholds the fame of Leinster."

Copies of these poems, in hand-writing nearly the same age as the original, are in possession of the Assistant Secretary.

ccxiii. At this time also flourished Mahon O'Higgin, a retainer of the O'Byrnes. He was author of the following pieces :

1. A poem in praise of Leinster, and of Felim, son of Feagh M'Hugh O'Byrne, one hundred and twenty verses, beginning " Cꞃᴇᴅ ᴅᴏ ᴄᴏꞃᵹ ᴄᴏᵹᴀᴅ ʟᴀıᵹᴇᴀɴ?" " What has impeded the war of Leinster?"

2. A poem shewing that it is a profitable employment to constantly praise God, and pray for his blessings, one hundred and seventy-six verses, beginning " Nᴀᴏɯ̃ᴄᴀ ᴀɴ ᴏᴃᴀıꞃ ıᴏɱꞃᴀᴅ Ðᴇ̃," " Praising of God is a holy work." This poem is, by some persons, ascribed to Mahon O'Hayne.

Copies in possession of the Assistant Secretary.

ccxiv. At the same time with the four last-mentioned writers lived Donald M'Eochaidh (M'Keogh), a retainer of the House of O'Byrne, of Ranelagh, county of Wicklow. He has left us a poem of forty-four verses on the return of Felim, son of Feagh M'Hugh O'Byrne, the chief of his tribe, from a journey he made to, the north. It begins " Cıꞃᴄ ꞃᴇɱ ꝼᴀıʟᴄᴇꞃı ᴀ ꝼᴇ̃ıʟıɱ," " Attend to my welcome, oh Felim."

Copies of this are in the Book of O'Byrne, in the library of James Hardiman, Esq. and in the collection of the Assistant Secretary.

ccxv. At this period also lived Fergal, son of Lughaidh (Louis) M'Eochaidh, or M'Keogh, the author of a poem upon seven of the descendants of John O'Byrne, of Ranelagh. In these are included

Feagh M'Hugh O'Byrne and his sons, and Conall and Cathaoir, his brothers. The poem begins "Móirseisior laoch lingeas troid," "Seven heroes that bound to battle."

Copies in the same collections as those mentioned in the foregoing article.

CCXVI. Cotemporary with these writers was DONALD, son of FEARGANAINM M'EOCHAIDH, or M'Keogh. He was author of an address to Brian, son of Felim O'Byrne, upon his return from a voyage to England, fifty-six verses, beginning "Fáilte romhat a Bhriain i Bhroinn," "Welcome to thee, Brian O'Byrne."

Copies as before.

CCXVII. At this period also flourished NIALL O'ROONEY, who was also a retainer of the O'Byrne's of Ranelagh, that so long contended against the English power.

He was author of the following pieces:

1. A poem in praise of Leinster, and its leader Feagh M'Hugh, one hundred and eighty verses, beginning "Mór cóir cháich air chríoch Laighean," "Great dues of all belongs to Leinster."

2. A poem on Feagh M'Hugh O'Byrne, one hundred and twelve verses, beginning "Mithidh triall a cceann Fhiacha," "It is time to go on Feagh's account."

Copies in the book of O'Byrne, in possession of the O'Byrnes of Cabinteely, in the library of James Hardiman, Esq. and with the Assistant Secretary.

CCXVIII. ANGUS, son of Dory O'DALY, lived at the same time with the above-mentioned writers. He was author of the following poems:

1. In praise of the O'Byrnes of Ranelagh, sixty verses, beginning "Dia libh a laochraidh Gaoidhil!" "God be with you, oh Irish heroes!"

Copies as before.

2. In praise of FELIM, son of FEAGH M'HUGH O'BYRNE, chief of the *Gabhail Raghnaill*, or O'Byrnes of Ranelagh, and of all the other septs of the O'Byrnes at the latter end of the sixteenth century. This poem consists of fifty-two verses, beginning "Rugas aimbreatha air Fheilim," "I gave false judgment on Felim."

Copy in the collection of the Assistant Secretary.

CCXIX. Donald Carrach M'Eochaidh (M'Keogh), also lived at this time. He was author of a composition, in verse and prose, in praise of the O'Byrnes of Ranelagh, particularly Felim, son of Feagh M'Hugh O'Byrne. It begins "ιοmδα υρραιm αιg cloιñ Cαταοιρ," "Many honours belong to the descendants of Cathaoir."

The Cathaoir here mentioned, was Cathaoir mór, monarch of Ireland in the second century, from whom the O'Byrnes are descended.

Copies as before.

CCXX. At this time also lived M'Amhlaoidh or M'Awley, chief of Duhallow, in the county of Corke. He was a religious man, and the reputed author of some prophecies, in Irish verse, said to refer to our times, copies of which are in the hands of almost every Irish reader.

CCXXI. Dermod O'Coffey, a poet of some distinction, also lived about this time. He was author of the following poems:

1. One hundred and fifty verses on the death of Owen O'Coffey and his wife, beginning "Dá nēll ορċρα οϝ ιαᴣ Uιϝmᴣ," "Two clouds of woe over Uisneach's land."

2. One hundred and sixty verses on the death of our Lord Jesus Christ, beginning "Dιόn cloιñe α nēcc α nαταρ," "The protection of the children is in the death of their father."

3. One hundred and fifty-six verses on the same subject, beginning "ϝιρ α beαṫα báϝ Tιᴣeαρnα," "The price of life is the death of a Lord."

4. One hundred and forty-eight verses, on Christ's satisfaction, beginning "Ϣαιρᴣ αϝ αιöne αnαᴣαιö bϝeιᴄιñ," "Alas, the pleading is against the Judge."

5. One hundred and fifty-six verses on Christ's goodness to man, beginning "Ϣαιρᴣ nαċ ᴄαιᴄιᴣ ᴣo ᴄeαᴣ ρίoᴣ," "Alas, that I had not recourse to the house of the king."

6. One hundred and sixty verses on the same subject, beginning "Deαcαιρ αιöneαϝ eαρcα ρίoᴣ," "Powerful the argument the tributes of a king."

Fine copies of all these poems are in the collection of the Assistant Secretary.

A. D. 1585.

CCXXII. NICHOLAS WALSH, Bishop of Ossory, was killed on the 14th of December this year, by a person of the name of James Dullard, who had been cited by the bishop for adultery. This prelate, with the assistance of John Kearney, treasurer of Saint Patrick's, Dublin, and Doctor Nehemiah Donellan, afterwards Archbishop of Tuam, began to translate the New Testament into Irish, which was afterwards finished by Doctor William O'Donell, Archbishop of Tuam.

CCXXIII. JOHN KEARNEY, treasurer of Saint Patrick's, Dublin, was the cotemporary and intimate friend of Doctor Walsh, above mentioned. He wrote and published a catechism in Irish, which was the first book ever printed in Irish types. He also, with the assistance of his friend Walsh, and Dr. Nehemiah Donellan, Archbishop of Tuam, began a translation of the New Testament into Irish. He died about the year 1600.

A. D 1586.

CCXXIV. About this time flourished MUIRCHEARTAGH O'COFFEY, author of the following poems :

1. On the salvation of man by the merits of Christ, one hundred and forty verses, beginning " Oligio liaig léigeaf a cafaio," " Perfection of physician is the cure of his friend."

2. On the death of Gearoid, or Garrett, Lord of Delvin, one hundred and forty-eight verses, beginning " Maig if baileaṁ oon oig bfóin," " Alas, that sorrow is attendant on the drink."

3. On William Nugent, who possessed great power in Delvin, one hundred and twenty-four verses, beginning " Oo gni clu áic oigfeaṫa," " Place of inheritance gives reputation."

4. On Christopher Nugent, Baron of Delvin, one hundred and eighty-four verses, beginning " Geall fe hiaflaċt ainm bafún," " The title of Baron is the promise of an Earldom."

Fine copies of all these poems are in the collection of the Assistant Secretary.

A. D. 1587.

ccxxv. At this time flourished Maolmuire, son of Conula Mc. an Bhaird (Ward). He was author of the following poems:

1. An address to red Hugh, son of black Hugh O'Donell, chieftain of Tirconell, who, in the year 1587, before he had attained the sixteenth year of his age, was decoyed into the hands of the English, carried to Dublin, confined in a tower of the Castle, and treated with great cruelty. In this poem, which consists of one hundred and ninety-six verses, beginning " ꞇomċ ꞃꞇ ꞇʹaꞇꞇꞃꝼꞇꞃꝼe a ꞀoꞋ ꝼꞃaꞃꞋ," " Support thy great afflictions, oh red Hugh," the author encourages his youthful prince to bear up against the persecutions of his enemies, and advises him to place his confidence in God, the defender of the just, and the chastiser of the wicked.

2. A poem, beginning " CꞃeaꞋ ꝼꞋaꞃaꞃꝼ oꞃam a ꞀoꞋ," " What hast thou found on me, oh Hugh," sixty-eight verses. It appears by this poem that the author had fallen under the displeasure of Aodh roe, with whom he remonstrates, asserts that he was always his faithful friend, even while he was in unjust captivity with the English, and accuses Aodh of injustice in opposing his interests.

3. A poem, beginning " Ꞁ oꞃꞋꞁ ꞇꞃꝼ aꞇa ꞇ aeꞃꞋꞃ," " O castle below, thou art solitary," one hundred and thirty-four verses, upon the deserted state of the castle of Donegal, after its being dismantled by Aodh roe O'Donell, for fear it should fall into the hands of the English.

Fine copies of these poems are in the collection of the Assistant Secretary.

A. D. 1588.

ccxxvi. Dubhthach (*Duffy*) O'Duigenan, flourished at this time, as appears by the twenty-third rann (stanza) of his poem in praise of Aodh, or Hugh, son of Feardorcha O'Neill, two hundred and forty verses, beginning " Cumam cɼoinic ɓo ċloiñ Neill," " Let us make a chronicle for the O'Neills." In this poem the author enumerates twelve chiefs of the O'Neills, who governed that tribe for a period of two hundred and sixteen years, from the time of Niall og, son of Niall mor, to the third year of Aodh, son of Feardorcha, which, according to this poem, was A. D. 1588.

A fine copy of this poem is in the collection of the Assistant Secretary.

2. Three hundred and sixty-eight verses on the History of the O'Donnells, beginning " leanam cɼoinic Clañ Ɠalaiᵹ," " Let us pursue the Chronicle of *Clann Dalaigh*." This poem gives a catalogue of twenty-five kings, or princes, who governed Tirconell for four hundred and one years, with the number of years that each prince ruled ; from the eighth year of Hugh roe O'Donell, A. D. 1600, in which year the poem was written, up to Eigneachan O'Donell, who became chief of Cineal Conall, or Tirconnell, A. D. 1199.

The O'Donells are called by the Irish Clann Dalaigh, and Muintir Dalaigh (Daly) from Dalach, their great ancestor, as they are called O'Donell, from his grandson Donall mor.

Copy of this poem is in the library of the Rev. Doctor O'Brien, Irish professor in the College of Maynooth.

ccxxvii. At this period lived IOLLAND O'DONELLAN, a Tirone bard, author of a poem on the O'Neills, particularly John, son of Conn. This poem consists of one hundred and thirty-two verses, beginning " Táinicc anam a ꞃEiꞃin," " A soul has come into Erin."

Copy in O'Gara's collection, in the library of John M'Namara, Esq.

A. D. 1590.

ccxxviii. At this time flourished CUCHONACHT, son of Maoilseachlainn O'Daly. He was the friend and companion of Aodh roe O'Donell, to whom he addressed the poem, beginning " Cioñuꞅ ɓo ꝼꞃccꝼiñꞃi Ⅎloɓ?" " How could I leave Hugh ?"

Copy in possession of Assistant Secretary.

ccxxix. At this time flourished CORMAC O'DALY, a Munster poet, who was the author of an elegy on the death of Donogh M'Carthy, one hundred and sixty verses, beginning " ꜰᴀᴅᴀ ᴀꞃ ᴏᴄꞃᴀꞃ ᴇᵹ ᴅᴏꝀᴄᴀᴅᴀ," " Long the death sickness of Donogh."

Copy in possession of John M'Namara, Esq.

ccxxx. Cotemporary with the above was DERMOD MAC AN BHAIRD, (Ward) who wrote an elegy on the death of Alexander, son of Conor roe M'Donald, chief of the M'Donalds of Ireland, one hundred and eighty verses, beginning " ꝼᴇᴀꞃᴏᴀ ᴀꞃ ᴄᴀᴑᴄᴇ ᴄʟᴀꝀ ᴅᴏ́ᴍᴏᴀᴑʟʟ," " Henceforward mournful are the M·Donalds."

Copy in the collection of the Assistant Secretary.

A. D. 1600.

ccxxxi. At the commencement of this century many fine poets flourished in Ireland, who found protection and patronage from the nobility of the country, as well amongst the descendants of the Anglo-Normans, as from the native Irish princes. Several of these poets, celebrated, in verse, the magnanimity and bounty of their respective patrons, or sung the valorous deeds, liberal actions, or pious lives of their ancestors. Some of them, not satisfied with exalting their heroes to the skies, drew comparisons between them and their cotemporaries, or between their respective ancestors, in which one party was degraded in proportion as the other was elevated. Amongst the most remarkable of this latter description of writers was TADHG, (or Teige) son of DAIRE MAC BRODY, generally known by the name of TEIGE M'DAIRE. He was principal poet to Donogh O'Brien, fourth Earl of Thomond, and, as his chief, was much favoured by the English government; and the Meathian, Ultonian, and Conacian princes were not so, but rather looked upon with a jealous eye; he was determined, so far as he could, to elevate the house of O'Brien above the tribes descended from Niall of the nine hostages, such as the O'Neills,

O'Donells, &c., or from his brother Brian, such as the O'Conors, M'Dermotts, O'Kellys, O'Rourkes, O'Reillys, &c. For this purpose he attacks the works of Torna Eigeas, a writer whose poems we have already described under the year 405. This drew an answer from Lughaidh O'Clery, a northern bard, who defended the memory of Torna, and supported the honor of the Heremonians. Teige, shortly after, replied to Lughaidh, and this induced others of the Ultonian, and some of the Conaght poets, to take part in the contest, which was carried on with a good deal of heat on both sides. The poems written on this subject are generally collected together, and are called the Iomarbaḋ, or contention of the bards, in which a great quantity of the ancient history of Ireland is recited in elegant verse. Of the poets who took a part in the *Iomarbadh*, or contention, Teige Mac Daire, Ferfeasa O'Cainte, Torlogh O'Brien, and Art og O'Keeffe, were most remarkable on the side of *Leath Mhogha* (Munster and Leinster); and Lughaidh O'Clery, Aodh O'Donell, Robert M'Arthur, Baoghalach (Boetius) roe M'Egan, Anluan M'Egan, M'Dermott of Moylurg, and John O'Clery, were the champions who supported the honor, and contended for the precedence of Leath Chuinn (Meath, Ulster, and Conaght).

Of the writers of this century we shall begin our account with

CCXXXII. TEIGE MAC DAIRE, who, as we have just now seen, began the contention of the bards, but whose poems were not entirely confined to historical subjects. The following pieces make the entire catalogue of his works that have come under our observation.

1. A poem of one hundred and twenty-eight verses, upon the birth of our Lord Jesus Christ, beginning "Deanaiḋ go ſúbaċ a ſíol Aḋaim," "Be joyful, Oh children of Adam."

2. A didactic poem, of two hundred and twenty verses, addressed to Donogh O'Brien, fourth earl of Thomond, upon his inauguration as chief of his tribe. It begins "Mór ata-air ṫeagaſg ḟlaṫa," "Much depends upon the instruction of a prince."

In this poem the author lays down rules for the guidance of his prince in the important affair of the government of his people. The precepts here delivered are merely a versified abridgment of our monarch Cormac's instructions to his son Cairbre Liffeachar, written about the middle of the third century of the Christian era, an account of which work we have given under the year 250. This piece of Mac Daire's has been published in the Transactions of the Gaelic Society of Dublin, accompanied with a Latin and an English translation, by the late Theophilus O'Flanagan, Esq.

3. A poem of twenty verses, addressed to the same prince as the foregoing poem, containing some further instructions for his general conduct. This poem begins " Ꝋo ceiꞇꞃe ꝛaiꞃ oꞃꞇ a Ꝺhoꞃċaꝺ," " My four stanzas to you, Oh Donogh." This also has been published, with an English translation, in the Transactions of the Gaelic Society of Dublin.

4. A didactic poem of one hundred verses, beginning " Ꞇaiꞃꞁiꝺ mo ꞃeaċna a ꞃíol mꞃꞃiaiꞃ," " Accept my warnings, Oh race of Brian," advising the O'Briens to avoid war and the enmity of the bards.

5. A poem of one hundred and forty verses, beginning " Ꝑꞃoiꞃ ꝺíolaiꞃ aꞃ ꝺeaċmaꝺ," " Now I pay the tithe," upon the death of seven males and three females of the house of O'Brien.

6. A poem of one hundred and forty-four verses, beginning " Olc ꝺo ꞇaꞃꞃaꞃ a Ꞇhoꞃna," " Ill hast thou argued, Oh Torna." In this poem the author endeavours to shew that the Munster tribes have a right to precedence before those of the other provinces; as the former are descended from Heber, the eldest son of Milesius, and the latter are the progeny of Heremon and Ir, two of the younger sons of that Spanish chief. He attacks Torna Eigeas, a poet of the fifth century, who, as we have shewn under the year 405, was the preceptor of Niall, monarch of Ireland, and Corc, king of Cashel; and who, in his poem, beginning " Ꝺáil caꞇa iꝺiꞃ Coꞃc iꞃ Ꞃiall," endeavours to reconcile these two heroes, who had quarrelled with each other, and shews that Niall had a right to respect and obedience from his opponent.

In the ninth stanza of this poem Teige asserts that Hibernia, the Latin name of Ireland, is derived from Heber, the great ancestor of the Momonian tribes. This poem of Mac Daire's was the cause of the iomaꞃbaꝺ, or contention of the bards, which was warmly carried on for some time, between the poets of Leath Chuinn and Leath Mhogha.

7. A poem of six hundred and eighty-eight verses, beginning " Eiꞃꝺꞃi Luꞃaiꝺ ꞃem' labꞃaꝺ," " Attend to my words, Oh Lughaidh," in reply to

Lughaidh O'Clery, who, in answer to Teige, had written a defence of Torna Eigeas, and asserted the superiority of the house of O'Neill over that of the O'Briens.

8. A poem of one hundred and twenty-four verses, beginning " Ꝺl lúᵹꝺıꝺ láḃꝛꝼaᵯ ᵹo ꝛéıᵯ," " Oh Lughaidh, let us speak mildly," a further reply to Lughaidh O'Clery's rejoinder to the foregoing poem.

9. A poem of ninety-six verses, beginning " Ꝺl óꝛꝼⁿe ⱡaḃꝛⱥꝼ ꝺⁿ ⱡꝺoı," " Oh man, who recitest the poem," in answer to Boetius roe Mac Egan's poem, beginning " ꝰⱥᵹ óꝗ ꝼeıceaᵯ ꝼeꝺꝛ ᵹꝺoıⱡ.*" In this poem the author declares his name, and defies his adversary to do so. He still insists on the right of Munster to precedence before the other provinces, and insists on his former argument, that the name Hibernia is derived from Heber, the eldest son of Milesius, from whom the O'Briens and other Munster families are descended.

10. A poem of forty-four verses, beginning " Ꝺ̃ı ᵹuꝺıꝛ ⱡeꝺᵯ ꞇ'uꝛċꝺꝛ ꝺ Ꝺloḃ," " Not dangerous to me are thy darts, Oh Aodh," in answer to a poem written by Aodh O'Donell, in defence of the honor and precedence of Leith Chuinn.

11. A further reply to Aodh O'Donell, six hundred and eighty-eight verses, beginning " Ꝺ̃ı ḃꝛeıꞇ oꝛᵯ ꝺo ḃꝛeıꞇ ꝺ Ꝺloḃ," " No decision to me is thy judgment, oh Aodh." In some copies of the *Iomarbadh* this poem is blended, by way of dialogue, with Aodh O'Donell's poem, beginning " ꝰeꝺꝛꝼꝺ ꝺo ꞇꝺᵹꝛꝼꝺıꝛ ꝺ Ꞇhꝺıꝺ̃ᵹ," so as to make the two poems appear but as one piece written by that author. In these copies M'Daire's poem begins at the second rann, and that and all the other ranns belonging to him are marked with Ꞇꝺ, the two first letters of his christian name.

12. A poem of two hundred and fifty-two verses, beginning " Ꝝo cceꝺḃ ꝺoꞇ ᵹꝺıꝛᵯ ꝺ ḃꝛꝺꞇꝺıꝛ," in answer to the Rev. Robert M'Arthur, a Franciscan friar of the Irish convent of that order, in Louvain, who had written in defence of Leath Chuinn, against M'Daire. In this poem the author desires the author to attend to the duties of his order, and tells him it is unbecoming in a clergyman to meddle in other matters.

13. A poem beginning " Ꝺ̃ı ꞇeıꞇıᵯ ꝛıꝺ ꞇꝺᵹꝛꝺ ᵯꝺoıꞇ," " I fly not before a boasting argument," one hundred and sixty-eight verses, in reply to a

* See page clv.

poem written by Baoghalach roe M'Egan, beginning "Fuiriḋ rem ṫagraḋa a Ṫaiḋg," "Wait for my argument, oh Teige."

14. A poem of one hundred and eight verses, beginning "Foiriḋ mo leisge a Leiṫ Ċuinn," "Await my indolence, oh Leath Chuinn." In this poem the author desires the poets of Leath Chuinn not to be impatient at his tardiness in replying to them. He says there is no indolence without cause, and his slowness in reply arises from the great activity of his mind. He tells them they have provoked his satire, but he is unwilling to satirize.

Copies of the above poems of M'Daire are in the collection of the Assistant Secretary.

15. A poem of two hundred and forty-four verses, beginning "Eascar Gaoiḋil éag aoin ḟir," "The fall of the Irish is the death of one man," on the death of Donogh, fourth Earl of Thomond, who died in the year 1624.

16. A poem of sixty verses, beginning "Ni traṫ ḋoḋ ḋol a Ḋiarmuid," "Untimely thy departure, oh Dermod," addressed to Dermod, son of Morogh O'Brien, dissuading him from leaving his people.

17. A poem of thirty-six verses, beginning "Roġa gaċ beaṫa beiṫ boċt," "The choice of lives is to be poor," on adopting a life of poverty.

18. A poem of one hundred and twelve verses, beginning "Aistraiġ ċugam a ċroċ naoṁ," "Come to me, oh holy Cross." An address to the Cross of our Lord Jesus Christ.

Copies of the four last-mentioned poems are in the library of John M'Namara, Esq.

CCXXXIII. Lughaidh O'Clery, the chief bard of Tirconnel, was the great opponent of the last-mentioned writer, and the most powerful advocate of all the bards of Leath Chuinn, for the honour and precedence of the descendants of Niall of the nine hostages, as well as the first to write in defence of Torna Eigeas. He was author of the following pieces:

1. A poem of three hundred and forty verses, beginning "A Ṫaiḋg na taṫaoir Tórna," "Oh Teige revile not Torna," in answer to Teige M'Daire's poem, beginning "Olc ḋo ṫagrais a Ṫorna," in which Teige

had attacked Torna Eigeas, the poet of Niall the Great, and endeavoured to show that the Momonian tribes were superior to the descendants of Heremon and Ir.

2. A poem of nine hundred and eighty-eight verses, beginning " Do crala aṅ ċaġnaiṡ a Caiöġ," " I heard all you have pleaded, oh Teige." In this poem the author brings many authorities from history, and from Irish proverbs, to prove that the Heremonian tribes were always considered superior to the Heberians. He insists that the name Hibernia, which Teige asserted was derived from Heber, is of no weight, as it is not the language of Ireland.

3. A poem of seventy-two verses, beginning " Na bṙoṫö meiṙe a ṁeic Daiṙe," " Provoke me not, oh son of Daire." In this poem the author says there are many better poets than himself in the country in which he resides, but as they are silent, he finds it necessary to take up the subject in debate. He declares his respect for the tribe of Cas, but truth and the honour of the Heremonians compel him to defend Torna Eigeas against the attacks of his adversary.

4. A poem of one hundred and twenty verses, beginning " 2ln cclṙne mē a ṁeic Daiṙe," " Do you hear me, oh son of Daire." In this the same subject is continued as in the foregoing poems. The author takes a review of the contest, and calls upon Teige to desist from a strife so unavailing to himself and those he endeavours to elevate above their usual rank.

Copies of these poems are in the collection of the Assistant Secretary.

ccxxxiv. Rev. Robert M'Arthur, D. D. a Franciscan friar of the Irish convent of that order in Louvain, took a part in the contention of the bards, on the side of Leath Chuinn. He was author of two poems, which he wrote while at Louvain, in defence of Torna Eigeas, and the rights of the Heremonians against Teige M'Daire.

1. A poem of one hundred and forty verses, beginning " Meaṙa a Chaiöġ öo Chaġnaiṙ ṗēm," " Worse, oh Teige, thyself hast argued."

2. A poem of seven hundred and eighty-four verses, beginning " Ze ṙaoil tu Chaiöġ naċ öeanna," " Though you think, oh Teige, it will not do." In this poem the author defends himself against the illiberal reflections of his opponet, contained in his poem, beginning " Zo cceaö öoc ġạm a bṙaċ ; and enters into many particulars of ancient Irish his-

tory, from which he deduces arguments to prove the princes of Leath-Chuinn should be, and in fact were, superior to the chiefs of Leath Mhogha.

Teige, in his abuse of the poet Torna Eigeas, asserted that he was not worthy of credit, or fit to be quoted, on account of his being a Pagan. He is contradicted by the reverend author, who enters into a panegyric on Torna, and insists he was a good Christian; in proof of which he adduces his poems.——See the account of Torna Eigeas, under the year 405.

Copies of these poems, written by John M'Solly in the year 1713, are in the collection of the Assistant Secretary.

ccxxxv. Baoghalach *(Boetius)* roe Mac Egan, took a part in the contest of the bards. He was author of two poems in defence of Leath Chuinn against the attacks of Teige M'Daire.

1. A poem of fifty-two verses, beginning " Mȧg oȷ feiceaṁ feaṟ ȝaṗil," " Woe to him who is obliged to defend a relation." In this short poem the author takes a view of the contest between Teige M'Daire and Lughaidh (Loo-ee) O'Clery. He accuses M'Daire of partiality to his relations, the people of Munster, and asserts, that " to slander the descendants of Conn of the hundred battles, the people of Meath, Ulster, and Conaght, he formed a fabulous history in bald verses, without permanence in foundation, and not found in poems nor in books."

> " Oo ċoiḃéim aiṟ ċlaṅaiḃ Cṟ̄ṅ.
> Oo ċom ṟē an ṟeanċṟṡ faḃṟ̄ll,
> 2l noṟaiṅ ṁaoil ȝan bṟaiṅe ṟe bṟ̄ṅ
> Ṅaċ fṟaiṟ a laoi no a leaḃȷ."

On the other hand, he asserts that O'Clery's reply to the calumnies of Teige was " written in the schools, and polished with learning and science."

It may not be improper to remark that this author was of a Momonian tribe.

2. A poem of one hundred and sixty-eight verses, beginning " Fṟṟiȝ ṟem ċaȝṟaṟa a Ṫaiȯȝ," " Wait for my argument, oh Teige." This poem

was written in reply to the poem of Teige M'Daire, beginning " 𝔄 óṙne labṁuṛ an laoi." (See No. 9, page 152.) The author desires M'Daire to defend his claims for the honor of Leath Mogha, by authority, if he can produce any. He denies that the repetition of Teige's assertions has any weight, and insists that one falsehood is not made more true by the telling of a second.

These poems are beautiful compositions, and contain many useful maxims.

Fine copies are in the collection of the Assistant Secretary.

ccxxxvi. Anluain M'Egan also took a part in the contention of the bards, and made use of his pen in defence of Leath Chuinn. He was author of the following pieces :

1. A poem of fifty-two verses, beginning " Naċ áiṫ an obáṙi á ṫaióṡ," " Is not this strange work for Teige." In this poem the author treats M'Daire with no great degree of respect. He says he should not contend with M'Egan, an acknowledged antiquary and scholar.

2. A poem, beginning " bṙéaṡaċ ṙm a bean," " That is false, Oh woman," addressed to a female, advising her to avoid vanity and falsehood.

Copies in the collection of the Assistant Secretary.

ccxxxvii. John O'Clery, a northern poet, took a part in the contention of the bards. To him we are indebted for the following pieces :

1. A poem of two hundred and seventy-six verses, beginning " Eiṙóiṡ a éiṡṙi banba," " Attend, Oh ye learned of Ireland." In this poem the author calls on the poets of Leath Chuinn and Leath Mhogha to desist from their disputes, to put an end to their panegyrics on the descendants of Heber and Heremon, and to do justice to the progeny of their brother Ir, to whose magnanimity the bards were indebted for the protection given them in Ulster, when they were expelled from all the other provinces in Ireland, in the time of Conor Mac Nessa, who, he asserts, was the first Irish Christian. He gives a particular instance of the bounty of Conor on this occasion, in his endowment of the poet Athairne of Binn Eadair, with a large portion of land, and bestowing on him one hundred and fifty milch cows, with their profits and increase. He shows that to

the race of Ir our country was indebted for its great law-giver Ollamh-fodhla, (the learned doctor) and for a long train of heroes, poets, and philosophers that grace the pages of Irish history; such as Fergus, son of Roy, Cormac Conluingios, Conor Mac Nessa, Conall Cearnach, Cuchullan Cumusgrach, Loingseach, Iriall, Fionntan, Diothorba, Rossa, Conghall, Cathbhaith, Conlaoch, Naise, Ainle and Arden, &c. He says, if the stars of heaven, the white sands of the sea, the blades of grass of the field, and the leaves of the forest be numbered, they will be nearly equalled by the numbers of the estimable progeny of Ir. He shows that twenty-five of the most potent of the Irish monarchs were of this family, and that in possession of seven of those princes the sceptre of Ireland remained for a great number of years, without the intervention of a prince of any other line; and that of this tribe also was the only female that ever held the reins of government in this country, Macha Mong-ruadh, the foundress of Emania; in after ages commemorated by a town built nearly on the same scite, and called after her Ard Macha, or, as it is called at this time, Ardmagh.

In this piece there are preserved a vast quantity of Irish history, and beautiful flights of poetry.

2. A poem of twenty verses, beginning " Cia ɣo beaꞃꞃaɣ ᵹ bꞃeiɼne," " Who is this that lops the Breifne," in praise of the families of O'Rourke and O'Reilly.

Fine copies of these poems are in the possession of the Assistant Secretary.

ccxxxviii. Mac Dermod, of Moylurg, wrote a few verses on the subject in debate between the bards. These verses claim no attention.

ccxxxix. Mac Con O'Clery, a northern poet, flourished at this period. He was author of the following poems:

1. In praise of the O'Neills, beginning " Sealɓ Eiꞃioñ aiᵹ aicme Neill," " The possession of Erin belongs to Niall's race," two hundred and thirty-six verses. This poem was written in the time of Torlogh Luineach O'Neill, and gives an account of several illustrious characters of the O'Neills' progenitors, who swayed the sceptre of Ireland, or were provincial chiefs after the destruction of the monarchy. Accounts of

several battles fought and other great actions performed by these heroes are detailed in the course of this poem. By the last rann but two, the poet shows that there were thirty-five generations from Torlogh Luineach, son of Niall Conallach O'Neill, up to Niall of the Nine Hostages, their great ancestors, from whom the tribe are named.

A valuable and beautiful copy of this poem is in the library of John Mac Namara, of Sandymount, Esq.

2. A poem of thirty-six verses, beginning "A bean na luꞃᵹan lꞅ̣me," "Oh woman of the naked legs."

This small piece has nothing to recommend it.

Copies in the collection of the Assistant Secretary.

CCXL. O'CLERY, the chief of his tribe, who flourished at this period, wrote a poem, consisting of one hundred and twenty-eight verses, in praise of Saint Francis, founder of the religious order of Franciscans. The poem begins "Do ċaiṫꝼiñ cáꞃa cꞃꞅ̣ꞇe."

Copy in the collection of the Assistant Secretary.

CCXLI. GIOLLA-IOSA O'DALY flourished at this time. He was author of a poem, consisting of one hundred and forty-eight verses, in praise of Felim and Redmond, two sons of Fiach M'Hugh O'Byrne, chief of all the septs of O'Byrne, in the time of Queen Elizabeth.

In this poem, which begins "Ꝼꞃeaṁa an ċoᵹaiḋ cꞃioċ Laiᵹ̇ean," "The root of the war is Leinster," the writer introduces some historical notices of transactions in the province of Leinster, in which the O'Byrnes were principal actors. He also describes Glen Molaur, and the castle of Feagh, son of Hugh O'Byrne, who so terribly annoyed the English in the latter end of the sixteenth century.

Copy in possession of the Assistant Secretary.

CCXLII. At this time also lived MUIREADHACH O'DALY. He was author of a poem of three hundred and ninety-six verses, on the noble family of Fitzgerald, beginning "Cánꝼꞅ̣ᵹ̇eaꞃ liom loꞃᵹ na ꝼꝼeaꞃ," "The race of men shall be sung by me." In this poem the author gives a particular account of the chief families that sprung from Maurice Fitzgerald, who accompanied Strongbow in his expedition to Ireland, on the invitation of Dermod Mac Morough, king of Leinster, in the year 1168. Of the principal branches of this noble stock are the princely House of Leinster, the White Knight, the Knight of Glenn, the Knight of Kerry, the Fitz-Gibbons, &c. &c. &c. The minor branches of these respective houses are also mentioned, and the names of their ancestors, in whom each tribe branched off from the main stock, are given; with some account of the principal actions of their lives, the castles they built, and the religious houses they founded.

Copy in the collection of the Assistant Secretary.

ccxliii. Maurice O'Maolconaire flourished at this time. He was author of a poem, consisting of twenty-eight verses, in praise of Owen O'Halloran, a harper. It begins "Oppery óg ainm Eogain," "Orpheus, junior, is the name of Owen."

Copy with Assistant Secretary.

ccxliv. Cu-Ulaidh Mac-an-Bhaird (Ward), flourished at this period. He was a retainer of the family of O'Donell, chiefs of Tirconnell, and wrote an elegy on the death of Graine, the sister of Aodh roe O'Donell, and wife of Art og, son of Torlogh Luineach O'Neill, two hundred verses, beginning "Frigeall foimrò fril Dalaig," "Remnant of the envy of noble Daly's blood." This much admired young lady died of the measles at Beal-atha-Seanaigh (Ballyshannon) shortly after the celebration of her marriage.

Copy in the collections of the Rev. Doctor O'Brien, and of the Assistant Secretary.

ccxlv. Feargal og Mac an Bhaird lived at this time, and to him we are indebted for the following poems:

1. A poem in praise of the Magennis's, Lords of Ibh-Eathach (Iveagh). This poem consists of three hundred verses, beginning "Lubgoirt fineamna fril Ir," "A garden of vines, the race of Ir."

Copy in the collection of the Assistant Secretary.

2. On the people of Scotland renouncing the religion of their forefathers, and denying the Real Presence of our Lord Jesus Christ in the Eucharist.

This poem consists of one hundred and four verses, beginning " ᴅuꞃꞃᴀꞃ m'eᴀᴄóꞃᴀ ᵹo h'Ꙇllbꞃꞃꞃ," " Sorrowful my journey to Alban (Scotland.)

Copy in collection of the Assistant Secretary.

3. A poem of one hundred and four verses, beginning " beᴀꞃuᵹᴀᴅ ꞃᴀꞃ uᴀꞃm ᵹo h'Єꞃꞃꞃ," " West from me blessings to Ireland," written whilst the author was in Scotland. The beᴀꞃuᵹᴀᴅ, or Benediction, is several times repeated, and addressed to different parts and persons in Ireland, particularly to Magennis, Lord of Iveagh.

4. A poem of two hundred and forty-four verses, beginning " ꟼóꞃ ᴅo mꞃll ᴀoꞃbꞃeᴀꞃ Єꞃꞃeᴀꞃᴅ," " Much has the pleasure of Ireland destroyed;" shewing that the pleasures of Ireland had invited invaders from different regions of the earth, and that the Nemethians, the Tuatha-de-danans, &c. had fallen on her fields; and that the Milesians had established themselves. The writer asserts that ancient prophecies will be fulfilled, and that O'Neill will be the Moses that shall deliver the Irish Israelites from the bondage of Pharaoh and the Egyptian host that oppressed and destroyed them.

5. A poem of one hundred and fifty-two verses, beginning " Ꙇꞃ ꞃlꞃoᴄᴅ ᴄꞃꞃuꞃ ᴀᴄᴀꞃᴅ Ᵹᴀoꞃꞃl," " Of the race of three, the Gathelians are," on the tribe of O'Farrel, descended from Ir, son of Milesius, whose progeny the author asserts was superior to those of either of his brothers, Heremon and Heber.

6. On the descendants of Niall of the Nine Hostages, one hundred and ninety-two verses, beginning " ꟼᴀꞃᴄ ᴅo ꞃꞃᴅꞃoᵹᴀᴅ ꞃól Nꞃll," " Well situated are the offspring of Niall."

This poem was written in the time that Torlogh Luineach O'Neill was chief of that tribe. The author asserts that Corc of Cashel submitted to Niall, and that from that time all parts of Ireland paid obedience to his race.

7. On the death of Edmond, son of Maolmuire Mc. Suibhne, chief of the M'Sweeny's of West Munster, a respectable branch from the great stock of the M'Sweenys of Derry and Donegal. The poem consists of one hundred and forty-eight verses, beginning " Cꞃᴀ ᴀᴅeꞃ ᵹꞃꞃ ꞃmᴄꞃᵹ Єᴀmoꞃ," " Who says that Edmond is gone."

Copies of the five last-mentioned numbers are in the beautiful and valuable book of O'Gara, in the library of John M'Namara, of Sandymount, Esq.

8. A poem, beginning "Mąg um diaiġ ċeanglais cumann," "After me, woe to him who contracts friendship."

9. A poem on the accession of James I. to the Crowns of England, Ireland and Scotland, one hundred and twelve verses, beginning "Tri coróine a ccairt Semais," "Three Crowns in the Charter of James."

Copies of the two last-mentioned poems are in the collection of the Assistant Secretary.

10. On the death of Aodh, or Hugh, roe O'Donell, who died in Spain, on the 10th of September, 1602, two hundred and seventy-six verses, beginning "Teasda Eire san Easbáin," "Erin died in Spain."

Copy in the library of Rev. Doctor O'Brien.

CCXLVI. EOGHAN ROE MAC AN BHAIRD (Red Owen Ward), flourished at this time. He was author of the following poems:

1. An address to Aodh roe O'Donell, upon his voyage to Spain, after the defeat of the Irish at Kinsale, in the year 1602. This poem consists of one hundred verses, beginning "Rob soireiḋ t'eaċtra a Aoḋ ruaiḋ," "Prosperous was thy voyage, Oh red Hugh."

2. A poem of ninety-two verses, beginning "Dána an turas triallṫar soñ," "Bold the journey that has been undertaken here," on Roderick, son of Aodh, son of Manus O'Donell's going to Dublin, and entrusting himself in the hands of the English, after the death of his brother, red Hugh, chief of Tirconnel, who died in Spain.

3. An elegy on the death of Aodh roe, or red Hugh O'Donell, prince of Tirconnel, one hundred and fifty-six verses, beginning "A bean fuair faill air an ffeart," "Oh woman that found society in the grave." In this poem the author recites the noble actions of his hero, and shows that his death is cause of grief to Erin, "from sea to sea."

4. A poem of fifty-two verses, beginning "Cia re bfailte fir̄ñ Eirne," "Who does the host of Erne welcome," upon Aodh roe, or red Hugh O'Neill, Earl of Tyrone, to whom the Irish of the North looked up as a leader against the English, after the death of red Hugh O'Donell, in the year 1602. The author says, this chief was foretold by Saint Columb

Kill, and by Saint Adamnan, or Adamnanus; no wonder, therefore, that he should be welcomed by the Irish as the worthy successor of the heroic red Hugh O'Donell.

5. Eulogium on Rory, son of Rory, son of Maolmordha M'Sweeny, one hundred and ninety-two verses, beginning " ꝺoꝶ an ꝼile ꝝiol Sꝛꝗbꝫ," " The prop of the poet, the race of Suibhne."

Copies of these poems are in possession of the Assistant Secretary.

6. Address to Niall garbh, son of Conn, son of Calbhach O'Donell, confined by King James in the Tower of London, ninety-two verses, beginning " ᲀl bꝝaiᵹe aᴄa a ᴄᴄoꝶ lonꝺon," " Oh captive that art in London's Tower."

7. On the imprisonment of the O'Donell's, Neachtan and Aodh, by the English, ninety-two verses, beginning " Ოaiꝝᵹ! aꝝ bꝝaiᵹe aꝝ macꝝaiꝺ muꝝbaiꝺ, " Alas! captive are the sons of sorrow."

8. Elegy on the death of Rory O'Donell, first Earl of Tirconell, who died in Rome, on the 8th of July, 1608. This poem begins " Ოaᴄ an ꝝealaꝺ ꝼuᵹ Eiꝝe," " Erin found good for a time."

9. On Hugh, son of Rory O'Donell, second Earl of Tirconell, two hundred and eight verses, beginning " ꝼoᵹuꝝ ꝼuꝝᴄaᴄᴄ ꝺoꝶ ᴄiꝝ ᴄuaiꝺ," " Near is comfort to the north country."

Copies of the four last-mentioned poems are in the library of the Rev. Doctor O'Brien.

CCXLVII. At this time flourished DERMOD OG O'MAOLCONAIRE, of whose writings the following have come to our hands:

1. A poem of fifty-two verses, in praise of the Blessed Virgin Mary, beginning " Ცꝝꝗ ꝝaᴄa ꝝoᵹa ꝺeilbe."

2. A poem of eighty verses, on the same subject as the foregoing, beginning " iomꝺa ainm maiᴄ aiꝝ Ოꝝꝗꝝe," " Many glorious names belong to Mary."

3. A poem of fifty-two verses, on the Resurrection of our Lord Jesus Christ, and his apparition to the Blessed Virgin Mary.

Copies of these poems, in the hand-writing of the late Most Reverend Doctor John Carpenter, R. Catholic Archbishop of Dublin, are in the collection of the Assistant Secretary.

CCXLVIII. DONOGH O'FIALAN (O'Phelan) a poet of Leinster, was cotemporary with the foregoing authors. He wrote a farewell address to the O'Byrnes of Bally-na-corr, beginning " beanoċṫ aıg baıle na coṗṗa," " Farewell to Bally-na-corr."

Copy in possession of the Assistant Secretary.

CCXLIX. At this period also flourished S. MAC COLGAN, a follower of the house of O'Neill, who wrote a poem on the journey of Art, son of Torlogh O'Neill, to London, one hundred and twenty verses, beginning " Rob ropaıṡ an ġéaṡra roın," " Happy is this eastern road."

This poem is sometimes ascribed to Owen roe, son of William Mac-an-Bhaird.

Copy in possession of the Assistant Secretary, who procured it from his old and very sincere friend, the late Reverend Father Paul O'Brien, Irish Professor in the College of Saint Patrick, Maynooth, and one of the Acting Committee of this Society, whose justly lamented death was announced to the author whilst writing the above account, on Saturday, 20th May, 1820.

CCL. At this time also flourished MAHON O'HIFFERNAN, author of a small poem, consisting of only forty-eight verses, beginning " A mıc! na meaḃraṡ éıġrı," " Oh son! commemorate not the learned." In this poem the writer advises his son not to praise the sages of his country, nor the descendants of Milesius, the ancient possessors of the soil. He tells him, if he must praise any one, it would be most his advantage to praise the English.

Copy in collection of John M'Namara, Esq.

CCLI. BRIAN, son of ANGUS MAC COINMHIDHE, the chief Ollamh or Professor of O'Neill in Poetry, lived at this time. He is mentioned with great respect by Teige dall O'Higgin, in his poem, beginning " Taınıg oıṡce go heaṙ caoıle."

We are unable to say where any of this poet's compositions are now to be found.

CCLII. DERMOD O'BRIAN, author of a small poem on the river Shanon, flourished at this time. This little piece consists of twenty-eight verses, beginning " ᱿l Sʜɪᴏɴᴀᴍᴅ ᖯʀɪᴀɪɴ ᖯᴏʀᴏɪᴍᴇ," " Oh Shanon of Brian Boroimhe."

Copy in possession of Assistant Secretary.

CCLIII. Donald, son of Thomas O'Higgin, was living in the year 1600, as appears by the poems of Fergal Mac an Bhaird. He wrote a poem, consisting of one hundred and sixty-four verses, on the election of Torlogh Luineach O'Neill, as chief of his tribe, A. D. 1567. This poem begins " ᵭo ᴛoᵹ Ϲɪʀᴇ ʀᴇᴀʀ ʀᴀɪʀᴇ," " Erin has chosen a guardian."

Copy in O'Gara's collection in the library of John N'Namara, Esq.

———◆———

A. D. 1602.

CCLIV. Maoilin og Mac Bruody, or Brodin, who, according to the Four Masters, was " the best poet and historian that was in Ireland in his time," died this year. He was the son of Conor, son of Dermod, son of John M'Broden, and succeeded to the office of Chief Poet to the tribes of Ibh Breacain and Ibh Fearmaic (the O'Gormans and O'Gradys) upon the death of his brother Dermod in the year 1563. He was author of the following poems :

1. Upon the O'Gormans, two hundred and seventy-six verses, beginning " ᵭᴇoʀᴀᴅ ʀoᵑᴀ ʀʟɪoᴄᴛ Ϲᴀᴛᴀoɪʀ," " Strangers here are Cathaoir's race."

This poem was written upon the election of Donald O'Gorman, as chief of his tribe. It traces the pedigree of the O'Gormans up to Cathaoir the Great, Monarch of Ireland, A. D. 174, and shows that from the same noble stock have sprung the O'Phelans, or O'Whelans, O'Dunns, O'Dempsys, Clan Colgans, &c. &c. From Cathaoir the pedigree is traced up to Hugony the Great; and it is mentioned, that from Conn of the hundred battles, the twentieth in descent from Hugony, are sprung the clann Colla; the clan Colman, kings of Meath; the O'Neills; the O'Conors of Conaught; the O'Rourkes; the O'Reillys; the O'Mealys,

&c. &c. &c. From Hugony the pedigree is carried up to Heremon, son of Milesius, who landed first in Ireland, A. M. 2935.

2. A poem of four hundred and four verses, beginning "Cᵣɲꝼιoꝺ crmaɱ ap claɲ ᴄaιl," "I will lay an obligation on the clann of Tail."

In this poem the pedigree of the O'Briens, from Conor, brother of Morogh first earl of Thomond, is traced up to Heber, the son of Milesius, and various other branches of the principal stock are noticed; amongst which the author counts the Plunketts, Powers, and Eustaces. He shows that forty-six of the ancestors of the O'Brien family were monarchs of Ireland since the introduction of Christianity.

3. A poem of two hundred and seventy-six verses, beginning "Cuᵹ ꝺaɱ ᴄ'aιꝑe Iɲꝛe na Laoιꝺ," "Give attention to me, Ennis of the poems."

This poem gives the number of years that elapsed, and the names of the princes of the House of O'Brien, that governed Thomond, from Cairbre O'Brien to the year 1588, when Donogh, fourth Earl of Thomond, was head of the O'Brien race, and at which period the poem was written. It also gives the names of nine princes of this family, who were kings of Cashel after the death of Brian Boroimhe, their illustrious ancestor.

Copies of the above three poems are in the collection of the Assistant Secretary.

4. A poem, beginning "Ƶaꝺꝛaɱ aɲ craιꝑᴄꝛι aιꝑ cloɱ Caιl," "Let us make this visit to the clann of Tail." Another poem on the O'Briens, M'Namaras, &c.

5. A poem, beginning "ᴀlιᴄιɲ mιꝛe a Ɱheᵹ Coċlaιɲ," "Know me, Oh Mac Coghlan," on the family of the Mac Coghlans, princes of Dealbhna Eathra, a district of the ancient kingdom of Meath, now the barony of Garrycastle, in the King's County.

6. A poem, beginning "O ceaċꝛaꝑ ᵹluaιꝛιoꝺ Ƶaoιꝺιl," "From four proceed the Gathelians."

These three last-mentioned poems are said, by the Four Masters, to be the productions of Maoilin og, but we know not where copies are now to be found.

The two following poems are ascribed to Maoilin, but the Four Masters, who were his cotemporaries, and who gave an account of the above six poems, not having mentioned these, we may conclude he was not the author of them.

7. A poem of one hundred and forty-four verses, beginning "*Lám veart Eirion ηb eačač*," "Bloody hand of Ireland, the race of Eochaidh," on Art, son of Aodh Magennis, whose birth, the poet says, was foretold by St. Bearcan.

8. A poem of one hundred and seventy-six verses, beginning "*Cóir jrl le feaṙam Ʒaoʋil*," "It is right to expect the establishment of the Irish," on John O'Donell.

Copies in possession of John Mac Namara, Esq.

CCLV. At this time also flourished BRIAN, son of OWEN *mhaoil (bald)*, O'DONALLAN. He is mentioned by Tadhg dall O'Higgin in his poem on the death of Maolmordha M'Sweeny, as his cotemporary and friend. He was author of the two poems following:

1. An address to Rickard og de Burk, upon his being elected Mac William, two hundred and twenty-four verses, beginning "*Caire ριοτ a Riocaiṙʋ óiʒ*," "Watchfulness be thine, Oh young Rickard."

2. A poem addressed to Celia, the widow of Mac William, desiring her to cease from lamentation after the death of her husband, one hundred and eighty verses, beginning "*Léiʒ čoρτ ʋo čɲᵖɣi a Shile*," "Throw by your grief, Oh Celia."

Copies of these poems are in the library of John M'Namara, Esq.

CCLVI. At this time flourished OWEN, son of DONOGH O'DALY, author of a poem of one hundred and eighty verses, beginning "*Do čɲτ a cloč crl ʋ'Eiριᵐ*," "The protecting rock of Erin has fallen," on Dermod O'Sullivan's going to Spain after the defeat of the Irish and Spaniards at Kinsale.

Copies in the collection of John M'Namara, Esq. and the Assistant Secretary.

CCLVII. TEIGE, son of DERMOD OG O'DALY, also lived at this time; he was author of an elegy on the death of Owen O'Sullivan. This poem consists of one hundred and forty-four verses, beginning "*Uaiʒneač a ʋeiɲτeaρ Dúnbaoi*," "It is said that Dunboy is solitary."

Copies in the collections of John M'Namara, Esq. and the Assistant Secretary.

CCLVIII. ANGUS MAC MARCUS was cotemporary with the four last-mentioned writers; he was author of a poem on Aodh, or Hugh roe O'Donell's voyage to Spain after his defeat at Kinsale, forty-eight verses, beginning " Ⱥnocꞇ aꞃ ꞃaiȝneaċ Eiꞃe," " To-night is Erin desolate."
Copy in collection of Assistant Secretary.

CCLIX. At the same time with the foregoing, lived JOHN OGE O'DALY, author of a poem in praise of Dermod M'Carthy, prince of Desmond, seventy-six verses, beginning " Ⱥnoiꞃ ꝺo cꞃioċnꞇȝeꝺ ceaꞃċuill na cꞃoꝺaċ," " Now is the circle of valour finished."
Copy in the library of John M'Namara, Esq.

———

A. D. 1605.

CCLX. CONOR ROE MAC AN BHAIRD (Ward), a northern poet, flourished at this time. He has left us a poem of two hundred verses, on the death of Aodh O'Donell, beginning " Cionaꞃ ꞇicc Eiꞃe ȝan Ⱥoꝺ," " How comes Erin without Aodh."
Copy in the MS. collection of the Assistant Secretary.

———

A. D. 1607.

CCLXI. In this year AODH O'DONELL wrote a poem of four hundred and thirty-six verses, in defence of Leath Chuinn against the attacks of Teige M'Daire. He enumerates a great catalogue of heroes descended from the loins of Heremon, and defies his opponent to produce a list of Heberians equally respectable. The poem begins " Ɱeaꞃa ꝺo ꞇaȝꞃaiꞃ a

Cḣaıoᵹ," " Worse hast thou argued, oh Teige." In the last rann but two of this poem, it is said " In the year of Christ one thousand six hundred and seven, the race of Conn were driven beyond sea, and their country taken from them." It was, therefore, some time in this year that the poem was written.

In some copies of the *Iomarbadh*, this poem, and Teige M'Daire's poem, beginning " Nı ḃpeıⱦ opam oo ḃpeıⱦ a 2loᵹ," are blended together, by way of dialogue, so as to make the two poems appear but as one piece written by the same author.

CCLXII. At this time flourished ART OG O'KEEFFE, who took a part in the contention of the bards, on the side of Leath Mhogha. He was author of the poem beginning " 2l ḟıp ⱦaᵹpaıſ an ċaınⱦ ḃaoⱦ," " Oh man, that urgest silly talk," sixty-eight verses, against M'Dermott and Aodh O'Donell, who had written on the side of Leath Chuinn.

Copy in the collection of the Assistant Secretary.

CCLXIII. At this time also lived TORLOGH O'BRIEN, of Cahirmannan, who wrote an answer to Aodh O'Donell, on his poem above mentioned. O'Brien's poem consists of thirty-two verses, beginning " 2l 2loᵹ óıᵹ na neaċ lraıⱦ," " Oh young Hugh, of swift steeds."

Copy in collection of the Assistant Secretary.

A. D. 1608.

CCLXIV. At this time flourished GIOLLA BRIGHID, alias BONAVENTURE, O'HEOGHUSA, a Franciscan friar of the College of Saint Anthony of Padua, in Louvain. He was author of the following pieces:

1. A Catechism, in prose, first printed at Louvain, A. D. 1608, and reprinted at Antwerp, in A. D. 1611.

2. A Catechism, or Abridgment of Christian Doctrine, in two hundred and forty verses, beginning " 2lⱦáıo ⱦpı ɒoıpᵹe aıp ⱦeaċ nɒē,"

" There are three doors to the House of God." This abridgment was reprinted at the end of Donlevy's Irish Catechism, in Paris, A. D. 1642.

3. A poem of thirty-two verses, prefixed to the Catechism, and address to the reader. It begins " ᴀ ꝼⁱꞃ leaᵹꞇa aꞃ leaꞃꞃaⁱꞃ ꝥⁱᵹ," " Oh man, read of the little book."

4. A poem of three hundred and fifty-six verses, beginning, " Cꞃuaᶁ lⁱoꝼ a ꞔoꝼꝥaⁱꞃ ᶁo ꞔoꞃ," " Sorrowful to me thy condition, oh my companion," addressed to a friend upon deserting the religion of his ancestors.

5. A poem on the vanity of the world, sixty-eight verses, beginning " Cꞃꞃaᵹ coꞃ ꞔloꝼe ᴀᶁaⁱꝼ," " Miserable the state of the sons of Adam." This is a translation from a Latin work of Saint Bernard's.

6. A poem of eighty-four verses, beginning " Ꝝaꝥ aⁱꞇꞃeaꞔaꞃ ꞃaⁱꝼ," " Accept my repentance." In this poem the author confesses his offences against his God, declares his penitence, and begs forgiveness. Written upon occasion of his renouncing the world, and entering on a life of poverty and mortification, in the order of Saint Francis.

7. A consolatory poem, addressed to Jane, wife of Richard Nugent, on the death of her husband, sixty-four verses, beginning " ᵭeaᴄaⁱꞃ ꞃuaꞃ aⁱꞃ ꞔꞃeaᶁ ccaꞃaᶁ," " It is hard to rest over the wounds of friends."

8. Reflections on the author's leaving Ireland, and on the death of his dear friend Aodh, or Hugh Maguire, sixty-eight verses, beginning " Cꞃꞃaᵹ aꞃ ꞇaꝼaꞃcꞃa a Єⁱꞃe," " Sorrowful is this vision, oh Erin."

9. A vision, in which he praises Roalb M'Mahon, one hundred and eighty-four verses, beginning " loꞃᵹꞃaᶁ ꝼ'aꞃlaⁱꞃᵹ a ꞃЄaꝼaⁱꞃ," " Wonderful my vision in Emania."

10. In praise of Felim, son of Feagh M'Hugh O'Byrne, and the province of Leinster, one hundred and eighty-four verses, beginning " Ceallaꞔ eⁱꝼᵹ ꞃaꞔ laⁱᵹeaꞃ," " A land of generosity is the province of Leinster."

Copies of all these poems are in the collection of the Assistant Secretary; some copies are in the library of John Mac Namara, Esq. and some others in the libraries of other members of this Society.

A. D. 1609.

CCLXV. Doctor NEHEMIAH DONELLAN, Archbishop of Tuam, died this year. He is said to have translated into Irish the New Testament and Communion Book, and to have printed them in A. D. 1603. Of this some doubts may be entertained ; but the work was printed in his time, and the expense levied on the people of Conaght.

See William Daniel, or O'Donell, under the year 1628.

A. D. 1610.

CCLXVI. At this time flourished TEIGE DALL O'HIGGIN, son of Cairbre, and brother to Maolmuire, Archbishop of Tuam. He was a poet of the county of Sligo, famous for the elegance of his encomiums, and the keenness of his satire ; and it is remarkable, that the first and the last of his productions are the most biting of his invectives. To the last of his poems is attributed the cause of his death. It is a satire on six persons of the tribe of O'Hara, who forcibly took some refreshments in his house, and so severely were the lashes of the poet felt by the delinquents, that they some time afterwards returned to his house, seized him, cut out his tongue, and otherwise abused him; of which barbarous treatment it is said he died.

On the 30th of June, 1617, an inquisition was held in Sligo, before Thomas Browne and another, by which it was found that " William, son of Corcashell O'Hara, and Owen O'Hara of Castlecarragh, Brian O'Hara, Art O'Hara, and Donald O'Hara, were attainted of the murdering Teige dall O'Higgin, his wife and child." The time in which this murder was perpetrated is not mentioned in the inquisition; but it was found that the murderers were possessed of some lands, which were consequently forfeited to the king.

To this writer we are indebted for the following poems :

1. An epigram on some pretender to learning, amongst his cotemporaries, whose name is, perhaps, justly forgotten. It begins " ꝼeaꞃ ꝺána

ᴀɴ ꜰєᴀꞃ ꝰᴏ ꞃᴉᴀꞃ," " A man of song, this western man," or, as the two
first words may be translated, " a man of impudence," which would, perhaps, be an appropriate epithet for a pretender to science.

This epigram has been published in Irish and English, in the Transactions of the Gaelic Society, and applied to Doctor Ledwich, by the late
Theophilus O'Flanagan, an accomplished scholar of Trinity College,
and a complete master of the ancient language and history of his country,
who, to the disgrace of his compatriots, lived neglected, and died in
poverty.

2. A genealogical poem on the O'Haras, princes of Luigne and Gai-
leng, two districts of the ancient kingdom of Conaght, now called the
baronies of Leney and Gallen, the first comprehended in the county of
Sligo, and the latter in the county of Mayo. In this poem, which consists of three hundred and twenty verses, beginning " Ꝺⁿ áⁱl lⁱƀ ꞃєᴀⁿċᴀꞃ
ꞃⁱl Ccєⁱn," " Is the history of the race of Cian pleasing to you ?" the
author traces the pedigree of Cormac O'Hara, chief of his tribe in the
reign of Queen Elizabeth, up to Cian, son of Olioll Olum, king of
Munster, who died A. D. 234, according to O'Flaherty.

A copy of this poem, in the hand-writing of John M'Solly, is in the
collection of the Assistant Secretary.

3. A poem of one hundred and eighty verses, on Drum Laigheann, an
old name of the hill of Cruachan, or Drum Druid, near Elphin, county
Roscommon. The name of this hill is sometimes improperly translated
Mount Leinster.

This poem begins " Ϻᴀⁱʒєᴀⁿ ꝺⁱᴏʒlᴀ ꝺꞃᴜⁱm lᴀⁱʒєᴀⁿⁿ," " A field of destruction is the ridge of Laighean," and gives an account of various battles fought there, and of the conjurations of the Tuatha-de-Dadans, in
their conflicts with the Milesians.

4. A poem on Torlogh Luineach O'Neill, two hundred verses, beginning " lᴏmƀᴀ ꝰᴏċᴀⁱꞃ ᴀⁱʒ ꞃⁱᴏl Ɲєⁱll," " Many are the privileges of
Niall's race." In this poem the author compares Torlogh to Noah, and
says, that as God had appointed Noah to preserve the race of man from
destruction in the general deluge, so he sent Turlogh, as a second Noah,
to preserve the Irish after the massacres and cruelties committed on them
by the English.

5. An address to Hugh, son of Manus O'Donell, on his going to Connaght, two hundred and twenty-four verses, beginning " Oɪɑ ꝺo beɑꞇɑ ɑ ṁeɪc Ɱhɑᵹnɑɪɾ," " Hail! son of Manus."

6. In praise of the Castle of Lifford, and of the son of O'Donell, and his wife, the daughter of John O'Neill, forty-four verses, beginning " ɪoɲṁuṁ bɑ-ɪle bɾuᵹh Leɪꞇbɪɾ," " Beloved seat, fair Lifford's Castle."

Copies of these two poems are in the library of Rev. Doctor O'Brien, and in the collection of the Assistant Secretary.

7. A poem of one hundred and sixty-four verses, beginning " Ɱɑᵹ ꝼeɑꞇɾɾ ꝺ ṁɪɾ ceɪꞇlɪnꝺ," " Alas! I looked on Enniskillen," " on the castle of Enniskillen, and the hospitality of Cuchonacht Maguire."

Copy in collection of the Assistant Secretary.

8. A poem of one hundred and ninety-six verses, beginning " Ⱥ Ɱóɪɾ cɾṁnɪᵹ ɑ̃n comɑ̃n," " Oh Mor, remember the obligation!" addressed to a woman, who, it appeared, had deserted him for a person of the name of O'Connor.

9. A poem of one hundred and fifty-two verses, beginning " Ꝺeɑnɑm cuɲꞇuɾ, ɑ Chɑꞇɑɪl," " Let us render an account, oh Cathal," addressed to Cathal O'Conor Sligo, son of Teige. In this poem the author boasts that he was the bed-fellow of his hero, and received from him an ample share of the spoils which he had carried away from the Mac Williams, (Burkes) M'Costelloes, (Nangles) Conallians, (O'Donells, O'Doghertys, M'Sweenys, &c.) and from the O'Neills.

A fine copy of this poem is in the library of John Mac Namara of Sandymount, Esq. and another in the collection of the Assistant Secretary.

10. A poem in dispraise of bad butter, twenty-four verses, beginning " ꝼuɑɾɑɾ ꝼeɪn ɪm mɑɪꞇ ó ṁnɑoɪ," " I got good butter from a woman."

Copy in the collection of the Assistant Secretary.

11. An epigram on the clan Mac an Bhaird, or tribe of Ward.

Copy with the Assistant Secretary.

12. A poem, consisting of one hundred and thirty-two verses, beginning " Ꝺɑoɪne ɾɑoɾɑ ɾɪol Ccollɑ," " The race of Colla are a free people," in praise of Cuchonacht (Constantine) Maguire, chief of Fermanagh, and eldest lineal descendant of Colla da Chrioch, son of Eochaidh Doimhlen, and grandson of Cairbre Liffeachar, monarch of Ireland, who

lost his life in the battle of Gabhra, near Tara, A. D. 294. Colla-da-chrioch, together with his two brothers, Colla Uais and Colla Meann, conquered settlements for themselves in Ulster, from the Rudricians, and destroyed Emania in the year of our Lord 347; since which period the descendants of the Collas have enjoyed large estates and great power in the province of Ulster, until the entire province was declared the property of King James the First, in the early part of his reign.

13. A poem exciting the native Irish to take up arms, and expel their English enemies, two hundred and eighty verses, beginning "Ó'ḟioṛ coġaíó coṁailteaṛ ṛíoṫċaın," " To a man of war, peace is preserved."

In this poem the author points out Brian, son of Brian, son of Owen O'Rourke, as the proper leader of the Irish against their oppressors, as his power was then acknowledged by the Ulster and Conaght tribes.

14. A poem in praise of the Mac Sweenys, two hundred verses, beginning " ıaó ḟéın éṁaıṛ aıṛ cloıṁ Néıll," " The race of Niall exceed themselves."

15. A poem beginning " Tainıġ oıóce ġo ḥeaṛ caoıle," " Night came to Narrow-water," one hundred and sixty-eight verses, on the death of Maolmordha Mac Sweeny, and two others of the author's friends and cotemporaries.

In this poem the author mentions Brian O'Conallan, Brian M'Coinmhidhe, and Conor O'Higgin, poets, and cotemporaries with the author, who were patronized by Maolmordha Mac Sweeny.

16. A poem beginning " ḟeaṛonó cloıṁe cṛíoċ banba," " The country of Ireland is sword land," two hundred and forty verses, in praise of the family of Burke, many of whom he names as conquerors in various battles in Ireland, England, and the Holy Land.

17. A poem of one hundred and fifty-two verses, beginning " Noólaıc óo éráóṁaṛ óo'n Chṛaoḃ," " Christmas we went to the Creeve," on a Christmas assembly of the poets at the Creeve, one of the hospitable mansions of Torlogh Luineach O'Neill.

18. A poem in praise of Richard, son of Oliver Burke M'William, two hundred and forty verses, beginning " Móṛ ıonġabaıl anma ṛíoġ," " Great prudence of the soul of a prince."

19. A poem of forty-eight verses, beginning " Sluaġ ṛeıṛṛ taınıġ óom tıġ," " A band of six came to my house."

This poem is a bitter satire on six persons of the tribe of O'Hara, who went to the author's house and took some refreshments against his inclination. The virulence of this satire was so keenly felt by the O'Haras, that they cut out his tongue, which probably caused his death, as we have seen before that five of the family were found attainted of the murder of Teige O'Higgin, his wife and child.

Copies of the thirteen last-mentioned poems are preserved in the valuable book of O'Gara, in the library of John M'Namara, of Sandymount, Esq.

CCLXVII. At this time also lived MAOLMUIRE, son of Cairbre O'HIGGIN, brother to the last-mentioned author. He was Archbishop of Tuam; and we are told by the Reverend Fergal O'Gara, in his collection of poems made in the Netherlands in the year 1656, and now in the library of John M'Namara, Esq. that this prelate died in Antwerp, on his return from Rome, but he does not mention in what year. To this author we are indebted for the following pieces :

1. A hymn in praise of our Lord Jesus Christ, consisting of one hundred and sixty-four verses, beginning " Do ᵹniō ɑoꞥ mɑc ionɑꞃ cloiꞥe," " One son supplied the place of many children."

2. A poem in praise of Ireland, written when the author was on the Continent, one hundred and thirty-six verses, beginning " 2ɭ ꝼiꞃ ċeiō ᵹo ꝼioō ꝼꞃꞥiō," " Oh man, who goest to the land of the West."

3. A poem of thirty-six verses, beginning " 2ɭ ċeɑċċɑiꞃe ċeiō ɑnoꞥ," " O messenger, who goest to the other side." This poem contains a beautiful description of a woman.

4. A poem of twelve verses, on Consideration, beginning " 2ɭ ꝼiꞃ ċꞃeɑbɑꞃ iꞃ ċꞃlɑċ," " Oh man, who cultivatest the hill."

Copies of all these poems are in the collection of the Assistant Secretary.

CCLXVIII. Cotemporary with the two last-mentioned writers, was CONN, son of JOHN O'NEILL, author of a chronological poem on his own tribe, from the death of Heremon to the departure of Hugh O'Neill from Conaght, in the year 1610. This poem commences with " Cɑ líoꞥ ꞃuᵹ iꞃ ōɑṁnɑ ċeɑꞥ," " How many kings and mighty chiefs."

Copy in possession of the Assistant Secretary.

A. D. 1612.

CCLXIX. FLANN M'COINMHIDHE lived at this time. He was author of a poem in praise of the Blessed Virgin, fifty-two verses, beginniug " breáġtaṛ beaṅ le ṛéaḋ ṛṅṛġe," " A woman is allured by gifts of kind-ness."

Copy in possession of Assistant Secretary.

CCLXX. At the same period as the foregoing, lived MAURICE, son of DAVID *duff* FITZGERALD. He was author of the following poems:

1. Forty-four verses, on receiving a present of a horse from Teige O'Brien, of Dumhach, beginning " fṛaṛaṛ eaċ naċ ḋṛaiḃṛeaċ ḋoiṅb," " I received a horse, not wicked nor peevish."

2. Forty-four verses on his ship preparing for a voyage to Spain. This poem begins " beaṅaiġ an loṅṛṛa a Chṛíoṛḋ caiḋ," " Bless this ship, Oh holy Christ."

3. Forty-four verses on his receiving a present of a sword from O'Logh-lin of Burren, beginning " ḋo bṛoṅaḋ ḋam cáṛa cṛlġ" " A sword was given by my friend."

4. Twelve verses on a French cat, beginning " Maṛcaṅ ġeaṛṛ, ġṛuama, ġeaṛáṅac," " Sour, sullen, complaining animal."

5. Forty-eight verses, enumerating things that were pleasing and dis-pleasing to him, beginning " Ríc liom ṛṛéaḋ ṛġiaṁaċ ṛġacáṅaċ," " I like a beautiful stately horse."

6. Advice to a young woman, beginning " Ġaḃ mo ceaġaṛġ a beaṅ óiġ," " Receive my instructions, oh young woman."

7. Advice to a young man, ninety-two verses, beginning " Caiṛe ḋuic a óġaiṅ fíṅ," " Be cautious, oh fair-haired youth."

Copies of all the above poems are in the collection of the Assistant Secretary. The poem, No. 2, has been translated and published by Miss Brooke, in her " Reliques of Irish Poetry."

A. D. 1617.

CCLXXI. On the 16th of December in this year, died ANGUS, or ÆNEAS *roe* O'DALY, as appears by an inquisition taken at the Old Castle in Cork, on the 18th September, 1624. By this inquisition it was found that "Angus O'Daly was seized, in his life time, of the towns and lands of Ballyorroone, containing three carrucates of land, value ten shillings per annum; and being so seized, did, on the last day of March, 1611, enfeoff Thadeus M'Carthy, Richard Waters, John O'Daly, and Farfasa O'Canty (Fearfeasa O'Cainte), and their heirs for ever, to the use of said Angus O'Daly, during his natural life, and after his death to the use and benefit of Angus O'Daly, junior, his son and heir, and the heirs male of his body lawfully begotten; and that the said feoffees, Thadeus, Richard, John and Farfasa, the foresaid premises, without the king's license being first obtained, together with Angus O'Daly, senior, did, by their deed, dated 10 April, 1617, enfeoff Carolus O'Daly, his heirs and assigns, in the western part of the land of Balliorroone aforesaid, with the appurtenances, containing one carrucate of land, under this condition, that, when the said Angus O'Daly, senior, his heirs or assigns, should pay said Carolus O'Daly, his heirs or assigns, the sum of thirteen pounds, then the said Angus O'Daly, senior, his heirs or assigns, should be at liberty to re-enter and possess said land and premises, as before the making of said deed. And that afterwards the said Angus O'Daly died on the 16th December, 1617," &c.

This poet is best known to the Irish scholar by the names of Angus na naor (Angus of the Satires), and Bard ruadh, or red Bard. He was author of the following pieces:

1. A long poem, in which he gives a satiric description of the chiefs of the principal native Irish families, and such of the descendants of the Anglo-Normans as had formed close connexions with the Irish. From this general abuse of the Irish tribes he exempts the Clann Daly, or O'Donells, because, as he says, he was afraid of their vengeance:

" Ɖa naoᵱuiñ clañ nƊálaıᵹ,
  Nıoᵱ ɓıón ɓaṁ ᵱıol ᵱeanáɓaıṁ;
  Clañ nƊalaıᵹ bᵲó ɓıon ɓaṁ,
  Aᵹuᵱ ᵱıol Aɓaıṁ o'Aoᵱaɓ."

" If I lampoon the Clann Daly, no shield to me is the race of old Adam : Let the Clann Daly protect me, I may satirize all mankind."

This poem was written in the reign of Queen Elizabeth, and it is said that Angus was specially employed for this purpose by the agents of the Earl of Essex and Sir George Carew.

Copies are in the hands of every Irish scholar.

2. A poem on the death of Donogh fionn M'Carthy, one hundred and sixty-eight verses, beginning " Ʈᴀɪɴɪc ᴌēɴ ᴅo ᴌeᴀᴄ Ꝏho̓ᴀ," " Misfortune has come over Leath Mhogha."

Copy in the collection of the Assistant Secretary.

CCLXXII. FERFEASA O'CAINTE flourished at this time, as we have seen by the Inquisition quoted in the preceding article. He was a Munster poet, and took a part in the contention of the bards, on the side of Teige Mac Daire and the Momonians, against Lughaidh O'Clery and the Northerns. He was author of the following poems:

1. One hundred and twenty verses against Lughaidh, beginning " Ɲᴀ coɪʒɪᴌ ᴌᴀ᙮ᴘᴀ, ᴀ ᴌuʒᴀɪᴃ," " Spare not speech, oh Lughaidh."

In this poem the author accuses Lughaidh of partiality, in his defence of the chiefs of Leath Chuinn, to the prejudice of those of Leath Mhogha. He insists that the descendants of Eogan mor and Cormac Cas are superior to the progeny of Conn of the Hundred Battles. He tells Lughaidh it is sinful to oppose this known truth, desires him to read over his books, and acknowledge his errors.

2. On worthless people, striving to make themselves respected by boasting and lies, forty-two verses, beginning " Ꝏoᴘ ᴅo ʒɴᴃ ᴅᴀoɪɴe ᴃɪᴃ᙮ ᴘēɪɴ," " Men make themselves great."

Copies of these two poems are in the collection of the Assistant Secretary.

3. On the death of Donald O'Keeffe, chief of the district of Ealla, and on that of his poet, Angus O'Daly, commonly called the Red Bard, or Angus the satirist, one hundred and eighty verses, beginning " ᴃeᴀɴ ᴅᴀ́ ᴄuꝏᴀ cᴘɪᴄ Eᴀᴌᴌᴀ," " A woman of two sorrows is Ealla's land."

4. A poem addressed to Ireland, to whom he promises a steady friend in young Teige Mac Carthy, presumptive chief of Desmond, or south Munster. This poem consists of one hundred and eighty-four verses, in

which he gives some good instructions to young Mac Carthy for his general conduct. It begins "Fuirliḋ go fóill, a Eire," "Wait awhile, oh Erin."

Copies of the two last-mentioned poems are in the library of John Mac Namara, Esq.

A. D. 1618.

CCLXXIII. At this time flourished TEIGE, son of Dermod O'DALY, author of an elegy on the death of Dermod O'Sullivan, who died this year, at the early age of twenty-five years, one hundred and forty-eight verses, beginning "Cia so caoineas críoċ Banba," "Who is this that Ireland laments?"

Copy with the Assistant Secretary.

Perhaps this writer may be the same mentioned under the year 1602, by the name of Teige, son of Dermod og O'Daly.

A. D. 1620.

CCLXXIV. In this year lived OWEN M'CRAITH, a Munster poet, author of sixty-eight verses, on the death of Donogh O'Brien, Earl of Thomond, who died this year, as appears by the twelfth rann of this poem. It begins "Tugaḋ an tár só air Eirinn," "This destruction came on Ireland."

Copy in the collection of the Assistant Secretary.

CCLXXV. At this time also flourished CUCOIGCRICHE, grandson of CONN O'CLERY. He was poet to the O'Donells, chieftains of Tir-Conell, and author of the following poems:

1. On Rory O'Donell being created first Earl of Tirconnel, nineteen *ranns*, each consisting of eight verses, beginning "Rug cobair air Conallċaiḃ,

ⱅⱃᵹ oᵯαn αⱳ eαⱃccáⱳⱂⱄⰱ," " Power has come to the Conallians, terror has seized on their enemies."

2. On the long and peaceful life of Torlogh, son of Cathbharr O'Donell, who, at the time this poem was written, had attained his seventieth year, one hundred and sixty-eight verses, beginning " ᵯo ᵯαllαⱍⱅ oⱳⱅ, α ⱳαoᵹαⱂl!" " My curse on thee, oh world!"

Copies of these poems are in possession of the Assistant Secretary, in an ancient paper manuscript, lent to him by his late dearly beloved and much lamented friend the Rev. Dr. Paul O'Brien, Professor of the Irish language in the College of St. Patrick, Maynooth.

cclxxiv. At this time also lived Donogh Cauch (blind) O'Mahony, a Munster poet, who wrote many songs, some of which are in the collection of the Assistant Secretary.

———

A. D. 1626.

cclxxv. On the 26th of September in this year, died Hugh Mac Cawell, a Franciscan friar, who had been Divinity Lecturer in the College of Saint Anthony of Padua, in Louvain, and afterwards R. C. Archbishop of Armagh. He was known in his order by the name of Aodh Mac Aingil, and under that name published his " Scαⱅαn ⱳαcⱳαᵯᴇⱳⱅe ᵯα ⱨⱘⰻⱅⱳⰻⱄe," or " Mirror of the Sacrament of Penance," printed at Louvain, in 1618, although Harris, in his additions to Ware, erroneously says it was printed after his death.

———

A. D. 1628.

cclxxvi. On the 11th of July this year, died Doctor William O'Donell, one of the first fellows of Trinity College, and treasurer of the Cathedral of Saint Patrick, Dublin, in which church he was conse-crated Archbishop of Tuam, in the year 1609. He is said to have been the translator of the Book of Common Prayer and the New Testament into the Irish language; but Mr. Beling, and others, say the latter was translated by Mortogh O'Cionga, or King. This was printed in the year 1603, in quarto, the charges of which were levied on the people of Co-naght. It was re-printed in 1687, at the expense of Robert Boyle, and in the year 1690 the entire Bible was printed in London, in quarto size, and in the Irish character; and at the same time, and by the same press, it was printed in eighteens, in the Roman letter, for the use of the *Gaoidhil*, or Gaels of Scotland. This was the only Gaelic translation the people of that nation had of the Sacred Scriptures, until about the year 1767, when a new translation of the New Testament was published in Edin-burgh. In the year 1787 a new translation of the Old Testament was published, in the same city. In these new translations the ancient and correct orthography of the Gaelic or Irish language was much debased. But in the last new translation printed for the Bible Society in London, in 1804, much greater changes have been made, which go far towards disguising the radices of the language, and to cut off the connection that until lately existed between the sister dialects of Eire and Alba.

In the year 1818 a new edition of the New Testament was published in London, by the British and Foreign Bible Society, on beautiful Irish types; but either through the ignorance or the negligence of the editor, or perhaps through both, the errors of this edition are innumerable. In the first three chapters of the Gospel of Saint Mathew, there are no less than sixty typographical errors, some of which materially affect the sense of the Evangelist. Of this a remarkable instance occurs in the 3d chapter and 12th verse of this Gospel, where our Blessed Saviour is represented as a female; thus, " ᴁᵹᴀ ʙᵹᴛl ᴀ ᴄᵹᴀᴈᴀᵹ ᴀᵑ ᴀlᴀᴍ," " Whose fan is in HER hand." Other errors, equally bad, or worse, frequently occur throughout the book; such as ꜰᴇᴀᵹ, grass, instead of ꜰᴇᴀᵹ, a man, &c. &c. which render this work totally unfit for the purpose intended by the publishers.

In London also, in the course of the last year, were published, in Irish, the books of Genesis and Exodus. The Irish Bibles printed in London in 1690, abound with errors, grammatical and typographical, all which, so far as these two books go, are suffered to remain in the text by the present editor; and he has added to the stock no small quantity of his own, and introduced words that never before appeared in any Irish book.

In Irish the preposition a, *in*, causes *eclipsis*, or suppression in the initials of all substantives immediately following it, except such as begin with the letter m or the *immutable* consonants l, n, or r. To nouns beginning with vowels it causes n to be prefixed; thus, a naizéin, in the deep; a néaóótċaiʒ, in despair; a niḟnioṅ, in hell; a noióce, in the night; a nuaizneaʒ, in solitude, &c. The present editor of the Sacred Scriptures knowing that n is always joined with such substantives in pronunciation, when preceded by the preposition, and seeing that it is so written in books, but not knowing the cause of such union, imagined that when the article an preceded a substantive beginning with a vowel, the n should be de-detached from the a and united with the substantive; and under this impression, whenever the article an, or the preposition and article óon, or óo an, occurs, in such a situation he invariably deprives the article of its n, and prefixes it to the substantive, and thereby renders such passages downright nonsense.

Of the kind of error here noticed, the first chapter of Genesis furnishes sufficient examples. Thus, in the sixth and seventh verses, Aʒuf aóubaint Óia, bioó *iormoilt* a meaóón na nuirʒeaó, &c.——Aʒuf óo niñe Óia a niornmoilt, aʒuf noiṅ na huirʒeaóa faoi a niornmoilt ó na huirʒeaóaib óf cioñ na hiornmoilte, aʒuf óo bi maʈ fin. Aʒuf ʒoin Óia óo niornmoilt neaṁ." This, literally translated into English, would be absolute nonsense; it would run thus: " And God said, let there be a firmament *(iormoilt)* in the midst of the waters, &c.—And God made *in a* firmament (a niornmoilt) and he divided the waters under *in a* firmament (faoi a niornmoilt) from the waters above the firmament, and it was so. And God called to, &c. heaven." The words óo niornmoilt here cannot be translated into any intelligible language; they should be written óo'n iornmoilt, if iornmoilt had any meaning. Verse 9. " Cruiñiʒcear na huirʒeaóa aca faoi neaṁ a neunáic aʒuf leiʒcean a nḟñr cinim leir." The n in nernáic is here properly prefixed, because the preposition a requires it; a nernáic, in one place; but it is improperly prefixed to ḟñr, land, for that should be preceded by an article, and not a preposition; a nḟñr, signifies *in the* land: it should be an ḟñr, the land.

Again, verse 14, " Aguſ a dubgt Dia, bioð lócṁaiṅ a niormoilt neiṁe do ṙoiṅ eidiṙ an lā aguſ a noiðce," &c.   Here the ṅ prefixed to iormoilt is right, because the preposition a goes before it; but it should not be joined to oiðce, as it is, because the sense requires the article.   A noiðce means *in a* night, but it should be written an oiðce, *the* night. " biṙ an lā aguſ an oiðce," literally means " between the day and the night." The word lócṁaiṅ, in this verse, is a proof of the absence of grammatical knowledge in the editor.   Lócṁain is an oblique case of lócṁan, light; and it should be here in the nominative case.   Moreover, even if the oblique case should be used, the orthography is wrong; it should be lócṁain.   The word *iormoilt,* used here for firmament, is one of those words adopted by this editor that never appeared before in any Irish book, ancient or modern, printed or manuscript, except in the late edition of the Scottish Gaelic Bible; and even there, not admitted into the text.

The great importance of correctness in an edition of the Sacred Scriptures, and the fearful consequences that may result from a depraved translation of them, will, it is hoped, be a sufficient apology for this digression from the original plan of this work.

A. D. 1629.

CCLXXVII. Died at Madrid on the 18th of November, this year, father FLORENCE CONRY, or O'MULCONAIRE, an Observantin Franciscan, in the sixty-ninth year of his age.   Through his solicitation Philip III. king of Spain, founded the college of Saint Anthony of Padua, in Louvain, for the Irish Franciscan Friars, and to this seminary, in the year 1654, his bones were translated from Spain by his countrymen.   His " Scáṫán an Cḣṙabuiḋ," or " Mirror of Religion," a Catechism, was printed in Louvain, in 1626.

A. D. 1630.

CLXXVIII. EOCHAIDH O'HEOGHUSA, Maguire's chief poet, flourished at this period, as appears by his poem on O'Donell, second Earl of Tirconnel. By the thirty-sixth *rann* of the first poem in the following list, it appears he began his poetic career so early as the year 1593, when he was but a youth. The ensuing catalogue contains all the legible poems that we have met with of this author's works, many of which have much merit, and none of them are contemptible.

1. Two hundred and twenty-eight verses, on the appointment of Aodh roe (or red Hugh) O'Donell, as chieftain of Tirconnell, after his escape from captivity in the Castle of Dublin, in the last week of December, 1592. This poem begins " Oiol ꝼꞃáτá ꝼláιτιοꝼ Eιꞃeáñ," " A reward exciting hatred is the sovereignty of Erin."

Copy of this poem in possession of the Assistant Secretary.

2. One hundred and twenty verses, in praise of Cuchonacht Maguire, Lord of Fermanagh, beginning " ꝼáꞅá leιᵹτeáꞃ Eáṁꞃꞃn án ᴄoꞃτuṁá."

3. A didactic poem, consisting of one hundred and seventy-two verses, for the instruction of Cuchonacht, or Constantine, Maguire, Lord of Fermanagh. This poem begins " Oeáᴄáιꞃ ιoñꞃáιṁ ná hoιᵹe," " Difficult the service of youth."

4. One hundred and twenty verses, on the sickness of Teige O'Brien, beginning " Oeálᵹ áτáláιᴅ oτꞃáꞅ Tháᴅᵹ," " A re-hurting sting is the sickness of Teige."

5. Eighty verses, lamenting the absence of Hugh Maguire, beginning " ꝼuáꞃ leám án oιᴅᴄeꞃι ᴅ'Ꞁloᴅ," " Cold I feel this night for Hugh."

6. Ninety-two verses on the sickness of his Chief, Cuchonacht Maguire, beginning " ꝼáᴅá ó m'ιñτιn á háṁáꞃᴄ," " Far from my mind its vision."

7. An address to Hugh Maguire, one hundred and forty-eight verses, beginning " Sláñ ꝼáᴅ loτ á láṁ Ꞁloᴅá," " Health to thy wound, oh hand of Hugh."

8. Seventy-six verses addressed to Hugh Maguire, beginning " Cuιꞃꝼeáᴅ ꝼo ιoñáᴅ Ꞁloᴅ," " I will implant this in thee, O'Hugh."

9. Two hundred verses, addressed to Teige, son of Brian and Mary O'Rourke, Lord of W. Breifne, beginning " Cazuɩ́ꝛ ꝛeꝺ meaꞃma a mɩc bhꞃɩaɩꞃ," " Contend with thy natural disposition, oh son of Brian."

10. An historical poem, addressed to Hugh Maguire, three hundred and forty-four verses, beginning " Faꝺa ꞃe huꞃcóɩꝺ Eɩꞃe," " Long is Ireland acquainted with injury."

11. A very beautiful historical poem, in which the author eulogises Owen og M'Sweeny, the son of Margaret, daughter of Aodh O'Donell, chief of Tirconell. This poem consists of two hundred and thirty-six verses, beginning " Roɩ̃ leɩ̀e aɩꞃ aꞃbꞃaɩꞃ Eɩꞃeaꞃ̃," " The uneasiness of Ireland is divided."

12. One hundred and fifty-two verses, lamenting the distressed state of Ireland, and calling on Hugh O'Neill to remember the glorious acts of his forefathers, and to redeem their ancient patrimony from bondage. This poem begins " Fꞃɩoc aꞃ ꞃaɩꞃꝛe aɩꞃ ɩꞁɩꝛ Fáɩl," " Devote this opportunity for the Isle of Fail."

13. One hundred and sixty-four verses on Brian, son of Hugh M'Mahon, chief of Uriell (Oɩꞃꝛɩalla) beginning " beaꝣ maɩꞃeaꝛ ꝺo macꞃaɩꝺ ꝣaoɩꝺɩl," " Few remain of the sons of Gathelus."

14. Ninety-six verses, on the hospitality and pleasures of the mansion and amiable family of Felim, son of Feagh M'Hugh O'Byrne, of Ranelagh, beginning " ɩoꞃ̃muɩꞃ ꞇeaċ ꞃe ꞇꞇuꝣaꝛ cúl," " Beloved is the house that I have left."

15. One hundred and sixty-eight verses, addressed to Hugh Maguire, beginning " Móꞃ aꞃ ꞇaɩꞃm ollaꞃ̃ Flaċa," " Professor (*chief Doctor*) of a prince, is a noble title."

16. Two hundred and sixteen verses, on the Maguires, and in praise of the wife of Con Maguire, beginning " Suɩꞃꝣeaċ ꞃɩꞃ a Eɩꞃe óꝣ," " Lovely that, oh noble Erin."

17. Eighty verses, against satirical writing, beginning " Maɩꞃꝣ ɩaꞃꞃaꝛ ɩomlaoɩꝺ cáɩꞃꞇe," " Woe to him who seeks satyric poems."

Copies of all the above poems, except the first, are in O'Gara's collection in the library of John Mac Namara, Esq. The first, and most of the rest, are also amongst the MSS. belonging to the Assistant Secretary.

18. Two hundred and sixteen verses on the O'Donells, beginning " ᴺɪ ᴄóṁᴄṗom ᴄóᵹaᵹ ᵬanᵬa," " Not equal is the war of Banbha, (Ireland)."

19. Forty-four verses, on O'Donell, Earl of Tirconnell, beginning " ɪonṁolᴄa malaɪṗᴄ ᵬᵹɪᵹ," " Commendable the exchange of profit."

Copies of these two poems are in the manuscripts of the late Reverend Doctor O'Brien, and of the Assistant Secretary.

20. Seventy-two verses, recommending a life of temperance, beginning " ᴀ ᵭuɪne na heaᵲláɪnᴄe," " Oh man of disease."

21. Twenty-four verses, advice to a female friend, beginning " ᴀ ᵬean ᵭᵲoɪᵭe ᴄompánᴄa," " Oh woman of the social heart."

22. Twenty verses, addressed to a friend, beginning " ᴀ ᵲɪn ᵭᵲoɪᵭe ᴄaᵲuɪṁᵴɪ," " Oh man of the heart I love."

23. Eighty-eight verses, addressed to Almighty God, beginning " ᴀᵽ ᴄᵲaoᵲaṁ ᵭaṁ a ᴅᵫé aᴄaɪᵽ," " By thy protection to me, oh God the Father!"

24. One hundred and twenty-four verses on Cuchonacht, or Constantine, Maguire, beginning " ᴄᵲeᵭ ṁuᵲᵹlaᵲ maᴄᵲaɪᵭ ᴇɪᵽne," " What is it that awakes the sons of Erne."

25. Sixty-eight verses, addressed to Con, son of John O'Neill, beginning " ᴏᵲaoɪᵭ leaᴄ a leaᵬaɪᵽ ᴄᵲᵫ̃," " A theme to thee, oh generous Conn."

26. One hundred and seventy-six verses, addressed to Cuchonnacht Maguire, beginning " ᵭo ᵲeᴄhaɪᵭ ᵲulaɪᵹ ᵹaoɪᵬɪl," " The forbearance of the Gathelians is seen."

27. Two hundred and thirty-two verses, addressed to the son of Richard de Burgo M'William, beginning " ᴍaᴄaɪᵲ ᴄoᵹaᵭ ᴄᵲɪoᴄ ᵬanᵬa," " Mother of war is the country of Banbha (Ireland)."

28. Eighty-eight verses addressed to Hugh, son of Cuchonacht Maguire, beginning " ᴍóᵽ an ᵲeaᵲᵹᵲo oᵽᴄ a ᴀoᵭ," " Great is thy wrath, oh Hugh."

Copies of the nine last-mentioned poems are in the collection of the Assistant Secretary.

This author wrote several other poems on miscellaneous subjects, imperfect copies of which are in the collection of the Assistant Secretary.

CLXXIX. Maurice O'Daly, O'Reilly's poet, flourished at this period. We have met with only one poem of his writing; this is in praise of

Tullagh Mangain, the hill on which the princes of the House of O'Reilly were inaugurated. It gives a Catalogue of the Kings or Princes of East Brefny to his own time, beginning "Mo ṫruaiġe mar a taoi a Thulaiġ!" "Alas, that thou art thus, oh hill!"

Copy in possession of the Assistant Secretary.

CCLXXX. At this time lived in Dublin, the Rev. FLORENCE GRAY, who had been a Divinity Lecturer in the College of Saint Anthony of Padua, in Louvain. Harris, in his additions to Ware, says he wrote an Irish Grammar.—We have not seen a copy of it.

CCLXXXI. At this time lived CONLA MAC GEOGHEGAN, an industrious collector of the antiquities of his country. He compiled, from the Book of Leacan and other ancient documents, a *Leabhar Gabhala*, or Book of Conquests; a *Reim Rioghraidhe*, or Catalogue of Kings; and a Genealogy of the Saints of Ireland, which were afterwards revised and enlarged by Michael O'Clery and others. He also wrote Annals of Ireland, from the earliest account of time, to the year 1466. He dates this book on the last day of June, 1627. It is now in the library of Trinity College, but we cannot say where his other works are to be found.

A. D. 1632.

CCLXXXII. In this year was begun to be compiled, in the Franciscan Convent of Dunagall, that noble repertory of Irish history, the "ANNALS OF DUNAGALL," otherwise called the "ANNALS OF THE FOUR MASTERS." The first title they took from the place in which they were written, but why they should be called by the second name is not easy to conceive, as there were in reality *six* persons concerned in the compilation of them. This we learn from the certificate prefixed to the work, signed by the two gentlemen who had been superiors of the convent whilst it was in progress.

To show from what works these annals were compiled, and the persons employed in the compilation, we here give a literal translation of the certificate above mentioned :—

" The Fathers of the Order of St. Francis, who sign their hands here-
" unto, testify that it was Ferrall O'Gara who induced the brother
" Michael O'Clery to collect the chronologers and learned men together,
" by whom this Book of Records and Annals of Ireland were written,
" (so much as they were able to obtain materials to write;) and that it
" was the same Ferrall who gave them a remuneration for their labour.

" This Book is divided into two parts, and from the beginning to the
" end it was written in the Convent of the Brothers of Dunagall, they
" giving attendance and supplying necessary food. In this Convent was
" begun and written the first Book, in the year 1632, at the time that the
" father Bernardin O'Clery was guardian.

" The chronologers and learned men who were employed in writing
" this Book, and in collecting the various Books from which it was com-
" piled, were Michael O'Clery; Maurice, son of Torna O'Maolconaire,
" who attended during one month; Ferfeasa, son of Loghlain O'Maol-
" conaire, (these two were from the county Roscommon;) Cucoigcrighe
" O'Clery, of the county Dunagall; Cucoigcrighe O'Duigenan, of the
" county Roscommon; and Conaire O'Clery, of the county Dunagall.

" These are the old Books they had in their possession : the Book of
" Clonmacnois, blessed by Saint Kiaran *Mac-an-tsaoir*, (son of the Artist;)
" the Book of the Island of Saints on Lough Rive; the Book of Senait
" Mac Manus on Lough Erne," (now called the Ulster Annals); " the
" Book of the O'Maolconaires; the Book of the O'Duigenans of Kil-
" ronan; the Book of Records of the Mac Firbis's, which they procured
" after they had written the greater part of the Book ; and from that
" Book they wrote whatever they found supplementary and necessary to
" them, which were not in the first Books they had procured; for the
" Book of Cluain-mac-nois, and the Book of the Island of All Saints
" contained nothing, except to the year 1227.

" The second Book of this work commences with the year 1208, and
" was begun to be written in the year of Christ, 1635, in which the
" Father Christopher (Donlevy), surnamed *Ultach* the (Ultonian), was

" guardian ; and this part is continued to the year 1608, when the Father
" Bernardin O'Clery was again Guardian. The above-mentioned Michael
" O'Clery, Cucoigcrighe O'Clery, and Conaire O'Clery, wrote the latter
" Book from 1332 to 1608. These are the Books from which the afore-
" said three compiled the principal part of this Book :—the Book of the
" O'Maolconaires, to the year 1505, which is the last year in that Book ;
" the Book of the O'Duigenans, from the year 900 to the year 1563 ;
" the Book of Senait Mac Manus, which comes to the year 1532 ; a
" fragment of the Book of Cucoigcrighe, son of Dermod, son of Teige
" *cam* O'Clery, from the year 1281 to 1537 ; the Book of Maoilin og
" Mac Bruody, (or Brodin) from the year 1588 to 1603 ; the Book of
" Lughaidh O'Clery, from 1586 to 1602. We have seen all these Books
" with those learned men after they came to us, and other Books of
" Records which it would be a delay to name. In proof of what we have
" above written, we have affixed our manual signatures in the convent of
" Dunegall, this 10th day of August, 1636.

> " BERNARDINUS O'CLERY, Guardianus Dunagallensis.
> " Br. MAURICE ULTACH (Dunlevy)."

This certificate is countersigned by Brother Michael O'Clery, Maurice
O'Maolconaire, Ferfeasa O'Maolconaire, Cucoigcriche O'Clery, and
Conaire O'Clery.

The dedication of this Book to Ferrall O'Gara, Lord of Moy O'Gara,
and Coolavin, and one of the knights elected to represent the county of
Sligo in the Parliament held in Dublin in 1634, was written and signed
by Michael O'Clery, by which it appears that he was the principal person
under whose direction this work was carried on. The original copy was
bound in two volumes folio, the first of which, commencing with the year
of the world 2242, and ending with the year of our Lord 1171, was in the
library of the late venerable Charles O'Conor, of Belanagare, and is now
deposited by his grandson, the Rev. Charles O'Connor, in the library of
the Marquis of Buckingham, at Stowe, together with many other valuable
Irish manuscripts. The second volume of the original, commencing A. D.
1335, and ending A. D. 1605, is in the library of Trinity College.

In this work there is a chasm from the year 1171 to 1335, which may be supplied from the continuation of the Annals of Tigernach, and from the Annals of Ulster. Copies of these Annals are not numerous. The first volume of the original is copied into two volumes quarto, in the library of Trinity College, which, with the second volume of the original, make the College copy complete. The late Chevalier Thomas O'Gorman had a complete set, from which the writer of this account was making a copy, which he had nearly completed, when the removal from Dublin, and subsequent death of his friend the Chevalier, prevented him from finishing it.

Besides the Annals of Dunagall, these writers collectively compiled the *Leabhar Gabhala,* or Book of Conquests; the *Reim Rioghraidhe,* or regal Catalogue, and a Genealogy of the Saints of Ireland. The Book of Conquests was compiled in the convent of Lisgoole, under the patronage of Brian roe Maguire, first Lord of Eniskillen. In this work the writers were assisted by Giolla Patrick O'Luinin, of Ard O'Luinin, in the county Fermanagh. The testimonies and approbations to this work are signed by Francis M'Craith, Guardian of Lisgoole, on the 22d December, 1631; and by Flann, son of Carbry Mac Egan, of Bally Mac Egan, in the county Tipperary, on the 31st August, 1631. The Reim Rioghroide was begun to be compiled in the house of Conall Mac Geoghegan, and finished in the Observantine Convent, at Athlone, on the 4th November, 1630. This work was carried on under the patronage of Torlogh Mac Coghlan, Lord of Dealbhna Eathra, part of the ancient kingdom of Meath, now called the Barony of Garry Castle, in the King's County.

Copies of the Book of Conquests are in the library of Trinity College, and in that of William Monck Mason, Esq. The original is in the collection of Irish manuscripts belonging to the Assistant Secretary.

Copy of the REIM RIOGHRAIDHE, or Regal Catalogue, and the Genealogy of the Saints, is also in the collection of the Assistant Secretary.

Besides the above works written by these authors collectively, there are other works executed by some of them individually.

CCLXXXIII. MICHAEL O'CLERY wrote, and published in Louvain, in the year 1643, a Vocabulary, in which many of the hard, or obsolete words in the Irish language were explained by words in common use in the modern language of our country. This work has now become exceedingly scarce. A copy of it was sold at the late General Vallancey's sale for six guineas. There is a MS. copy in possession of the Assistant Secretary.

This writer also translated into Irish the Rules of the Religious order of St. Clare, in the year 1636.

Copy in the Marquis of Buckingham's library, at Stowe.

CCLXXXIV. CUCOIGCRICHE O'CLERY, besides the part he took in the compilations of the Annals, &c. wrote a life of Aodh roe O'Donell, chief of Tirconell, who invited the Spaniards to invade Ireland in the early part of the reign of James the First.

The original copy of this work is in the library of William Monck Mason, Esq. and a transcript of it is in the collection of the Assistant Secretary, who has now nearly translated into English, with an intent to publish, this invaluable piece of Irish history.

Perhaps this author may be the same as the Cucoigcriche O'Clery, which we have mentioned under the year 1620.

CCLXXXV. CUCOIGCRICHE (son of Toole *buidhe*) O'DUIGEANAN, one of the writers of the Annals of the Four Masters, &c. was also the author of a poem, beginning " ꝛloin ꞅciaꞇ coꞃnaṁ na cceall," " Only protecting shield of the churches," on the return of Teige O'Rody from London, in 1641.

CCLXXXVI. CCLXXXVII. CCLXXXVIII. Of works written by FEARFEASA O'MAOLCONARE, CONAING O'CLERY, and MAURICE O'MAOLCONAIRE, we know no more than the part they took in the compilation of the Annals of the Four Masters, the *Reimrioghraidhe, &c.* unless we suppose the last-named writer to be the same as the Maurice O'Maolconaire we mentioned under the year 1600, at page clix.

———

A. D. 1636.

CCLXXXIX. In this year CATHAL MAC MUIREADHAIGH, or MAC MUIRICH, as he is called in the Erse dialect, wrote his poem on the Mac Donalds, one hundred and twelve verses, addressed to Colla Ciotach Mac Donald, beginning " Saoᴄ líom ᴅo ċoꞃ a Cholla," " Trouble to me is thy state, oh Colla."

This poem, in the hand-writing of the author, is in the library of Trinity College, class H. No. 54.

Mr. Astle, in his " Origin and Progress of Writing," plate 22, specimen 6, gives a fac simile of this author's hand-writing, and erroneously says it was taken from an Erse manuscript, written in the 15th century.

A. D. 1639.

ccxc. THEOBALD STAPLETON, an Irish priest, was author of a Latin and Irish Catechism, which he published at Brussells, this year, in Roman letter, and a quarto form. It is now a very scarce book, but there is a copy in the library of Trinity College.

A. D. 1640.

ccxci. At this time flourished OWEN ROE M'AN BHAIRD, a Franciscan friar, author of the following poems :

1. One hundred and eight verses, beginning " 2l ꝼíꞃ ꝼeaċaꝼ uaiᴄ an ċnáiṁ !" " Oh man, who beholdest the bone !" Reflections on the vanity of this world.

2. Two hundred and thirty verses, beginning " Ꝁlac a ċompaiꞅ compaiꞅ cóṁaiꞃle," " Accept, my friend, a friend's advice." Instructions for a holy life.

3. On the pleasures of a religious life, and on the habit of the order of Saint Francis, sixty verses, beginning " íoꞅṁꞃꞅ Cꞃíoꞅ co colꞅ heiṁneaċ," " Sweet is the girdle with painful stings."

4. On receiving news of young O'Donell's return, sixteen verses, beginning " ᴉoᵰᵯᵹᴖ ᵲᵹᴖᴉbeᵰ ᵲᵹᴀoᴉᴄᴇoᴘ ᵲᴜᵰ," " Pleasant news reported here."

Copies of all these are in the collection of the Assistant Secretary.

ccxcii. At this time lived EDMOND M'DONOGH, author of a short poem, on the evil propensities of the flesh, twenty-eight verses, beginning " ᴍo ᴄᴇᴀᵹᴀᵲᵹ ᴅᴀ ᵰᵹᴌᴀᴄᴅᴀ ᴀ ᴄᵲᵲᴘ!" " My advice, if taken, O body!"

Copy in the library of John M'Namara, Esq.

———

A. D. 1641.

ccxciii. FERGAL *Muimhneach* ODUIGENAN was author of a poem on the return of Teige O'Rody from London, in this year, forty-eight verses, beginning " ᴍᴀᴉᴄ ᴄᵲᴀᴄ ᴅo ᴄoᴉᵹeᴀᴄᴄ ᴀ Chᴀᴉᵹ!" " You came in good time, oh Teige!"

Copy in collection of Assistant Secretary.

———

A. D. 1643.

ccxciv. At this time flourished the Right Reverend THOMAS DEASE, R. C. Bishop of Meath, and one of the Supreme Council of the confederate Catholics. The following poems, written by him, have come down to our times:

1. Advice to a young lady, forty-eight verses, beginning " ᵹᴀb ᴍo ᴄᴇᴀᵹᴀᵲᵹ ᴀ ᴉᵰᵹᴉᴖ ᴏᴉᵹ," " Accept my counsel, youthful fair."

2. Beginning " ᴍᴏᴘ ᴅᴇᴉᵯᴖᴉᴘᵹᴀᴅ ᴖᴀ ᴄᴄoᵯᴘᴀᴖᴀᴄ," " Much is affirmed of the associates."

3. One hundred and forty-four verses, beginning " Rᵰᴇᴀᵲ ᴍo ᴄᴉoᵯᴖᴀ ᴀ Shᴇᴀᵯᴀᴉᵲ," " I have made my will, oh James."

Copies of all these are in possession of the Assistant Secretary.

A. D. 1645.

ccxcv. In this year the Rev. Anthony Gernon, a Franciscan Friar of the college of St. Anthony, in Louvain, published his Ραρριċαγ αη 2lηma, or Paradise of the Soul, a catechism, containing instructions for a Christian life. This author was living in 1667.

This is now a very scarce book, but there are copies of it in possession of William Monck Mason, Esq. John M'Namara, Esq. and the Assistant Secretary.

A. D. 1649.

ccxcvi. Somhairle Mac an Bhaird flourished at this time, as appears by the last *rann* but one of his elegy on the death of Aodh buidhe O'Donell, who died in this year. This poem consists of two hundred and eighty verses. beginning " Neαρċ ʒαċ ċiρe αιρ Ċiρ Chonαill," " The energy of every country is in Tirconell."

Copies of this poem are in the books of the late Rev. Paul O'Brien, and in the collection of the Assistant Secretary.

A. D. 1650.

ccxcvii. About this time died the Irish Herodotus, the Rev. Geoffry Keating, D. D. By an inscription over the door of the church of Tubrid, in his native county of Tipperary, it appears that that edifice was founded by the Rev. Eugene Duhy, vicar of Tubrid, and Doctor Geoffrey Keating, in A. D. 1644. He was a pious and learned priest, and author of many works in his native language, both verse and prose. We here insert a list of such of his compositions as have come under our observation.

1. A History of Ireland, from the earliest account of time, to the Anglo-Norman invasion. The title of this, in the original, is " Ρορυγ

ᵹeaᵹa aiᵹ Eiᵹiñ," " Rudiments of knowledge on Ireland." A faulty translation of this work, in folio, by Dermod O'Conor, was published in London and Dublin, in 1723. It has been republished in two volumes octavo, by Christie, Dublin, 1809. A new and correct translation of this work, as far as the Christian Era, was published in one volume octavo, Dublin 1811, with the original Irish on opposite pages, by the late Mr. William Haliday. It is to be lamented, that a lingering sickness and early death prevented this highly talented young gentleman from finishing his translation.

2. A treatise on the Mass, called " Eoċaiᵹ ᵹciaṫ aη Aiᵹᵹioñ," " A key to the shield of the Mass."

3. A moral treatise on Death, called " Cᵹi bioᵹᵹaoiṫe aη báiᵹ," " Three pointed shafts of death."

4. A poem in praise of Ireland, written while the author was on the continent, twenty-four verses, beginning " Ɯo beañaċt leaṫ a ᵹᵹibiñ," " My blessing with thee, oh writing."

5. A poem in praise of Teige O'Coffey, a celebrated performer on the harp, thirty-six verses, beginning " Cia aη ṫᵹaoi le ᵹeiñteaᵹ aη cᵹᵹṫ," " Who is the sage by whom the harp is struck."

6. A poem on the miseries of Ireland, twenty verses, beginning " Oη ᵹᵹeoil ᵹo cᵹaᵹ Ɯaᵹ ᵹail ηι ċoᵹlaiᵹ oiᵹċe," " From the news that pains Moy-Fail (Ireland) I sleep not a night."

ccxcviii. At this time lived Teige roe O'Conor, author of a poem in dispraise of a harper, forty-four verses, beginning " Saoi le ᵹeaᵹbuᵹ Eoiη ṁic Eoiη," " A sage in harshness is John Mac John."

Copy in the collection of the Assistant Secretary.

ccxcix. The Father Thomas M'Rory flourished at this time. He was author of an elegy on the death of Owen Roe O'Neill, Commander in Chief of the Forces of the Confederate Catholics, who lost his life by a pair of poisoned boots, in A. D. 1649, one hundred and fifty four verses, beginning, " Ɔo ċaill Eiᵹe a cēile ᵹiᵹe," " Ireland has lost her true companion."

This poem was translated into English by the Hon. Arthur Brownlow, in the year 1700.

Copies of both the original and translation, are in the manuscript collection of the Assistant Secretary.

CCC. DERMOD O'SULLIVAN flourished at this period. He was author of a poem, containing forty-eight verses, on the former and then present state of Ireland. It begins " Níon bnioʒač ꞃ̃ɲ a ccꞃioėaib Eibiꞃ móiꞃ," " We were unacquainted in the districts of mighty Heber."

CCCI. CONOR O'RIORDAN was cotemporary with the last-mentioned author, and wrote an answer to his poem, consisting of forty-four verses, beginning " An čán ꝺo bíoꝺaꞃ ʒaoiḃil a nEiꞃ̃ beo," " When the Gathelians were alive in Erin."
Copies of both these poems are in possession of the Assistant Secretary.

CCCII. CIAN O'HEICHIARAN lived at this time; he was author of a poem on the deaths of the Earl of Tirone, and of Henry, son of Owen roe O'Neill, one hundred and sixteen verses, beginning " Cainic cꞃioė aiꞃ olc nEꞃion," " An end has come to the misfortune of Erin."
Copy in possession of the Assistant Secretary.

CCCIII. About this period lived PATRICK O'DONELLY (Donghaoile) author of an ironical elegy on the death of Owen Liddy. This poem consists of ninety-two verses, beginning " buan an eaꞃbaiʒ báꞃ Eoʒam," " The death of Owen is a lasting loss."
Copy in possession of the Assistant Secretary.

CCCIV. At this time also lived TORLOGH OG M'DONOGH, author of a poem addressed to a friar who had forsaken his religion, thirty-six verses, beginning, " A bꞃačaiꞃ Eom ma ča ꝺo čꞃiall, " Oh brother John, if thou art going."
Copy in possession of the Assistant Secretary.

CCCV. At this period also flourished Doctor JOHN O'CONELL, Roman Catholic Bishop of Ardfert, or Kerry. He was author of a metrical account of some facts relating to the History of Ireland, beginning " Anꞇaiꞃ ꞃmꞃamim aiꞃ ꞃaoiċiḃ na hEiꞃeaꞃ̃," " When I reflect on the nobles of Ireland."
Copies of this poem are in the hands of every Irish scholar.

A. D. 1652.

cccvi. David O'Bruadair *(Broderick)*, a native of the county Limerick, lived at this time. He was author of the following poems, and of some others that we have seen, but do not know where they are now to be found.

1. Sixty-eight verses, beginning " *la luġnaṙa ṙpiunaið luéð ṙaiðḃeaṙa*," " On Lammas-day the people of riches pull."

2. Two hundred and four verses, on the Irish surrendering their arms, and on the beheading of King Charles the First. This poem begins " *Cṙéaċt ðo ðáil me am'aṙṙċaṡ ġalaiṙ*," " I received a wound in my state of sickness." This poem was written in 1652.

3. Twenty-four verses, addressed to our Lord Jesus Christ, beginning " *Aðṙaim ċa a ċaiðḃṙe aṙ ccṙú*," " I adore thee, oh pride of our blood."

4. Twenty-eight verses on the same subject, beginning " *Go ḃṙáċ a meic ṙuġ Oṙṙṙe mioṙḃṙleaċ*," " For ever is the Son that Mary miraculously bore."

Copies of the two first poems are in possession of the Assistant Secretary, the two latter are in the library of John Mac Namara, Esq.

5. A poem, beginning " *Ge aimḃṙeaṙaċ ṙeañaiṙe naṙ ṙiaṙ a ġlṙṙn?*" " Though the flayer be ignorant is not his knee crooked?"

6. Beginning " *A ṙiġ na cṙṙṙe ðo ṙiṙiṙe*," " Oh God of the world that made it."

7. Beginning " *Ðo ḃi ðṙṙe éiġin ṙoiṙ an ṙé ṙi*," " There was a certain man before this time."

8. Beginning " *Iṙ uṙċṙað cian ðam iað a naċṙú ṙliġ*," " It is long a misery to me they to be falling in the way."

9. Beginning " *Oṙċið ṙoiċim ġo Siol Ccaṙċaiġ*," " It is time I should go to the Mac Carthys."

The four poems last mentioned I have not seen; the first lines were sent to me by a friend, but he did not mention the subjects on which they were written.

This writer also made a copy of the *Leabhar Irse* of the O'Maolconaires, now in the library of Trinity College.

He was living in the year 1692.

A. D. 1655.

CCCVII. FEARGAL OG MC. AN BHAIRD, lived at this period. He was author of the following poems:

1. An elegy on the death of John O'Donell, who, according to the last rann but one of this poem, died in the year 1655. It consists of two hundred and thirty-two verses, beginning " Ɗo coɪɲneaɓ ceaɲuɼ èlaɲ Ccɼɲ," " The authority of the sons of Conn was raised."

2. One hundred and sixty verses on the descendants of Ir, son of Milesius, particularly on the Magennises. This poem begins, " Ɪɲɪal coɓɲaċ cloɪɲe hɪɲ," " Irial, treasure of the sons of Ir."

3. One hundred and eighty-six verses on the family of O'Ferrall, beginning " ɼan ɲaċ ɪmɲɪɓ aɪcme Ɪɲ," " In prosperity proceed the race of Ir."

4. On the O'Donells, particularly Calbhach, son of Manus, two hundred and forty-eight verses, beginning " Cɲeoɪn aɲ ceaɲuɼ Claɲ Ɗálaɪʒ," " Powerful the authority of the Clann Dalaigh."

5. On Dominick O'Donell, two hundred and forty-eight verses, beginning " Ʒaɪɓle ɼoɓla ɼɼl Choɲaɪll," " Props of *Fodhla* (Ireland) are the race of Conall."

Copies of all these poems are in the library of John Mac Namara, Esq. Numbers 1, 3, and 4 are in the collection of the Assistant Secretary.

A. D. 1660.

CCCVIII. At this time lived CIAN O'MAHONY, author of a short poem, beginning " Ɑ óɼɲe leɪʒ ɓo ċex ʒo cneaɼɓa ɼɼaɪɲc ɓaɲ," " Oh man, gently and pleasantly read your text to me."

Copy in collection of the Assistant Secretary.

CCCIX. MAURICE O'DUGAN lived near Benburb, in the County Tyrone, this year. He was author of the following poems, beginning

1. "Gluais do ċablaċ go mear meanmnaċ," "Set your fleet in motion cheerfully, spiritedly."

2. "Bhi Eoġan air buile agus triur air an duine," "Owen was in a rage, and three on the man."

3. "Faraoir ċaill Eire a céile fírċeart," "Erin has lost her lawful spouse."

4. "Foḋla an bean a meaṫ is ċraiḋ sad faoṡam," "Fodhla (Ireland) is a woman in decay, and her strength is gone."

This author is also said to have been the writer of the Coolin, beginning "Eiriġ ad suiġ a braċail is gleus daṁ mo ġearrán, "Arise from thy seat, boy, and prepare my horse for me."

The four last-mentioned poems I have not seen; the first lines were communicated to me by a friend, but he does not mention the subjects on which they were written.

A. D. 1662.

CCCX. In this year the Rev. RICHARD PLUNKETT, a poor Brother of the Franciscan Convent at Trim, in the county of Meath, wrote a Latin and Irish Dictionary, now in Marsh's library.——There is also a copy in the library of Trinity College, Dublin.

A. D. 1661.

CCCXI. In this year RICHARD MAC GIOLLA-CUDDY, OR ARCHDEKIN, an Irish Jesuit, printed at Louvain an Essay on Miracles, in English and Irish. He died about the year 1690.

A. D. 1676.

cccxii. Rev. Father FRANCIS O'MOLLOY, a native of Meath, a Franciscan Friar, and Lecturer in Divinity in the College of Saint Isidore, in Rome, published in that city, in this year, an Irish Catechism, under the title of " *Lóċṙan na Cċṙeıoṁeaċ,* " or " Lamp of the Faithful," and in the following year he published in the same city his Irish-Latin Grammar. These books are scarce, but copies are to be found in the library of Trinity College.

A. D. 1680.

cccxiii. JOHN O'DUININ, a Conaght poet, lived at this period. He was author of an elegy on the death of Gearoid, or Garrett, son of Teige O'Rody, and father of Teige oge O'Rody, who died on the second day of August, in this year, eighty-eight verses, beginning " *Ṫṙuaġ an maıoṁṙı aṙ maıcne hIṙ,* " " Sad is this breach on the sons of Ir."
Copy in possession of the Assistant Secretary.

cccxiv. CARROLL OGE O'DALY also lived at this period; he was author of a Vision, consisting of twenty-eight verses, beginning " *Aṁ leaba aṙéıṙ oo ṙaoıleaṙ ṙéṁ a ṫeaċṫ,* " " In my bed last night I thought with myself there came."
Copy in possession of the Assistant Secretary.

A. D. 1681.

cccxv. Most Rev. Doctor OLIVER PLUNKETT, R. C. Archbishop of Armagh, who was executed in London on the 1st of July in this year, upon a charge of high treason, of which he was completely innocent, has left us a small poem, in the Irish language, on Tarah, where the ancient monarchs of Ireland held their court. This poem begins " Ⴈ Ⴒheaṁaıɼ na ɼíoᵹ ɔob aṅaṁ leaⱅ," " Oh Tarah of the Kings, it was rare with you."

Copy in collection of the Assistant Secretary.

A. D. 1690.

cccxvi. At this period flourished WILLIAM O'KIARAN, a native of the lower part of Meath, bordering on Cavan. He was author of a poem, consisting of thirty-six verses, on the three Marys, *i. e.* Mary the mother of our Lord Jesus Christ, and her two sisters, Mary the mother of James and John the Evangelist, and Mary the mother of Jacob and Mathias. This poem begins " Saᵹaɼⱅ ɔo bí ɼeaċɔ oıle," " There was a priest in other times."

Copy in possession of the Assistant Secretary.

cccxvii. At this time also flourished OWEN O'DONELLY, an Ulster Bard. He was author of the following poems:

1. An elegy on the death of Brian, son of Colla M‘Mahon, who died in Dublin, according to this poem, in the year 1690. It consists of one hundred and twenty verses, beginning " Ⴒɼom na ᵹaıɼⱅaɼa a leıⱅ Chɼın," " Sad these shouts, oh Leith Chuinn."

2. A poem, beginning " Ⴒɼ̇ıɼɼeaċ ɔaṁ aıᵹ eıɼᵹe lae," Woeful to me the rising of the day."

3. One hundred and twenty verses, in answer to Dermod, son of Lewis Mac an Bhaird, who had praised the descendants of Ir, and set them up as superior to those of his brothers Heber and Heremon. This poem begins " Iɼ náɼ an ɼᵹeɼlɼa ⱅeaċɔ ɔa ⱅıᵹ," " Bad is this news that came to your house."

Copies in the collection of the Assistant Secretary.

cccxviii. TEIGE O'DUININ lived about the time of the battle of the Boyne. He was author of a poem, consisting of sixty verses, beginning

" Iᵧ lén liom leaᵹaö na bᵱlaċa iᵧ na bᵱioᵱᵧaᵧle," " Sorrowful to me is the defeat of the princes and the true nobility," on the miserable state of the Irish, after being deserted by King James II.

Copy in the collection of the Assistant Secretary.

cccxix. At this time also flourished Dermod *roe* O'Muireadhaigh, or O'Murray, author of a poem addressed to a Priest of the name of O'Phelan, who renounced the church and married a wife. This poem consists of thirty-two verses, beginning " ᵹo ᴄaᵱᵹö ᵹlᴦaᵧ aᵧ ᵧᴦan an ᴄᵧaoᵹail ᵹan ᵧᵹiċ," " Quickly pass on from this worldly sleep, without delay."

A. D. 1691.

cccxx. At this time flourished Dermod, son of Lewis Mac an Bhaird, a native of the county of Down. He is said to have written many poems, but the two following are the only pieces of his composition that have come under our observation.

1. A poem in praise of the descendants of Ir, son of Milesius, sixty-eight verses, beginning " 2l Choᵱmaic, cᵧṁniᵹ an ċóiᵱ," " O Cormac, remember the right."

2. An Elegy on the supposed death of Teige O'Rody, one hundred and forty verses, beginning " ᵱioᵱċᵧaö ö'eiᵱinö ᴄuᵱuᵧ ᴄhaiöᵹ," " Unfeigned grief to Erin is the journey of Teige."

The subject of this poem:—Teige O'Rody, having left Fiodhnach, in the county of Leitrim, his paternal inheritance, in the year 1689, and removed into the county of Clare with his family, it was generally reported through the lower Conaght and Ulster that he was dead, although he lived for some years afterwards. On hearing this report, Mac an Bhaird wrote the Elegy above mentioned; from the last *rann* but one of which it appears that it was written in the year 1691.

Copies of these poems are in possession of the Assistant Secretary.

A. D. 1696.

CCCXXI. At this time flourished PATRICK OG MAC AN BHAIRD, author of the following poems :

1. A description of Fiodhnagh of Maighrein, in the present county Leitrim, the ancient patrimony of the O'Rodys, and an eulogium on Teige, son of Garrett O'Rody, chief of his tribe, one hundred and thirty-six verses, beginning " 𝔄 ꜰɪꞃ ꜩⱥɪꞃⱦɪⱡ Cɥꞃíꞇ℮ Cɥꞃꞃⱥ," " Oh man, who travelled over the country of Conn," (Ireland).

Copy in the collection of the Assistant Secretary.

2. On Donogh, son of Maolmuire M'Sweeny, one hundred and eighty-six verses, beginning " Cꞃⱥ ꞃⱥꞃⱥ ⱥ ⱥⱥⱦⱡⱥꞇ℮ Eɪꞃ℮ⱥꞃ," " Part of the shares of Erin's trouble."

Copy in the library of John M'Namara, Esq.

CCCXXII. At this time also flourished JOHN BALLAGH O'DUIGENAN, author of an Epistle to Teige O'Rody, twenty-eight verses, beginning " ⱦ℮ⱥꞃⱥⱦ ꞃⱥⱥⱥ ⱥ ꞃꞃꞃ ⱦꞃⱥɪⱦ℮," " Blessing from me from the love of my heart."

Copy in possession of the Assistant Secretary.

A. D. 1700.

CCCXXIII. CONOR O'CORAGAN lived at the commencement of the 18th century. He was author of a vision, in verse, beginning " Ⱦⱥ ⱦɪⱥꞃ ⱥ ꞃℯɪꞃ ⱥ ꞃⱥⱥⱡ ⱥⱥ ⱡℯⱥⱦⱥ," " I was last night sleeping in my bed."

CCCXXIV. At this time also lived the Father THOMAS O'CLERY, Parish Priest of Kill Ann, in the county of Cavan, and author of the two poems following :

1. A recipe for the gout, forty-four verses, beginning " 𝔄ɪꞇꞃℯ ⱥⱥⱥ ⱥⱥ ⱬⱥⱡⱥꞃ," " Thy disease is known to me."

2. An epistle to a friend, beginning " ⱦ℮ɪꞃ ⱥⱥ ⱦℯⱥⱥⱥⱦ ⱬⱥ Ⱦⱥⱥⱥɪꞃ," " Bear my blessing to Thomas."

Copies in possession of the Assistant Secretary.

CCCXXV. THOMAS O'CONUGA also lived at this time. He was author of a short poem in praise of the descendants of Ir, beginning " Ceαrt ꝺealḃa ꝺuꞇraꞓꞇ molꞇa."

Copy in possession of the Assistant Secretary.

CCCXXVI. At this period also flourished JOHN *mór* O'RAGHALLAIGH, or O'REILLY, son of Owen Cláragh O'Reilly, a respectable farmer in the village of Crossarlough, on the borders of Lough Sheelan, in the county of Cavan. This writer was intended for the priesthood; and for the purpose of education was sent, by his parents, to the county of Kerry, where he made great progress in the classics. On his return to the county of Cavan, having given offence to some person, he was waylaid, and attacked by six men, armed with bludgeons, one of whom he killed with a single blow, in his own defence. Though acquitted, by the law of the land, of the crime of murder, he was, by the canon law, disqualified for the priesthood. Unwilling to remain longer on the scene of his misfortune, he returned to Kerry, and there married a young woman of the name of Egan, by whom he had Owen O'Reilly, a celebrated poet, of whom we shall hereafter speak. John mór was the author of several poems, which, but few years ago, were recited by the common people in his native county; and it is said that copies of many of them are to be found in the county of Kerry. We have seen but one poem, the production of this author, in which he regrets his absence from his native soil. It begins " Iꞏ ꝼaꝺa liom naꞓ ꞇꞇéiöim o loꞓ léin ꝟo loꞓ Siꝟlin," " Tedious to me that I go not from Lough Lein to Lough Sheelin."

CCCXXVII. At this time also flourished TEIGE *an Gadhra* MAC EGAN, author of a poem against lying and flattering bards, forty-eight verses, beginning " 2l luꞓꝺ ꞓumuꞏ ḃꞏeuꝟ ꞏan ꝺán," " Oh ye who form lies in verse."

Copy in possession of the Assistant Secretary.

CCCXXVIII. NIALL M'CANNADH, or M'KENNA, a native of the Fews, county of Armagh, a poet and musician, lived at this time. He removed to Mullaghcrew, in the county of Louth, where he is said to have composed some poems and songs, of which we have been favoured with the first lines of a few, by a friend :

1. " ᴍᴏ ᴍile ꞃlán oꞃꞇꞃe ꞃioꞃ a Ƈhꞃᵫꞇa."
2. " Ꝥluaꞃ liom ꝛo beaꞇꞇ, a ꞇéaꝺ-ꝛꞃaꝺ bi ꞇeaꞇꞇ."
3. " Ꝛimiꞃ ꝺeaꞃ ciꞃn, le aꞃ leiꝛiꞃ mo ꞃún."
4. Ni meaꞃamꞃa ꝼéin, na bꝼaꝺ ꞇuꞃa ꝺiol."

He is said to be the author of the songs " Sheela bheag ni Choindbealbh-an, or Little Celia Conlan," and the " Old Triugha." The words of these songs may have been written by him, but the music is certainly of an age long prior to his time.

cccxxix. At this time flourished RANDAL M'DONALD, a poet of the county of Donegal. The following first lines of so many poems written by him were sent to the compiler by his friend, the late Rev. Paul O'Brien, but the subjects on which they were written are not mentioned. They begin

1. " Ꝛ ꞇaoim ꞃiꝛ an ꞇꞃolꞃꞃ, an bꞃollaiꝛ ꝛil iꞃ báine cꞃuꞇ."
2. " Ƈꞃe cꞃꞃꞃle ꝛan ꞇꞃꞃle le ꞃianꞃa ꞃꞃlꞇ."
3. " Ꝺo ꝛaeꞇe aꞇa ꞇáñ aꞃ me ꝼañ le ꝛeuꞃ-ꞇꞃꞃꞃe."
4. " Ꝛ Ƈhoiꞃꞃꝺealbaiꝛ ꞃ Néill, ollam na ꞇꞇeuꝺ."
5. " beiꞃ beañaꞇꞇ ꝛo ꞇaꝼaiꝛ uaim ꞃioꞃ ꝛo ꞇiꞃ Conaill."

A. D. 1701.

cccxxx. PETER, son of Fearfeasa, son of Maoilseaghlainn O'MAOL-CONIARE, lived at this time, an elderly man. He was the poet of the O'Rody's, and author of the following poems :

1. Two hundred and twenty-four verses, beginning " Niamaꝺ na hꞃaiꞃle an eaꝛna," " Wisdom is the beauty of nobility," on the O'Rodys, tracing the ancestors of Teige, son of Garrett O'Rody, up to Ir, son of Milesius. By the concluding verses of this poem it appears that Fion-

guala (Penelope) daughter of Donogh, son of John *riabhach* (swarthy) son of John *geimlioch* (captive) M'Namara, was the wife of Teige O'Rody.

2. Sixty verses, beginning " Irinioc Chrioṛc ra coraib Chaiös," " Armour of Christ protect the feet of Teige," on Teige O'Rody being ill with the gout, in the month of March, 1696.

3. Sixteen verses, beginning " 2l ṁeic Ȝeaṗóib an ȝlóiṗ ȝloin," " Oh son of Garrett, of sincere speech," on Teige O'Rody's withholding his usual new-year's reward from the poet.

4. On the marriage of Calbhach O'Maoileaghlainn with Mary, daughter of Mahon, son of Donogh M'Namara, and niece of Teige O'Rody's wife, seventy-two verses, beginning " 2l nainm Chrioṛc an ceanȝalṛo," " In the name of Christ, this league."

This marriage was celebrated on the 7th of July, 1701, in the house of Teige O'Rody, where the bride was bred up from the eighth year of her age, in 1692, until the day of her marriage.

5. On the miserable state of the ancient Irish nobility, beginning " Cṛraȝ maṗ bo cṗeacab cṗíoc Chṝṅ," " Alas, that the country of Conn is plundered."

Copies of all these poems are in the collection of the Assistant Secretary.

cccxxxi. The Father Patrick O'Cuirnin also lived at this time. He was author of a poem, consisting of eighty verses, on Teige O'Rody, beginning " Deiṗḃ̄ṛrṗ bo'n ṛaiṛle an eaȝna," " Wisdom is sister to nobility."

Copy with the Assistant Secretary.

The Rev. Doctor O'Conor, in his catalogue of the Irish Manuscripts in the Marquis of Buckingham's library, at Stowe, mentions two other poems by this author, one written in the year 1726, and the other in 1734. We have not seen copies of them.

A. D. 1703.

cccxxxii. At this period flourished William M'Carton, a poet, of Ulster extraction, though said to have been a native of Munster. The

The following lines, furnished by my friend the late Doctor O'Brien, are the first of so many poems, or songs, written by him:

1. " ᴀɴ leoᵹan na Coiᵹe Ulaᵭ,"—(written on 28th April, 1703.)

2. " Ro ſᴄɾiocaᵭ ᵭom pɾimpiᴄ 'ɾᵭo pian mo lam."

3. " ᴀ leaᴃaiɾ ᴃiᵹ ᴄɾa ᵭo ᵭail ᵭam ɾᵹlᴄ aiɾ ꝼianaiᴃ."

4. " Ꟁo Ꝓein mo ᴄuɾꝒein, mo ᴄɾɾᵹe, mo leun, mo ᴄɾeaᴄ."

5. " Ɲioɾ ᴃoiɾᴃe an ꝼɾɾɾioꞆ ɾin a naɾᴄɾᵹiᴃ ᵹɾeiᵹ."

A. D. 1704.

CCCXXXIII. EDMOND O'CASSIDY, a Conaght poet, flourished at this time. He was author of the following poems :

1. Forty-eight verses in praise of Teige O'Rody, beginning " Ca ᵭɾeam iſ ꝼeaɾɾ 'na ſliocᵭ 1ɾ," " What tribe is better than the race of Ir."

2. One hundred and four verses, beginning " Cꝶim comaiɾle le Ꝺia," " I receive counsel from God." The same subject as the foregoing.

3. Twelve verses on the recovery of Elise, the sister of Teige O'Rody, from the small pox, in the month of June, 1704. This small poem begins " Slan ꝼa eiɾᵹe Eliſe," " Hail to thy rising, Elise."

4. One hundred and twenty verses, on the race of Ir, beginning " Ꟁo na mionca ᴄɾiall ᵹo Ꞇaiᵭᵹ," " More than often turn to Teige."

Copies of the above poems are in the collection of the Assistant Secretary.

Doctor O'Conor, in his account of the Stowe manuscripts, mentions another poem by this author, beginning " Ꞇɾom ᴄɾᴃaiᵭe aiɾ ɾiol Ccolla."

CCCXXXIV. At this time also lived JEOFFREY, son of Torlogh O'Rourke, author of four epigrams on Teige O'Rody, and his wife Fionguala, daughter of M'Namara. They begin

1. " ᴀn ᴄɾaoᴃ ᴄɾꝶɾa uaim ᵭo'n ᴄɟaoi, " The fragrant branch from me to the sage."

2. " ᴀn ᴄɾaoᴃ ᵹlaſ ᴄa ᵭiᴃɟi ó ꝼeaɾꝶᴃ ᴄɾic ꝼail," " The green branch is to you from the men of Fail's fair land."

3. " ᴀ ɟaoi le ɾᵹaoilᴄeaɾ ᵹaᴄ noᵭ," " Oh sage, by whom every difficulty is dissolved."

4. " ᴀᴛᴅ ᴘᴏᴍᴀ ᴅᴏ ᴍᴀ ᴍᴍᴀɪᴃ ᴀᴘ ᴛᴇɪᴄ," " This share to the women belongs."

Copies in possession of the Assistant Secretary.

cccxxxv. At this time lived, far advanced in years, TEIGE, or THADY O'RODY, of Crossfield, in the county of Leitrim, Esq. the lineal representative of the O'Rodys, princes of the territory of Fiodhnach Moy Rein. He was an excellent scholar, well skilled in the Greek and Latin languages, and intimately acquainted with the language, history, and antiquities of his native country; although the author of the Curiosities of Literature represents him as one scarcely knowing his own language, and totally ignorant of all others. He was the intimate friend of O'Flaherty, author of the Ogygia; and also the friend and correspondent of Sir Richard Cox, author of the History of Ireland, as appears by a memorandum at the head of one of the volumes of the Seabright collection of Irish MSS. now in the library of Trinity College. He was a great patron of learning and men of science; and to him the poets of his day devoted many of their best compositions, as is fully proved by the works of several of those just now mentioned, and by others whose names are forgotten. We have not met with any of his compositions in Irish, except a poetic Epistle, in reply to that of John Ballagh O'Duigenan, mentioned at page ccii. O'Rody's Epistle consists of fifty-six verses, beginning " ᴃɪᴍ ᴛᴇ ᴍᴇᴀᴄ ᴀ ᴍᴏᴛᴀᴃ ᴘᴇɪᴍ, " Sweet to a man is his own praise."

A fine copy of this poem, as well as some of the Latin poems of this author, are in the collection of the Assistant Secretary.

A. D. 1706.

cccxxxvi. In this year the Rev. Father FRANCIS WALSH, a Franciscan Friar, and Lecturer in Divinity in the College of St. Anthony, at Louvain, wrote an Irish Vocabulary, in which the common words of the Irish language are explained by more ancient and difficult words.

Copy in the collection of the Assistant Secretary.

A. D. 1707.

cccxxxvii. At this time lived the Rev. Father Anthony Cuillean, a Franciscan friar, to whom we are indebted for the two following pieces:

1. An epigram on Father Patrick Darry's refusing entertainment to Father Bon. O'Cuillean, Provincial of the Order of St. Francis. This begins " Riñir aɡur ni ðeaᵱnair," " You have done, and you have not done."

2. On the death of Hugh M'Dermott, who died at Shrule, in 1707, twenty verses, beginning " Níoᵱ baicᵱe 'na beaᵹa ðom Aeóɤa acð clú," " There was not known, in his life of my Hugh, but report."

Copies in possession of the Assistant Secretary.

A. D. 1708.

cccxxxviii. At this time, and for some years after, lived the Rev. Father Paul M'Aodhagan, or M'Egan, a Franciscan Friar. In the general persecution of the priests in the year 1708, he was confined in the Black-dog prison, at Corn-market, near Newgate. He was author of the following poems:

1. Forty verses, beginning " leaɡað leoin ó'ᵱ ðeacaiᵱ eiᵱɡe," " Afflictions came, from which 'tis hard to rise," on the losses sustained by the Irish in their adherence to king Charles and king James II.

2. Forty-four verses, in answer to the poem of John O'Neaghtan, or O'Norton, No. 4, page ccxiii. In this poem he desires his friend to repent of his faults, and amend. It was written on the twenty-sixth of February, 1708, and begins " Cᵱeall ðon cᵱñ̃e ma ᵹiɡ hañɤacð," " The space is short in which the world delights."

3. A vision, twenty-eight verses, beginning " Aiᵱlinɡ beaɡ aiᵱ Eiᵱe ðo conðaiᵱc me ɡan ɡo," " A small vision on Erin I beheld without a lie."

4. The moans of Paul M'Egan, fifty-two verses, beginning " Ðuᵱᵱain ðᵱñ̃ ɡac lá ꝗ ᵱɡañᵱað," " Woful to us each day's dispersion," on the miserable state of the Irish, both clergy and laity.

5. Verses on the author's want of snuff, from his prison to his friend William Taaffe, beginning " O cpíochaó ɣan ɾnaoiɾ-ɾmn̄c, ɣan cɾoñaɾ, ɣan cɾēan," " From the end without snuff, without pleasure or happiness."

6. An epigram on a person of the name of John Kelly, who had renounced the Roman Catholic religion, and drew his sword on the author. This composition begins " Maɾ aɾ clouóiom aicniɣeaɾ cɾeuóiom," " If by a sword the faith is known."

Copies of all these, and some letters of this author, in Irish, are in possession of the Assistant Secretary.

A. D. 1710.

cccxxxix. Cathal O'Heislionan lived at this period. He was author of the following poems :

1. Twenty-four verses, addressed to Torlogh O'Donell, on his coming to Dublin, beginning " ɾáilce ön̄c ɣo hƩlca-cliac," " Welcome to thee to Dublin."

2. Forty-four verses on the recovery of the Duke of Berwick from a fit of sickness, beginning " Ʃóƀaɾ ɣáine ó'Ini ɾáil," " Cause of joy to Inis-fail (Ireland)."

Copies in possession of the Assistant Secretary.

cccxl. At this time also lived the Rev. Philip Brady, known by the names of Parson Brady, and *Philip Ministeir*, a clergyman of the county of Cavan. He was a man of great wit, a good scholar, and particularly well versed in the language of his country. Many of his epigrams and witty sayings, and some short poems of his composition, are recited by the common people in the counties of Meath and Cavan, which it is to be wished some competent persons would commit to writing. He translated into Irish some of those Sermons which were published by Richardson in 1711.

Copies of some short poems of his writing, particularly one addressed to Torlogh O'Carolan, are in the collection of the Assistant Secretary.

A. D. 1712.

cccxli. Fiachra M‘Brady, a witty school-master, of Stradone, in the county of Cavan, and a tolerably good poet, lived in this year, as appears by some of his poems.

He was author of the following pieces:

1. A humorous poetical description of his travels, beginning " Nač τρυαᵹ liḃγe ċáιηδē, ᵹaċ buaιηeaδ δa δτáρlaιδ," " Do you not grieve, my friends, for the troubles that befel."

2. A vision, beginning " Choñaιηc me aιγlιnᵹ aιη mo leaba maη δo ċιfιñ bean," " I saw a vision on my bed, as if I saw a woman."

The first of these poems was published in the Anthologia Hibernica for October 1793, and in the same Magazine for December 1793, was published a translation of it into English, in the same measure as the original. In the same month was published number 2, with a promise of a translation, but it was never published.

3. A confession of his faults, beginning " Ḡniδιm διómuγ, bγιγιm γaoιηe διa δoṁnaιᵹ," " I indulge in pride, I break the holidays and Sabbath."

Copies of these, as well as some smaller poems and songs by the same author, are in the collection of the Assistant Secretary.

Three more poems by M‘Brady were in possession of the late Doctor O'Brien, the first lines of which he communicated to the compiler, but did not mention the subjects on which they were written :

1. " Imċιan fáιlτe όᵹτ mo δáιl."
2. " Iγ fιoγáċ δo ċηιoċaιḃ foḃla."
3. " Iγ τηιaṁγηeaċ γιñe an δηeιm na nδηeaγ."

cccxlii. Aodh, or Hugh Mac Gowran, of Glengoole, in the county of Leitrim, author of the *Plearaca na Ruarcach*, or Revelry of O'Rourke, flourished at this period. Dean Swift published a verse translation of this poem from a literal translation into English, made purposely for him. A fuller, and better translation into English verse, from the original, was published in Dublin, about thirty years ago, by a neglected genius of the name of Wilson. This poem begins " Pleaηáca na

Rrapcaċ a ccᵑmne ᵑle óᵑne," "The revel-rout of the O'Rourks is in the memory of all men."

Copies are common in the hands of every Irish scholar.

He also wrote a poem on losing his horse at a time that he went into the county of Roscommon, to woo the daughter of O'Duigenan. This poem consists of twenty-four verses, beginning " *ᴀ ᵹheaᵱᵱám leᵢᵱ ċaill-eaᵧ mo ᵱeaᵱc,*" "Oh *Garran*, by whom I have lost my love."

Copy in the collection of the Assistant Secretary.

cccxliii. James M'Cuairt, or Courtney, commonly called Dall M'Cuairt, a native of Criamhthan, in the county of Louth, flourished at this time. He was author of the following songs and poems :

1. On Brian O'Byrne's horse, Punch, beginning " *b'ᵱeaᵱᵱ liom ᵹeaᵱᵱán bhᵱiaın ᵑ bhᵱoiñ,*" "I wish I had Brian O'Byrne's horse."

2. Two hundred and ten verses on the battle of Aughrim, and the death of Somhairle M'Donald, beginning " *San Eaċóᵱᵑm an äiᵱ aᴄäıɓ na comñaıɓ,*" "In Aughrim of Slaughter, there are found."

3. On a great match of foot-ball played at Slane, on the banks of the Boyne, between the young men of the counties of Meath and Louth, eighty-eight verses, beginning " *ba haıᵹeanᴄa cᵱoıɓeamuil mo macnaıᵹᵢ anioᵧ,*" "High-spirited, courageous, were my friends above."

4. On the merits of Christ, and the salvation of man, one hundred verses, beginning " *1ᵧ claoıóᴄe ċuıᵱ ᴀóám ᵱe na clañuıɓ,*" "Adam entailed destruction on his children."

5. On the Blessed Virgin Mary, one hundred and seventy-six verses, beginning " *ᴀ blaɓ na ᵱᵱaᴄᵱıaᵱc 'ᵧa nᴀıᵑᵹeal,*" "Garland of the Patriarchs and the Angels."

6. Addressed to Torlogh O'Carolan, on his return to Meath from Conaght, eighteen verses, beginning " *Ɗá milliuın ɓeaᵹ ᵱáılᴄe óıɓ, ó äᵱuᵧ Ɱeaóba ıᵑᵹean Eaċaċ,*" "Twelve millions of welcomes to you, from the mansion of Meave, daughter of Eochaidh."

7. Twenty verses on the Passion of our Lord Jesus Christ, beginning " *ᴀ óᵑne naċ léıᵱ óᵑᴄ cᵱeaċᴄa cᵱoıɓı ón ɓall,*" "Oh man, who from blindness seest not the wounds of his heart."

8. Fifty-two verses addressed to our Lord Jesus Christ, beginning " *1aᵱᵱaım ɓo beañaċᴄ ᵹan ᵱeıᵱᵹ,*" "I beseech thy blessing without anger."

9. A small poem beginning " ⁿⁿⁿ ⁿⁿⁿ ⁿⁿⁿⁿⁿ ⁿⁿⁿ ⁿⁿⁿ ⁿⁿⁿⁿⁿ," " Every poor sinner without a guide."

10. In praise of Aña ní Ꝯheic an ᵹabán, or Nancy Smith, forty-eight verses, beginning " If mián leamƴa ƈƿáct aiƿ ƴᵹéiṁ na mna," " I desire to treat on the beauty of the woman."

11. A song, beginning " A Cƿƿiaṁƈáñ ƿíoƴ aƈa mo ṁiáñ," " In Creevin below is my desire."

12. A song on Rose O'Reilly, beginning " Sí mo Ꝛóiƴ bhƿéiƿneáƈ ᵈon pƿóƿ Ꝛaᵹallaiᵹ," " She is my Rose of Brefny, of the race of O'Reilly."

The following first lines of so many different poems, or songs, were communicated to the compiler, from memory, by his friend, the late Doctor O'Brien:

13. " Eiᵈiƿ ᵈá ƈiƿ caiłƿeaƿ me ƈoiᵇƈe."

14. " Chaill me lem' iomaiƿce eineáclan mo ƴuaƿcáiƴ."

15. " Ꝯo ᵈá ƿoƴᵹ, mo ᵈá ƿaᵈáƿc, mo ᵈá Ohƿoiceáᵈ aiƿ ᵹaƈ abáiñ."

16. " A Ꝛuᵈƿaiᵹ, naƈ cclƿƞ ƈa an caoƈ."

17. " Ƈa ƴcáƈa ᵈaiƈe, ᵈualáƈ, aiᵹ aƴƈaƿaᵈ leaƈ ᵹo ƿuaƿ-laᵹ."

18. " Cƿaᵈ éiᵹcion ᵹaƈ ƈiƿe, uaiƴle Eiƿioñ aiƿ ᵈibiƿƈ."

19. " Fáilƈe aᵹúƴ ƿiƈƈe ᵈ'ᵈn lanáṁain."

20. " Ꝯo ƈuƿaƴ ᵹo Ƈullaƈ o Ꝯeaƈ."

21. " Naƈ buaƿƈa ƈuaiᵈ mo ƴuáin a ƿéiƿ ᵈoṁ."

22. " Ce naƈ maiƈ iƴ leuƿ ᵈom na leabáiƿ Ꝣaoiᵇilᵹe."

23. " A ƈeaƈƈaiƿe ƈéiᵈ ᵹo ƿeaƿƿan an Ꝯhaiᵹƿe."

24. " Naƿ ƴƈaᵈ na ᵹaƿƈa, no ᵹƿeaᵈaᵈ láṁ."

25. " Fáilƈe ᵈo'n Eun iƴ biñe aiƿ ƈƿaob."

26. " A bóin a biᵈ aiᵹ boᵹa ᵈeaƿᵹ."

27. " Cuƿ cƿƞeaᵈ aiƿ ᵈo ƴluaiᵹƈe."

28. " A ƈuiƿƈ na ƿéile, ca'ƿ ᵹaᵇ m'ƒáilƈe."

29. " Na ƈaᵹaiƿ oƿm a ƿiᵹ na ƿañ."

Copies of the first ten poems are in the collection of the Assistant Secretary. It is much to be regretted that the remainder, and some others that we have seen, are not collected, and deposited in some public library. They are possessed of much poetic merit.

A. D. 1713.

cccxliv. Francis Nugent, a native of Mullingar, in the county of Westmeath, lived at this time. He was author of two short poems addressed to Father Paul M'Egan.

Copies in possession of the Assistant Secretary.

A. D. 1714.

cccxlv. Thomas O'Conduibh, a native of the county Clare, lived at this time. He was author of a poem on the death of Donogh O'Loghlainn, of Burren, who died this year, sixteen verses, beginning " Oιċμα, δeaμ, δoñċaծ ċaoιm, O'loċlaιñ a ccμē μιnτe," " Sorrow, tears, gentle Donogh O'Loghlainn in the clay is stretched."

Copy in possession of the Assistant Secretary.

A. D. 1715.

cccxlvi. John O'Neaghtan, or Norton, lived at this time in the county of Meath, a man much advanced in years. He was author of many original pieces, and translated several others from the Latin language into Irish. Amongst his works are to be found the following :

1. A poem of forty verses, beginning " 2lᶠ τμom δo ċoծla ᏯᎠhᖟμe móιμ." " Heavy is thy sleep, Oh glorious Mary." By a memorandum prefixed to this, it was written shortly after the battle of the Boyne, when the author was deprived of all his property by the English soldiers, except one small Irish book, which they left with him, because they could not read it.

2. Sixty-four verses on the imprisonment of the Rev. Doctor Patrick O'Donelly, a Roman Catholic Bishop, beginning " Olc an μᴣeul δo μᴣaoιl a ñē," " Bad is the story reported yesterday."

3. " Forty-four verses, on the imprisonment of Father Paul M'Egan, and five other priests, beginning " Ɑ ꝼeɑɲc ιꝼ ɑᵐɲɑċꞇ ᵹɑċ ɲɑoιꞇ," " Oh love and delight of every sage."

4. " Forty-eight verses, beginning " Ƈʜuᵹɑꝼ oɲꞇ m'ɲꞁe ɑᵐɲɑċꞇ," " I gave you all my love," on the affection he had for Father Paul M'Egan, to whom he here confesses his faults. This was written in February 1708.

5. Forty verses, on forgetting his gloves in the Dominican chapel of Cook-street, Dublin, beginning " Ɑ ċꞁɑɲ ɲιn ꝼɲɑιꝺ nɑ ᵹcocɑιɲιᵹ," " Oh ye Priests of Cook-street."

6. Sixteen verses, lamenting the expulsion of Father Paul M'Egan from the Chapel of Thomas-street to Kilmainham, beginning " Ƈɑ nɑ ꝺɲꞁe ɑιᵹ ꝼeɑɲɑꝺ ꝺιꞁιoᵐ," " The elements are pouring a flood."

7. Verses in reply to Father Paul M'Egan's verses, No. 5, page ccix, beginning " Ɑn Ꝑóꞁ bɑ ꝼιne nɑ ꝼιḃꞃe, ιꝼ bɑ ceɑᵐ ꝺo ċꞁéιɲ," " The Paul that was elder than thou art, and was head over clergy."

8. On the pride and ostentation of the English, and the weakness and dejection of the Irish, forty-four verses, beginning, " Ɑn ċɲíoċ ꝼo buꝺ nɑoᵐꞇɑ ιꝼ bɲꝺ ꝼéιꞁe cáιꞁ," " This country that was so holy and so generous."

9. Against some of the clergy who had gone to Mullingar to take the oath of abjuration, forty-eight verses, beginning " Ꝺá ꝼeɑɲ ꝺēɑᵹ ιꝼ pιobɑιɲe," " Twelve men and a piper."

10. On the generosity of Father Paul M'Egan, sixteen verses, beginning " Ɑn Cáιɲneɑċ ꝺo bɲoᵐ ιonɑɲ," " The priest who gave his coat."

11. On the clergy that were imprisoned for their religion in the Black-dog, forty-eight verses, beginning " Ƈɑbɑιɲ mo beɑᵐɑċꞇ ɑ ṗáιɲéιɲ," " Bear my blessing, oh paper."

12. On the vanity of the world, seventy-two verses, beginning " bɑoꝼ ιꝼ ꞁéιᵐe ιꝼ ɲɲeɑꝼbɑιꝺ céιꞁꞁe," " Folly, simplicity, and want of sense."

13. On the diversity of tastes and opinions, thirty-six verses, beginning " Ƈɑ Cɲɑċ 'neιꝼꞇeɑċꞇ Ɑꝼɑιꞁ," " The Cuckoo listens to an ass."

14. Sixteen verses, in answer to Father Paul M'Egan, beginning " Ɑn moꞁɑꝺ ɲɑιꞇ ꝺo ꝼɲɑɲɑꝼ," " The praise which I received from thee."

15. On the sea-fight between the English and French, and the ship-wreck of the English Admiral, Sir Cloudesly Shovel, after the engagement, seventy-two verses, beginning "Ɗo ḃⱤⰟ₣ moⱤꞏᴄḃⰟⰰꞇ mo SlⱤⰰⱪⰰⱮᴅ."

16. One hundred and thirty-six verses, written during the author's courtship with Una, or Winifred O'Brian, (to whom he was afterwards married), inviting her to a walk to hear the chorus of the birds. This poem begins "Ⱁⰰċ₣Ⱬⰻ̃ ₣ⰰⱀ ccoⰻⱡⱡ leⰰꞇ," "I would go to the woods with thee."

17. Twenty-four verses, written after the death of Una O'Brian, beginning "Ⱅⱨⱶⱬ me ⱳeⰰⱤc mo ċⱡeⰻꞵ 'ⱳmo ⱬⱤⰰꞵ," "I gave the love and affection of my heart."

18. On the death of Catherine Cruise, wife of Teige O'Naghten, and mother to Father Peter O'Naghten, of the Society of Jesus, twenty verses, beginning "CⰰⰻꞇⱤⰻⱀⰰ ⱀⰻ CeoⰻⱤⰻⱳ ⰰⱀ óⰻⰷꞵeⰰⱀ ꞵuⱳ áⰻⱡⱡe," "Catherine Cruise, the young woman who was beautiful."

19. On the banishment of the clergy, forty-eight verses, beginning "Ɱo ꞵⰻċⱳⰻ ⰷo ⱀeuⰷⰰꞵ, mo leuⱀ ⰻⱳ mo ċⱤⰰꞵ," "My deadly loss, my woe, my affliction."

20. On the death of Mary, queen of James the Second, fifty-two verses, beginning "₣ⰰċ éⰰⰷⱀⰰċ mo ꞵeoⱤ ꞵⱤáⰷ ⰷⰰoꞵⱡⰰⰻꞵ ₣ⰰ ꞵⱤóⱀ," "The grievous cause of my tears has left the Irish under affliction."

21. A song, consisting of three *ranns*, or stanzas, of eight lines each, beginning "Slárⱀ ⰷⰰ mⰰⱤꞇⰰⱀⰰċ, ⱡárⱀ ꞵo ċⰰⱤⱤꞇⰰⱀⰰċꞵ," "Lasting health, full of charity."

22. On the accession of King George the First, sixty-eight verses, beginning "Ⱬⱀ ₣eⰰꞵ ⱀⰰ ⱨ℈oⱤⱤⰰ ₣áⱡꞇeⰻċ."

23. Thirty-six verses, addressed to Ireland, beginning "ⱮóⱤ ꞵo ċⱤⰻⱤ ⰻⱳ ꞵo ċáⰻⱀ," "Great is your fatigue and your amercement."

24. Instructions to his nephew Aodh, or Hugh O'Neaghtan, twelve verses, beginning "SⰰoⰻⱡꞇeⰰⱤ ⱡⰻ͂e ⰷuⱤ mⰻⱤe ⰷⰰⱀ ⰰⰻⱤꞵ ⰻ ⰰⱀ póⰻꞇ," "It is considered by us that drunkenness is madness without pleasure."

25. Epistle to a friend in Dublin, forty-four verses, beginning "Ɱo ꞵeⰰ͂ⰰċꞇ leⰰꞇ ⰰ ⱣáⰻⱣeⰻⱤ," "My blessing with thee, oh paper."

26. On the upstart race that had gotten possession of the estates and properties of the ancient inhabitants of the country, one hundred and

fifty-six verses, beginning " ᾰη cᵹ̄péıɲ ɤeαη 'ɤα cᾰıllıuɲ," " The old cooper and the tailor."

27. Answer to father Paul Mac Egan, sixteen verses, beginning " ᾰη beαñαċc ɤ αıc ɲo ꜰɤαɲαɤ," " The salutation that I received from thee."

28. On the Duke of Berwick, forty verses, beginning " bɲαc buαóα ɲα ᵹcαċ," " Victorious hand of the battles."

29. A poem in imitation of those attributed to Ossian, twelve hundred and ninety-six verses, beginning " Sᵹó ꜰɲᵹ̄m ɤıoɤ α Phᾰoɲᵹᵹ," " Sit with me, Oh Patrick."

30. Aingliota's address to Goll Mac Morna, twenty-eight verses, beginning " Ƶoıll moɲóαlαċ ɲα mboɲb mbeαɲc," " Triumphant Goll, of mighty deeds."

31. Another address to Goll, by Aingliota, sixty-four verses, beginning " Cıα cαɤᵹαɲ αη ceαñ, " Who wounds the head."

32. A poem, beginning " 1ꜰ cūmαᵹ̄ lıom ımċeαċc cɲᵹeαɲ," " Grievous to me, is the departure of the five."

33. A poem, beginning " Óαoñαċó, Cɲıoñαċc, Cɲᾰóbα," " Humanity, Prudence, Devotion."

34. Forty-four verses, beginning " So óıb ꜰlᾰıηce Ⲙhαᵹαıó lᾰıóıɲ," " Here's to the health of powerful Moggy."

35. A poem, beginning " Cuɤα ᵹıollα ɲα meıɤᵹe," " Thou servant of drunkenness."

36. A poem, beginning " ᾰη ꜰoıɤeoᵹ bɲóeαċ ᵹo cⓜ̄ce," " The grateful lark certainly."

37. On seeing his wife, Una or Winifred O'Brian, in a dream, after her death, one hundred and eight verses, beginning " Ƶluαıɤ α būıɤ cɲαċ 'ɤbeıɲ me leαċ," " Come soon, oh death, and take me with you."

38. Aingliotta to Iollan, " O ıollαıη móıɲ ɲα ꜰꜰeαɲc."

39. Three hundred and forty-four verses, beginning " Óo bı Luóαɲcɲoⓜ̄ mαc Lobɤɤ," " There was Ludarcroinn M'Lobe."

40. Forty-eight verses, beginning " ᾰ Luɤıηα, mıle mαllαċc oɲc," " Oh Lucina, a thousand curses on you !"

41. The thanksgiving of the people of Tom M'Lobe, thirty verses, beginning " bɲóeαċαɤ leıɤ αη m̄αcαıɲ," " Thanks to the mother."

42. Ninety-six verses on the lamentable state of the ancient Irish,

beginning "A ḟaiṫle Eiriоn ṫearc mo ċum," "Oh nobles of Erin, love of my heart."

43. A Fenian Tale in prose, written in the year 1717, beginning "Do ḃi Fionn calmṫreaṫaċ," "Fionn of mighty valour was."

44. History of Edmond O'Clery, a fictitious story, written, it would appear, for the purpose of turning into ridicule persons learning the English language. This tale abounds with genuine humour.

Copy in possession of the Assistant Secretary.

This author also translated many of the Church Hymns, from the Breviary, into Irish verse.

Copies of the poems from No. 8, to No. 28, inclusive, are in the library of William Monck Mason, Esq. Copies of most of those, and of all the rest, are in the collection of the Assistant Secretary.

CCCXLVII. THOMAS O'CLERY, a poet of the county of Cavan, lived at this time. We do not know but he may be the same as Rev. Father Thomas O'Clery, of whom we gave some account under the year 1700. He was author of the following poems:

1. An elegy on the death of Aodh, or Hugh, son of John O'Reilly, forty verses, beginning "Do ċaill an Chaban a blaṫ," "Cavan has lost her blossom."

2. Twenty verses, on Rory M'Mahon, chief of Oirgialla, being routed by an old woman of the name of O'Reilly, armed with a distaff. This poem begins "Lá da raiḃ Rúḋraiġ aig toruiġeaċt creaċ," "On a day that Rory was in pursuit of prey."

Copies in possession of the Assistant Secretary.

A. D. 1720.

CCCXLVIII. At this time flourished the Rev. OWEN O'KEEFFE, a native of the county of Cork, who, before he was ordained a priest, presided for some years at the Bardic assemblies held annually at Charleville, in that county. He was author of the following poems, and some others, to which we cannot now refer:

1. Fifty-six verses on the death of his son Arthur, who, like himself, was in holy Orders. This elegy begins "An tán nach faicim fear," "When I do not see a man."

2. On a visit to a friend at Rathkeale, beginning Triallaim son go Rath Chathail," "I proceed to Rathkeale."

Copies in the library of John M'Namara, Esq.

3. On the battle of Aughrim, beginning "Air ttreasgaradh a nEachdhruim do shíol Eibhir," "On the destruction in Aughrim of Heber's race."

4. A poem, beginning "Mo bhrón, mo mhilleadh, m'ainéis, mo leún go buan," "My grief, my destruction, my sorrow, my lasting distress."

Copies of these two latter poems were in the library of the late Rev. Paul O'Brien.

CCCXLIX. WILLIAM O'BRIEN, Great-grand-father to the late Rev. Paul O'Brien, Irish Professor in the College of Maynooth, lived at this time. He was a native of the county of Clare, but having married the sister of Betagh of Moynalty, in the county of Meath, he settled in that county. He was author of the following poems:

1. On the going of his brothers-in-law, John and William Betagh, to France, in the year 1720, beginning "A Bhiadhtaig an tréin is na ndeighmhic ríg go mór."

2. On the same subject, beginning "Crapaim lá léin ort Eire mhealltaig."

3. On his wife, the daughter of Betagh, beginning "An ioctar tire ata si, an ingin is áille snuadh."

4. On the death of his wife, beginning "Is agam a bhídh an spéir bean bo deise fá'n an ngréin.

CCCL. JAMES *ban* M'NAMARA, the near relation of the last-mentioned writer, accompanied him from Munster, and settled with him in the county of Meath. On the departure of their friends, the Betaghs, from Ireland, M'Namara wrote two poems, of which we here give the first lines:—

1. "Creach mo chroidhe síol-chlann Eibhir."

2. "D'imthig ar nuaisle, mo nuair, tar bóchna."

Copies of the poems of these two writers were in the library of Rev. Paul O'Brien.

A. D. 1721.

CCCLI. JOHN, son of Philip O'FEARGHAOILE, or O'FARRELLY of Mullagh, in the county of Cavan, lived at this time. He was author of a valuable work called "Seancaſ an ꝺã bhꞃeıꝼne," or "History of the two Brefnys," which his wife, in a fit of jealousy, committed to the flames; part of it, however, was saved, and is still extant. He also wrote some poems, of which we here give the first lines:

1. On his wife burning his book, beginning "Ɑ leabaıꞃ na ꞃeuꝺ ꞃeunmaꞃ."

2. On jealousy, "Nı cöölãñ an coꞃ-ʒꞃıan, ꝺ'euʒmuſ a cëıꝺ 'eın cumaın."

3. Beginning "Nı ꞃaıb abal aıꞃ ʒeuʒ no ſmeuꞃ aıꞃ blaꝺ na nꝺꞃëaſ."

4. Beginning "Ca cöıꞃ-ꝺlaoʒ caſ ſıoꞃ-ꝺeaſ nac áıle an ʒꞃıan."

5. Begins "Ɑ ꞃıʒ na cꞃꞃñe, an cum ꞃꞃñe ꝺo laʒ-claonaꝺ."

A. D. 1722.

CCCLII. JOHN O'NEILL lived at this period. He was a native of Tullagh-O-Meath, near Carlingford, and author of some poems said to possess much merit. I have been favoured by my friend, Doctor O'Brien, with the first lines of three of them, which he could repeat from memory:

1. "Cꞃeꝺ é ꝺo cuman ban ſꞃóıl."

2. "Ca ſaoıce ſleıbce Cacaıꞃ lın gan aoıbneaſ ʒan ʒáıꞃe."

3. "Ɑ Chullaıʒ ı Mheac, caꝺ é an ʒꞃaımſe oꞃc."

A. D. 1725.

CCCLIII. BRIAN *duff*, son of Turlogh, son of John O'REILLY, a native of Stradone, in the county of Cavan, flourished at this period. He was author of the following productions:

1. A romantic tale, in verse and prose, called " Eαċτρα ṁeιċ na míoċoṁ-ṁαιρle, "Adventures of the son of Bad-counsel."

There is a copy of this Tale in the library of Trinity College, class E. No. 4; another in the library of John M'Namara, Esq.; and another in the collection of the Assistant Secretary.

2. A vision, ninety-six verses, beginning " Ðo bíóς lá αιρ maιðṁ go ðeaċρaċ ðeuρaċ," " I was one day, in the morning, severely afflicted."

A friend of the compiler's has furnished him with the first lines of two other poems:

3. Ɑ luaċ αιρgιð ċoρóṁ Ɑlban agaς a ċρaob na ρub."

4. Ɑ ċuρaιð na ρuaιg, beιρ buað gaċ báιρe."

Copy of No. 2 is in the collection of the Assistant Secretary.

A. D. 1726.

cccliv. A poet and musician called Colla mac Shean, or Johnson, a native of Mourne, in the county of Downe, flourished at this time. The late Rev. Paul O'Brien, who was a living magazine of the poetry and language of his country, furnished the compiler with the first lines of six poems composed by this author:

1. " Ɑιρ ςlιab an Ɑoιbneaς τa mo ṁιaṅρa."

2. " Ɯo nraιρςe na cιn a ςραρað gan ċιoṁ."

3. " Ɑιg ðul go baιle-áτa-clιaċ ðaṁ."

4. " Ɯa ċeιð τu a ðeaρcaṁτ ςcéιṁe."

5. " Ɑ nðún a ċoις Coιlle aιg ιmeall na Cρáιge."

He is also said to be the author of the song called " *Moll dubh an gleanna.*"

ccclv. Owen O'Raghallaigh, or O'Reilly, son of John *mór* O'Reilly, of whom we gave some account under the year 1700, flourished also at this period. He was an opulent man, much celebrated for his wit and talents, and resided at Sliabh Luachra, in the county of Kerry. He is said to have written many poems, copies of which are numerous all through the province of Munster, though but few of them have come under our observation. The following are all that we can at present refer to:

1. A reverie, or vision, beginning " Ꝃile na ꝣile ꝺo conꝺaipc aip fliꝣe, a nuaiꝣneaf."

2. Thirty-two verses, beginning " Ciꝺc ꝣꝗpc if cpeiꝣiꝺ if piꝺnꝣoin ꝣan leiꝣiof."

3. A translation from the Latin of Donat, Bishop of Fesuli's description of Ireland, sixteen verses, beginning " mif fa peim a ccein fan iapcap ca."

Copies of the above poems are in the possession of the Assistant Secretary, as also an imperfect copy of a description of a shipwreck, which this author was witness to on the coast of Kerry. This poem has much merit; we give one *rann* as a specimen of the rest:

> " ꝺoꝺ eaꝣnac impc na cple pe ꝺaop-puacap,
> " mꝺaꝺ na coine pe fꝗpneaꝺ na ꝣaoc ꝣuaipnein,
> " Caoꝺ na loinꝣe 'fa fꝗfion aip cpeun-luapꝣaꝺ,
> " 2iꝣ eiꝣeaꝺ cꝗcim ꝣo ꝣpiniol ꝣan ꝺail fuapcailc."

The following translation may serve to give some faint idea of the beauty of those lines:

> " The roaring flood resistless force display'd,
> " Each whirling blast the swelling surges sway'd;
> " The vessel burst! alas! the crew she bore,
> " Scream'd in the deep, and sunk to rise no more!"

CCCLVI. At this period also flourished PHILIP O'REILLY, a poetic genius of the county of Cavan. He was author of a poem, consisting of ninety-six verses, in praise of Miss Peggy Deane, a young lady of Galway. This poem has a good deal of merit. It begins " la ꝺ'apabaf a ccacaip na Ꝣailꝺe," " One day that I was in the city of Galway."

A. D. 1730.

CCCLVII. At this time lived Brian *rabhagh* O'Clery, a native of Moy-bologue, in the county of Cavan.

Rev. Doctor O'Brien supplied the compiler with the first lines of two poems composed by this author.

1. " Τα δο βραιξε ξεαl ξαn αιδβειl."
2. " 2l cómαρρα δεαnαιδ δειρc."

A. D. 1734.

CCCLVIII. Patrick Lindon, of the Fews, county Armagh, lived at this period. He was author of several songs that are much admired. Like most of the poets of his day, the principal part of his compositions depend only on memory for their preservation. It is much to be regretted that they are not committed to writing, whilst they are yet to be had. The following are the first lines of so many songs of this bard's, which are all that we can now recollect:—

1. " Moιδιm ρεαρδα όn άmρο ξο hάιmριρ δα ττιρcαιδ αn βάρ."
2. " Nα lειξ δο ρύn le Δαοιδ."
3. " Nαc άιτ α nόρ-mεαnξ α ξlαc ρύδ Ρόιρ nιc α βhαιρδ αñ α ceαñ."
4. " Inξεαn δεαρ nα mbán-cιαc ιρ αιlne ιοnα lιξε βρραcτ."
5. " Olραδρα ρlάιmτε α βραιξε ιρ ξlειξle cρυτ."
6. " Τρε cρρle ξαn τυρρle le ριαnρα ρρlτ."

A. D. 1736.

CCCLIX. Feardorcha O'Farrely, of Mullagh, county of Cavan, flourished at this time. He was author of several poems and songs, of which we are now able to collect no more than the four, of which the following are the first lines :

1. " Sirbail me crōg coige na póola, ir an Mhiōe gan clár."
2. " Cáil ōo mo meanbull nac mē biō man Cheanball."
3. " Bhiō mē lá ōear ēigin ain malaiō aoibin Alonaig."
4. " Bein beañać raim ríor go baile na ccraob."

<hr>

A. D. 1738.

CCCLX. TORLOGH, or TERENCE O'CAROLAN, a celebrated poet and musician, died on Saturday, the 25th of March, in this year. Some accounts of the life of this bard have been published, by different authors, but all are erroneous, so far as relates to the place of his nativity, and some circumstances belonging to the early part of his life. The biographers of O'Carolan say, " He was born in the village of Nobber, in the county of " *West* Meath, on the lands of Carlanstown, which were wrested from " his ancestors, by the family of the Nugents, on their arrival in this " kingdom, in the reign of Henry II."——" He must be deprived of " sight at a very early period of his life, for he remembered no im- " pression of colours." In these two short extracts there are nearly as many falsehoods as lines ; and yet these errors have been repeated in a History of " Irish Worthies" lately published in London. This is inexcusable in an editor who had the means of obtaining better information. It would be a deviation from the plan hitherto pursued in this work, to give a circumstantial account of the life of any writer mentioned in it, but as the name of O'Carolan is known all over Europe, as a musician, it must be gratifying to his numerous admirers to know the real place of his nativity, &c. This the writer of this work is enabled to do, from his own knowledge of the spot on which the bard was born, and from the communications of his friend, the late Rev. Paul O'Brien, the great-grand-nephew of O'Carolan.

Torlogh O'Carolan, then, was not born in Nobber, nor is Nobber on the lands of Carlonstown ; nor is Carlonstown in the county of *West*meath ; neither did the Nugents ever wrest those lands from the ancestors of O'Carolan; nor was he deprived of sight so early in life as to have no recollection of colours. Nobber is a small town in the county of *East-meath*, on the estate of Lord Gormanstown, and near nine miles from Carlanstown, a village in the same county, on the estate of Sir Henry Meredyth, two miles from Kells, and distant at least ten or twelve miles from the nearest part of the county of Westmeath. Having shewn where our bard was not born, let us proceed to facts, and show where he really was born.

TORLOGH O'CAROLAN, the son of John O'Carolan, an industrious farmer, was born in the year 1670, in the small village of *baile nuaḋ*, or Newtown, in the parish of Kilmainham Wood, three miles and a half from Nobber, and seven miles from Carlanstown. At a proper age he was sent to school to Cruisetown, a village in his own neighbourhood, and not in the county of Longford, as erroneously asserted by some of his biographers. Here he formed an early acquaintance with Miss Bridget Cruise, of the respectable family of that name, from whom the village and the adjoining townland are called; and here commenced that tender attachment which he afterwards manifested to her in the first, and some others of his poetical and musical compositions. On entering the fifteenth year of his age he was seized by the small-pox, in which it was the will of Providence that he should lose his sight. Hence it is evident that he could not be ignorant of the difference in colours, and that he might have formed tolerable ideas of beauty, which afterwards served him in his description of those persons that he celebrated in his verses.

The musical compositions of O'Carolan are numerous, and his poetic pieces were not much less so. Of the first, no complete collection has been yet published, and but few of the latter have been committed to writing. Not above forty years ago, hundreds of persons were to be found in the lower part of the county of Meath, and in other places, who could sing, or repeat from memory, innumerable songs composed by O'Carolan; but that generation is gone, and the poetry of O'Carolan is forgotten. The following imperfect catalogue gives the first lines of all his poems that we have seen written, or can now recollect.

1. On Miss Bridget Cruise, beginning " Ⱥ ḃⱃiᵹiᵭ ḃeuⱃaċ iſ oⱃꞇ mo ḃeuⱃⱃa," Oh well-taught Bridget, to you my verse belongs."

2. On Bridget Cruise, "Ta na céaba feap gaṡoa," "There are a hundred brave men."

3. On Cathaoir M'Cabe, beginning "Naṫ oo ceiroe féin oṗc," "The reward of your own art on you."

4. A song, beginning "Iṡ brapʄta le ṡeal, ta an taob ṡo o'an talaṁ," "There is trouble for a while on this side of the earth."

5. On Grace Nugent, "Iṡ miañ liom tpáéṫ aip blaṡ na ḟiñe," "I wish to treat on the blossom of whiteness."

6. On Mrs. Nugent, "Tpa teíʄim féin ṡiap go hlaipimṡe an ṡeal ṡo," "When I go to westward to Westmeath at this time."

7. On Con O'Neill, "Go bpuaċ loċ neaċaċ a ġlraiṡ me apéip," "To the verge of Lough Neagh as I wandered last night."

8. His receipt, "Maṡ tiñ no ṡlán oo táplaiṡ me," "If sickness or health happen to me."

9. Epigram, "Mo ċpeaċ a Dhiapmṫṡo ṫ ḟhloiñ," "My sorrow, oh Dermod O'Flinn."

10. On the supposed death of Cathaoir M'Cabe, "Iṡ tpráġ ṡin miṡe, aġaṡ me a ttṫḟpeaċ a nṫëiġ mo ċṫil," "I am miserable, and in grief, after my friend."

11. On Mr. O'Conor, of Belanagare, "Go maṡ ṡlán beo bliaṡnaċ."

12. On Mrs. O'Conor, of Belanagare, "Iṡ miañ liom tpáéṫ an raipṡe," "I desire to treat at this time."

13. On the death of his wife, Mary Maguire, "Iñcleaċt na heipeañ na Ʒpëiʒe 'ṫna Róma," "The intellect of Erin, of Greece, and of Rome."

14. On O'Conor Faly, "Ua Conċobaip mile ṡlán leat," "O'Conor, a thousand healths to you."

15. On the marriage of Conor O'Reilly with the daughter of O'More, beginning "Súo ı ḟéipin oeaġṁna aille," "There is a gift for thee, Oh good and beauteous fair."

16. On Colonel Irvin, "Naċa me aip craipt gan ṡpáṡ," "I will go visit without delay."

17. On Mrs. Cole, "Iṡ raoiteamṫil 'ṡaṡ ṡaiṁ i," "She is generous and courteous."

18. On Miss Mac-Neill, "Mo ċuaipt go baile ı Sʒanláin," "My visit to Ballyscanlan."

19. On Catherine Oulaghan, "La léin ortí nac éadtrom a siublañ sí."

20. On himself, "Ní ḟfuil mo ṡaṁail do ṡiol Eaba," "There is not my like of the race of Eve."

21. On O'Reilly of Oristown, "Tóigtear mo seolta agas ġleustar mo ċoṁdálta liom."

22. On Philip M'Brady, "Fáilte ċugad añ mo ḋáil," "You are welcome to me."

23. On Mrs. French, "Is miañ leam labairt air óg mnaoi," "I wish to speak on a young woman."

24. On Mable Kelly, "Ce b'é a bfuil se a ngár do," "Whoever he be that is near thee."

The songs of *Plearaca na Ruarcach* and *Tigherna Mhuigheo* are also ascribed to Carolan, but, we believe, improperly.

A. D. 1739.

CCCLXI. **Cathaoir M'Cabe**, a native of the county of Cavan, and a poet, the intimate friend and companion of O'Carolan, survived him for some time. He is said to have written several poems and songs, of which we know no more at present than the two following:

1. A reply to Torlogh O'Carolan, who had composed some ludicrous verses on him, beginning "Ní'l ó Gailbe fear dá ċapull go Dún Pháduaic," "There is not a man worth two horses from Galway to Downpatrick."

2. On the death of his friend O'Carolan, in which he particularises the year of his death. These few lines begin "Riñeas smaointe ad ṁeasas nar ċuis náire."

Copies of these poems are in the collection of the Assistant Secretary.

A. D. 1740.

CCCLXII. **Andrew M'Curtin**, a wandering bard of the county of Clare, lived at this time, and conceiving himself neglected by the gentry of the country, he composed a poetic address to Donn of Duagh, or Donn of the Sand Pitts, an imaginary being supposed to preside over the fairies of that part of the country. In this poem the bard begs that Donn will take him into his service, as he is deserted by mortals; and in his praising the hospitality of the Chief of the Fairies, he obliquely censures the parsimony of the gentlemen of the country. It begins " beaṅṙᵹaó óoiṁiṅ öṙꝺ ꝺ Ŏhoṁ ꞃꝺ Ŏꝺ1ƀċe," " Deep salutations to thee, oh Donn of the *Sand-pits*, (literally, of the *Kieves* or Vatts)."

From the merits of this piece, we regret that we are not able to point out where any more of the effusions of its author are now to be found.

Copy in the collection of the Assistant Secretary.

CCCLXIII. At this period also flourished the Right Rev. JAMES GAL-LAGHER, R. C. Bishop, first of Raphoe, and afterwards translated to Kildare. He received a part of his education in Paris, but finished his studies in Rome, where he was a member of the College de Propaganda fide. In the year 1735 he published sixteen sermons in his native language, which he reprinted at this time, with the addition of a seventeenth sermon, " On the Joys of Heaven." These Sermons have gone through eighteen editions; the last of which was corrected, and prepared for press, by the author of this work.

A. D. 1742.

CCCLXIV. TEIGE O'NEAGHTAN, or NORTON, was a schoolmaster in Dublin, and a good Irish scholar. We are indebted to him for the following productions; the most important of which is—

1. An Irish-English Dictionary, which he commenced on the 30th of May, 1734, and finished in the year 1739. This book is now in the library of Trinity College.

2. A collation of the Punic Speech in Plautus, with the Irish. This tract, in the hand-writing of the author, is now in the library of William Monck Mason, Esq. a Member of this Society. It is dated 12th August, 1742, many years before General Vallancey published his

Collation of that Speech, which first procured for him the reputation of an Irish scholar.

3. A poem, consisting of twenty-four verses, beginning "Oubaıⁿc cⁿıocaı̇ne aıʒ a ṗaıb maoın," "Said a miser who had riches," on an old miser who gave a hen to a boy to carry to his house, instead of which the boy took it to his tomb.

4. Thirty-two verses, by way of prophecy, beginning " Roıṁ an Noȯlⁿc a n'eⁱⱼⁱⁿ áⁱn," " Before the Christmas in noble Erin."

5. Forty-four verses, on Betty Meares, beginning " Ca ̇oeⁱⱼeaċċ ⱼoⁱll-ⱼıʒeaⱼ ⱼe ʒⁿēⁱn," " What beauty is illumined by the sun."

6. Seventy-six verses, on the great frost, which commenced on Saint Stephen's day, 1739. This poem begins " Ɱa bⁱ bⁿóⁿ ⱼo ṁóⱼ ʒan ceⁱⁿⁱoll," " If great woe were without a shade."

7. A prayer, consisting of twenty-eight verses, beginning " A Ṗáȯⱼⁿc naoⁱⁿ̇ca ⱼa bⁿıʒⁱ̇o ̇oeⁱ̇oʒⁱl," " Oh holy Patrick, and white-toothed Bridget."

8. An elegy on the death of Anne Tipper, ninety-six verses, beginning " Oċóⁿ! oċóⁿ! oċóⁿ! m'ēaʒⁿac!" " Alas! alas! alas! my cause of grief."

9. A visit to Conn Magee, a student in Trinity College, forty-eight verses, beginning " Coⁿ ċⱼoⁱ̇oe Ɱ̇hac-Aloȯa áⁱn," " Conn of my heart, noble Magee."

10. On the drunken folly of Dominick O'Quigly, seventy-two verses, beginning " Chomⱼáⁱn ċⱼoⁱ̇o a ċⱼ̇o mo ċom," " My heart's companion, my dear kinsman."

11. On the recovery of Conn Magee from a fever, seventy-six verses, beginning " Ɱⱼⱼʒaⁱl a Ȯhe! mⱼⱼʒal mē!" " Awake, oh God! awake me."

12. On the word *Alleluja*, thirty-two verses, beginning " Ȯon Aⁱlle-lⁱⱼʒaⁱȯaȯ ⁱⱼ aoⁱⁿeaⱼ," " In Alleluja is joy."

13. On the death of Conn Magee, on the 9th of October, 1741, sixty-four verses, beginning " Uⁱ Eⁱȯeⁱn ⱼⁱⁿ̇ cⁱa bⱼⱼⁱ Coⁿ," " Son of Eiden fair, where is Conn?"

14. Sorrows of Banbha (Ireland), one hundred and twenty-four verses, beginning " Ɱⁱⱼⁱ banba an bean boċc," " I am Banbha, the distressed female."

15. On the death of Esther Brasil, wife of George Ratigan, two hundred and eight verses, beginning " *báy eiyṫiṗ ṁ bḣṗeaṙail báin,*" " The death of fair Esther, daughter of O'Breasail."

16. Twenty-eight verses against lust, beginning " *baoy an ḋṗḟiṙ ḋan ḋean ḋan ḋṗaḋ,*" " Lechery is folly, without delight, without love."

17. On the pride of the Irish nobility, two hundred and thirty-six verses, beginning " *ḋeilċniṙ, ḋleiḋil, áillṙn, óḋ,*" " White-skinned, fair, beautiful, young."

18. On the death ·of Cardinal Fleury, eighty-four verses, beginning " *ṁiaǹ ḋaṫ móṗoáṫṫ claoiḃeaǹ cṗó,*" " Death destroys every desire of greatness."

19. On the wickedness of the tongue, fifty-six verses, beginning " *ḋiḃ ball beaḋ an ṫeanḋa ṫá,*" " Though the tongue be a small member."

20. In praise of the tongue, fifty-six verses, beginning " *ǎn beul ḃeaṗṫaṙ bṙiaṫṗa Đe,*" " The mouth that delivers the words of God."

21. Seventy-two verses in praise of a young woman of the name of O'Moore, beginning " *ṅḋaiṁilm laoiḋiṙ ṙ ṁḣóṗồa.*"

22. On the return of Francis O'Sullivan from London to Dublin, after taking his degree of Doctor of the Canon Law, thirty-six verses, beginning " *Ǎl leaḃṗaiḃ noṫ leiḋṫeaṗ liṁ,*" " In the books that are read by us."

23. On seeing an Englishman hanging on a tree. " *Ṙaṫ oo ṫoṗáo oṗṫ a ċṗoiṁ,*" " Increase to thy fruit, oh tree."

24. A poem, beginning "*ṁoṫ maioṅe eiṗḋe a ċṙồ,*" " In the dawn of the morning arise, my love."

25. Sixteen verses, made extempore whilst waiting for his father, in company with Catherine Cruise, to whom he was going to be married, beginning " *ḋaḃ mo ồíon a ṁic Đe,*" " Be my protection, oh Son of God."

Copies of the poems from No. 2 to No. 22, both included, are in the library of William Monck Mason, Esq. in the hand-writing of the author. Copies of the three last-mentioned poems, and most of the others, are in the collection of the Assistant Secretary.

ccclxv. Cotemporary with the last-mentioned writer, was the Rev. ANDREW DONLEVY, Superior of the Irish Community at Paris, who, in the year 1742, published, in that city, a Catechism in the Irish and English languages.

A. D. 1750.

ccclxvi. At this time lived, far advanced in years, Hugh M'Curtin, a native of the county of Clare, a Poet, Historian, Grammarian, and Lexicographer. We can at present give no larger account of this author's Irish works than is contained in the following list:

1. An elegy on the death of Donogh O'Loghlin, of Burren, in the county of Clare, seventy-two verses, beginning " Eaᵹ Ðhoñċaᴅa ıſ ᴅol ᴅaoıṅe," " The death of Donogh is the way of men." This was written in 1714.

2. On the death of Lewis O'Brien, who died in France, in the year 1715, sixty verses, beginning " ıoṁᴅa eaſbaᴅ aıſ Eıſıñ," " Much is the loss to Erin."

3. On the death of the Rev. Edmond O'Byrne, addressed to Teige O'Neaghtan, sixty-four verses, beginning " 2l Ċhaıᴅᵹ ſ, Neaċcaıṅ 'ſa ċaſſᴅ na héıᵹſı," " Oh Teige O'Neaghtan, oh friend of the learned."

4. On the ship of O'Loghlin, of Burren, twenty verses, beginning " beañaıᵹ an báſc blaċſñſce béalċumċa," " Bless the nice-formed, well-fastened bark."

Copies of these poems are in the collection of the Assistant Secretary.

5. An English-Irish Dictionary and Grammar, in quarto, printed at Paris, in 1732. The Grammar had been published some years before, in duodecimo. By a poem, written by M'Curtin, and prefixed to the Dictionary, it would appear that that work was compiled by the Rev. Conor O'Begley, although the Title-page says it was the joint production of O'Begley and M'Curtin. This work has now become scarce, but there is a copy in the library of Trinity College, and other copies in possession of different members of this Society.

ccclxvii. At this time flourished William *buidhe* O'Kiaran, of Oristown, county of Meath. He was author of the following poems, and others to which we cannot now refer:

1. On O'Reilly, of *Baile Othra*, or Oristown, beginning " 2lıᵹ Ráᵹallaċ bhaıle Oċſaıᵹ."

2. On his wife, who, it appears by the poem, was continually railing at him, beginning " Iᴦ Obaɪᴦ Shíle beɪᴛ aɪᵹ abaᴘᴛaɪᵬ a ᴄoɪᵬᴄe oᴘam."

3. A poem, beginning " 2l Ꮯᴛaɪlᴛeaɲ ɲa loᴄ."

ccclxviii. In this year were published proposals for printing an English, Irish, and Latin Dictionary, by a Mr. Crab, a school-master, of Ringsend, near Dublin. This book was never printed, but found its way into the library of the late General Vallancey, and at the sale of that gentleman's books, after his decease, was purchased for Doctor Adam Clarke, at the price of forty guineas.

With this author we shall end this account of the writers of our country who have written in their native language. For, although several versifiers have appeared in later times, whose productions possess a considerable degree of merit, they are not to be compared to those of their predecessors, nor do they tend to elucidate the History, Manners, or Customs of ancient Ireland, and therefore do not come within the views of our Society.

Of this latter description of the Poets and Writers of Ireland, we cannot, however, avoid mentioning the names of the few following :

Denis M'Namara, a school-master, of the county of Waterford, who, about the year 1755, set off for the Newfoundland fishery, *to better his fortune by labouring work*, but being driven back, on the next day, by some adverse cause, returned to his old trade of teaching. On his return a Mr. Power, one of his patrons, humourously insisted on an account of his voyage. M'Namara complied, and wrote a mock Æneid, in which there are some lines by no means inferior to any of Virgil's. The shout of Charon, as described by the Irish bard, thus :

" Ꭰo léɪᵹ ᴦe ᵹáɪᴘ óᴦ áᴘᵬ ɪᴦ béɪceaᴄ,
" le ᴘᴘaɪm a ᵹoᴛa ᵬo ᴄᴘɪᴛeaᵬaᴘ ɲa ᴦᴘéaᴘᴛa,
" Ꭰo ᴄᴘalaᵬ aɲ ᴄᴘɲ͠e é 'ᴦ cᴘᴘ lᴘᴘɪo͠ ᵹēɪm aᴦ."

is, perhaps, superior to the Cyclops' roar of the Mantuan poet.

Denis Mahony, a lyric poet and satyrist, who lived in the city of Cork, about 1755.

Rev. John O'Brian, cotemporary with O'Mahony, a lyric poet, who wrote against O'Mahony.

John M'Donald, better known by the name of *Shane Cláragh*, a good poet, who presided at the Munster Bardic Session, held at Charleville, in the county of Corke, in 1755.

William O'Brian, of Ros-na-Riogh, county Meath, who wrote some very excellent songs, lived about 1760.

John Murphy, a distinguished Munster poet, who lived about the same period.

Right Rev. Doctor John O'Brian, R. C. Bishop of Cloyne, author of an Irish-English Dictionary, printed at Paris in 1768.

Michael Cumming, author of the " Adventures of Torlogh, son of Storn," a beautiful composition, written in elegant language, and in which the author shews himself a man well skilled in Universal History, Geography, &c.

——— Merriman, author of the humorous and witty, though indecent poem of " Cúipc an meoḋain oiḋce," or " The Midnight Court."

Art M'Covey, of the Fews, county Armagh, author of some poems and songs. He was living in 1774.

Cotemporary with M'Covey was ——— M'Auliffe, a blacksmith, near Glanmire, county Corke, author of some poems, in one of which he describes the river Funshan in a storm, where his " Ġlian ġoċaċ láiḋiṙ u ġcaiċioṁ na ḋcoñ," is not inferior to Homer's description of the rolling waves, in the 4th Book of the Iliad.

John Toomey, a Munster poet, who lived about 1790.

Patrick O'Brian, of New Grange, near Slane, county of Meath, lived in 1790; was author of several good songs, &c.

To these might be added the names of Pierce Fitzgerald, Donald O'Brien, Timothy O'Sullivan, and several others, whose compositions display, in smoothly-flowing verses, much fancy and poetic talent.

In addition to the works we have now described, whose authors we know, there are great quantities of other works, still extant, whose authors are unknown or forgotten ; they consist of Laws, Annals, Chronicles, Poetry, Divinity, Astronomy, Medicine, and other branches of Literature, and tend to exhibit the skill of the ancient Irish in the Arts and Sciences, and to elucidate the History and Antiquities of our country. A description and account of those documents, it is intended, shall occupy some future Number of the Transactions of the Iberno-Celtic Society.

END OF PART I.

A. O'NEIL, Printer, Chancery-Lane, Dublin.

INDEX.

THE END.